ON THE VERGE OF NOTHING

ON THE VERGE OF NOTHING
Pessimism's Impossible Beyond

Gary J. Shipley

Foreword by Scott Wilson

Nine-Banded Books

Published by

Nine-Banded Books
PO Box 1862
Charleston, WV 25327
U.S.A.
NineBandedBooks.com

ISBN: 978-1-7356438-3-0

Copyright © 2021 Gary J. Shipley

Cover image: from *100 Scenes* by Tim Gaze

Image on page 3: "Yearning" by RC Miller
Cover design by GJS

All rights reserved. No part of this book may be reproduced or transmitted in any form or by any means, electronic or mechanical, including photocopying, recording, or by any information storage and retrieval system, without written consent of the publisher, except where permitted by law.

Earlier versions of parts of this work have appeared in the following places: "Dreaming Death: the Onanistic and Self-Annihilative Principles of Love in Fernando Pessoa's *The Book of Disquiet*," in *Glossator*, vol. 5 (2011); "A Commentary on Eugene Thacker's Cosmic Pessimism," in *Continent* 2.2 (2012); "Smithereens: On Robert Walser's Microscripts," in *The Black Herald*, issue 4 (2013); and "Non-Terminator: Rise of the Drone-Gods," in *Sustain/Decay* (Void Front Press, 2017).

Printed in the United States of America

The only attitude worthy of a superior man is to persist in an activity he recognizes is useless, to observe a discipline he knows is sterile, and to apply certain norms of philosophical and metaphysical thought that he considers utterly inconsequential.

—Fernando Pessoa
The Book of Disquiet

And when he heard the Princess say that life was a dreadful business, it gave him a feeling of solace as if she had spoken to him of Odette.
"Yes, life is a dreadful business! We must meet more often, my dear Princess. What is so nice about you is that you're not cheerful. We might spend an evening together."

—Marcel Proust
Remembrance of Things Past

CONTENTS

Foreword by Scott Wilson   ix

Introduction: Pessimism's Impossible Beyond,
Or the Junkies of Futility   1

Chapter 1. On Cosmic Pessimism:
Some Preliminary Comments and Aphorisms   35

Chapter 2. Dreaming Death: The Onanistic
and Self-Annihilative Principles of Love
in Fernando Pessoa's *The Book of Disquiet*   47

Chapter 3. Nonhuman Materialisations:
The Horror in the Detail of the Cockroach   79

Chapter 4. Non-Terminator:
Rise of the Drone-Gods   97

Chapter 5. Smithereens: Depressed Survival
in Robert Walser's *Microscripts*   117

Chapter 6. Incompleteness as a Tunnel:
Death, Escape and Paradox   127

Chapter 7. Pessimism and Performance Art:
A Speculative Contract   143

Foreword

Beyond the Pessimism Principle,
Or How to Become the Drone-God That You Are

> I like to imagine the idea of pessimism as self-help.
> —Eugene Thacker

I. The Pessimist's Inspection House

Pessimism is the tenor of our times, even if it is rarely fully embraced. Gary J. Shipley's important book not only embraces pessimism, it offers a way to make life liveable not in the modality of morose resignation, but with enthusiasm. This is an achievement, even for pessimists who regard all achievement as ultimately futile. While Shipley is no doubt correct that avowed pessimists are a "select few"—they are mostly philosophers, after all—their reflections on pessimism are nevertheless symptoms of a general underlying condition. We are all pessimists now, assumed if not avowed. This is not just because of anxieties about the future of the planet in the Anthropocene, the global economy, political instability, the future of AI and so on. Rather it is because of the primacy of a certain structure of affect predicated on suffering—in the West, at least—that informs attempts to address contemporary anxieties about the state of affairs (the planet, the economy, politics).

As Shipley underscores, the basic tenet of pessimism concerns the problem of suffering, and its single guiding principle demands the maximal diminution of suffering. As Shipley acknowledges, the emphasis on suffering places pessimism (especially moral and ethical pessimism) squarely in the tradition of utilitarianism. Jeremy Bentham, after all, famously placed suffering as the ground for the claim that non-human animals should be granted the same moral consideration as humans—still the founding principle of animal rights. "The question is not," writes Bentham in *An Introduction to the Principles of Morals and*

On the Verge of Nothing

Legislation (1789), "can they reason? nor, can they speak? but, can they suffer?" Why should the law refuse its protection to any sensitive being?

The greatest philosopher of pessimism is not Arthur Schopenhauer, it is Jeremy Bentham. This is not widely acknowledged, but Shipley hints at it in his book, and his logic points there. Yet while Shipley accepts the connection pessimism has with utilitarianism, he has two significant reservations. First, Shipley points to Karl Popper's reformulation of a "negative utilitarianism (which seeks to reduce or eliminate suffering rather than the classical utilitarian preoccupation with promoting happiness)." Second, Shipley of course points out that for the radical pessimist nothing in life has any utility whatsoever. I think the first objection can be addressed by differentiating the positions of Bentham and John Stuart Mill, the true founder of Utilitarianism. Bentham is actually closer to Popper in this regard than to Mill. In his elaboration of his moral philosophy, Mill required the Romanticism of Samuel Coleridge to ameliorate Bentham's materialism that eliminated every consideration other than pleasure and pain and thus for Mill disclosed a "deficiency of Imagination" that lacked all sympathy for human nature.[1] While it is true that the founding maxim of Bentham's moral principle of right and wrong is "the greatest happiness of the greatest number,"[2] Bentham's concept of happiness is very minimal indeed and concerns the relative diminution of suffering and the eradication of the threat of violence through ubiquitous surveillance. Bentham's idea of happiness is close to Sigmund Freud's understanding of pleasure: "the agreeable feeling of not too much excitation." For Bentham and Freud, happiness or pleasure consisted in a state of regularity or homeostasis: no alarms and no surprises. We need to remember that Bentham's Inspection House or "Panopticon" was his practical architectural mechanism for establishing the greatest happiness in society. Essentially it is a piece of hardware designed to house and implement software (a logic) that could automatically assess the moral status of any act, thereby enabling the regulation of suffering.

---

[1] John Stuart Mill, "Bentham," in *John Stuart Mill and Jeremy Bentham: Utilitarianism and Other Essays*, ed. Alan Ryan (Harmondsworth: Penguin, 1987), 148.
[2] Jeremy Bentham, "An Introduction to the Principles of Morals and Legislation," in Ryan, *John Stuart Mill and Jeremy Bentham*, 65.

Foreword

The design of the Inspection House was a direct response to the horrifying violence and ineptitude of sovereign law that reigned at the time. Mill writes that what animated Bentham in his codification of law was to systematically eradicate "modern corruption grafted upon ancient barbarism."[3] This "barbarism" is memorably evoked by Michel Foucault's description of the botched execution of the regicide Damiens at the beginning of *Discipline and Punish*.[4] For Bentham, the panoptic surveillance machine *protected* the prisoner, worker, pupil or patient from the neglect, incompetence, corruption and often sadism of the prison warder, factory owner, teacher and doctor, all of whom would be equally subject to the disciplinary gaze of the central tower. Bentham was bemused by the objections his panoptic apparatus provoked at the time; the idea that constant surveillance would constitute a punishment worse than death. He believed that those who had nothing to hide had nothing to fear from constant inspection. For Bentham himself, such surveillance would be "a matter of indifference" or "even of comfort" if he "feared abuse of power by his gaoler."[5] Today we hear the same sentiments expressed by state

---

[3] Mill, "Bentham," 134.

[4] It is characteristic that Foucault should alight on Bentham's apparatus as the source of the greatest maladies of the modern age of power. In his own views on suffering, Foucault's enthusiasm for "the art of unbearable sensations" was evident in both his life and writing (Michel Foucault, *Discipline and Punish* [Harmondsworth: Penguin, 1986], 11). Foucault's own position is as far away from the pessimist as it is possible to get. From his enthusiasm for *l'eclat des supplices*—the splendour and explosive ritual of death by torture—to his expression of regret that he'd never had the opportunity to try Sade's prescribed methods, it could be suggested that Foucault indeed was, in the words of Gilles Deleuze, "a sadist" (See James Miller, *The Passions of Michel Foucault* [London: Harper Collins, 1993], 212–13; Michel Foucault, *Foucault Live*, [New York: Semiotext(e), 1989], 82; Gilles Deleuze, *Two Regimes of Madness: Texts and Interviews 1975–1995* [New York: Semiotext(e), 2006], 131). A sadist is much like an optimist in her interest in anticipating the future. The sadist typically suspends time through an anxiety-producing threat of violence, so that she can enjoy anticipating the suffering that will constitute for her a favourable outcome. A masochist, by contrast, is more like the pessimist in that he knows for sure that suffering is coming (it's in the contract) and takes a certain satisfaction in the knowledge of its inevitability.

[5] J. Semple, *Bentham's Prison: A Study of the Panopticon Penitentiary* (Oxford: Oxford University Press, 1993), 144–145.

security services and online service providers all the time, and most seem to agree. Bentham's utilitarian principles, coupled with behaviourism, underlie the contemporary system of surveillance capitalism wherein the data gleaned from "behavioural surplus" feeds the machine-learning that has enabled the implementation of ubiquitous, predictive computing. "Recommender" algorithms close the gap constitutive of market uncertainty and smooth out the anxieties associated with choice, foreclosing desire—an index of suffering relative to the "lack" that it implies—with the perpetual supply of goods you never knew you wanted.

For Bentham, "utility"—or rather work—was not a means but an end. It was not important that the worker produced something useful, it was important that work constituted an activity that provided its own mode of satisfaction. *Work, utility, efficiency was nothing in the end other than a project through which suffering could be limited.* But with contemporary capitalism, of course, the concept of utility does not even apply to products. As Jean-Joseph Goux wrote of "postmodern capitalism" in the early 1990s: "Is it useful or superfluous to manufacture microwave ovens, quartz watches, videogames or, collectively, to travel to the moon and Mars, to photograph Saturn's rings, etc.?"[6] With online capitalism, most of the objects are in any case insubstantial; like the concepts of "need" and "utility" themselves, they are "fictions," in Bentham's sense, in which economic "reality" is made out of panoptic algorithms designed to ameliorate suffering.

Bentham's "Panopticon" is an 18th century piece of software engineering and a stupendous work of pessimist art, perhaps the first of its kind. As such, it fits Shipley's criteria for "post-pessimist" creation that shapes something out of our "terror of existence" by "reprocessing it as various forms of art and literature . . . even with the very worst aspects of human life." In *On the Verge of Nothing*, Shipley closely examines and demonstrates how the art and literature of pessimism has been "actively engaged in neutralising its negative effects though a creative program" even while accepting the central premise of pessimism. But Bentham's example also shows that it is not the *realisation* of the creative program that is the main point. Bentham's Inspection House was never to be realised in his lifetime; it was a

---

[6] Jean-Joseph Goux, "General Economics and Postmodern Capitalism," in *Bataille: A Critical Reader*, ed. Fred Botting and Scott Wilson (Oxford: Blackwell, 1998), 28.

Foreword

failure, even though its general principles have enthused sociologists and behavioural psychologists for generations. More crucial was Bentham's obsession with the design that he continued to refine to his death. Bentham's fixation on his panoptic pleasure-machine was a form of "intoxication," comparable to Shipley's "junkies of futility" whose pursuit of pointless pleasures constitutes a "nullification" of pessimism's negative effects.

In his examination of Eugene Thacker's aphoristic elegies to pessimism, the fictions of H. P. Lovecraft, Thomas Ligotti, Franz Kafka and Clarice Lispecter, Robert Walser and performance art, Shipley discloses a logic to pessimistic production that, I suggest, involves three stages: pleasure-pessimism, surplus pessimism, and post-pessimism; which is itself a mode of satisfaction-pessimism wherein a state of tonal intensity provides a superior form of homeostasis: the immoderate satisfaction of the Drone God.

II. Pleasure-pessimism, surplus pessimism, post-pessimism

There are then three main types of pessimism evident in Shipley's commentary on his chosen writers. They each exemplify a particular mode of suffering—and life—in a singular way. They do not represent any kind of progression (what would it mean to say that suffering progresses?) and aspects of each of the three modes of life are evident in all the writers and artists.

The first, *pleasure-pessimism*, is evident where the writer, like the neurotic who loves her symptom, finds a certain contentment in pessimism. As Shipley notes, "depressives make bad pessimists" and they rarely commit suicide. Pessimism is a form of auto-affection: only I, and a "select few" like me, know the truth about the futility of the world, and that gives me a form of comfort. Nothing is going to surprise me. Pessimism is a given. Pleasure-pessimism arises from interpreting the world, and one's place in it, and is thus situated at the level of meaning, or "understanding." The search for meaning stops when we are content with an answer, or maybe even if we think there can be no answers. When we think we have understood something— even that there is nothing to be understood—we are content. So, the answer "there is no meaning to life" is still an answer. Since for the pessimist suffering is life, the meaning of the meaning of life is situated precisely at the level of affect which becomes contentment with the truth of suffering. Inertia is proper to pleasure-pessimism and its writing, which is thick with the meaning of non-meaning, able to support an *infinite resignation*. The meaning of non-meaning is so secure it is even supported by the "cosmic pessimism" of the world-without-us.

But, as we have argued, with pleasure-pessimism, meaning is situated at the level of affect which for Thacker is a general sense of gloom spiced with spite. The narcissism of the pessimist is not generous. Thacker writes: "There is an intolerance in pessimism that knows no bounds. In pessimism, spite begins by fixing on some particular object—someone one hardly knows too well; a spite for this person or all humanity . . . a spite for a noisy neighbour, a yapping dog … the meandering idiot on their phone etc."[7] This is the pessimism of the troll, angry at the stupidity of the Other's existence, whose noisiness so disturbs the pleasure of troll-like solitude that one has to write something spiteful, or at the very least write something about spite in order to re-establish the harmony of his gloomy equilibrium.

Shipley knows perfectly well that the inertia of pleasure-pessimism constitutes a dead end. This is the initial premise of his book, and his desire to locate a way past the impasse. We will come back to this and particularly to pessimism's sonic dimension and the function of noise.

For the pessimist, the word "life" is virtually synonymous with the word "suffering," a correlation that can prove consoling provided that the equation is confined by natural or scientific laws. Thacker quotes Fernando Pessoa's resignation concerning "the futility of all effort, given that we're ruled by implacable laws which nothing can repeal or obstruct."[8] But "law" is not synonymous with "life"; laws are just ways of accounting for life in mechanical or mathematical terms. Laws are no longer given by God, they are perceived regularities, numerical constants, abstractions, statistical averages. In this regard, life may be meaningless, but it is not *senseless*. Indeed, scientists precisely make some sense of life with the help of their mathematical instruments. For the pessimist who is not content with the comforts of maths, however, no one knows what life *is*—least of all the biologist whose deathless assessments of bio-chemical processes are unsatisfying. Here the register shifts further away from contentment with the lack of meaning

---

[7] Eugene Thacker, *Infinite Resignation* (London: Repeater Books, 2018), 14.
[8] Thacker, *Infinite Resignation*, 24.

Foreword

(which concerns the subject) towards an affect that concerns the body as locus of anxiety. Anxiety is of course the primary affect for Freud; anxiety never lies, the others being displacements. For the pessimist afflicted with anxiety, no one knows anything about the life of suffering other than that one experiences it; we have a "sense" of it in the body that is different to the sense made of it by the biologist. The state of inertia shifts from the imaginary relation to non-meaning to the circulating, self-referential routines of scientific discourse. For the pessimist, then, this sense of the body in the experience of non-knowledge necessitates that she split her suffering from the register of pleasure, and locate it in the beyond-of-discourse. Gloominess gives way to anxiety, apprehension, and incomprehension.

In his chapter "Nonhuman Materialisations: The Horror in the Detail of the Cockroach," Shipley draws on Franz Kafka, Clarice Lispector, Georges Bataille and others who evoke the human horror of phobic objects and animals like insects in order to suggest that life is essentially *formless* and thus unknowable. Shipley quotes Bataille's short piece "Formless" from the journal *Documents*. Bataille writes, "affirming that the universe resembles nothing and is only *formless* amounts to saying that the universe is something like a spider or spit." From a mathematical or discursive perspective this is of course nonsensical. To say that the universe is something like a spider or spit is *precisely* to give it a form, the form of a spider or spit. It only makes sense from the perspective of the arachnophobe whom the presence of a spider reduces to a state of abjection beyond all rational control or determination. Phobic objects (frequently animals) are for Freud an effect of the question that being raises about the world before the subject became individuated as a subject. Phobias crystallise and defend a subject's sense of individuality in its pessimism about the very universe that has given rise to it—a universe that is always threatening to return it to the formlessness of non-being. Phobia is an anxiety that occurs the moment a discrete body apprehends the vulnerability of its existence in the presence of a voracious outside that would return existence to the continuity of intimate violence (there are plenty of mothers who eat their offspring).

In the literary tradition cited by Shipley (from Lovecraft to Ligotti), the type of individuation supported by the auto-affection of pleasure-pessimism is confronted with, and pushed towards, an unpleasant excess in which life and suffering are conflated in a particular object that marks a certain limit beyond which it is impossible to step. As forbidding as it is, it nevertheless offers itself as an exit beyond discourse. The phobic object is a defence, but also an exit-sign. As we know, in literature the sign "There Be Dragons" is an invitation to seek the New World. Other signs for the exit are the "horror" or the "weird" or historically the "sublime" and indeed the "impossible." In this chapter, Shipley focusses on the extra-discursive world of animals, evoking the Deleuzian trope of "becoming-animal." For Shipley, however, becoming-animal is "a transitory measure to facilitate becoming neither." Rather, "something neither human nor animal is hidden inside and ridiculing the presumption that any such scrutiny might reveal its nature." This element of the exterior that is nevertheless "something inside" points to the path of ex-sistence, the path any writer must take if he or she wants to broach the genuinely new or different. Creativity occurs in relation to that which lies outside the discursive world of being. The difference occurs, however, from the *relation* that the writer has with the outside, the effects of which, as Shipley suggests, can only be felt inside—in Bataille's sense of "inner experience," the particular nature of which is not available to anyone else.

As we have seen, to say that pessimism tells the truth that life is pointless, useless, meaningless and a locus of suffering is actually to confer an order to it, pretty much along the lines of science which extracts meaning, intentionality and purpose retroactively as the chance or statistical effect of certain laws, regularities, consistencies. For another kind of pessimist, however, life is always in excess; its truth lies in a surplus that escapes law, regularity and so on by returning to a chance or even a miraculous experience of the outside that does not give itself up to narrative coherence. The surplus that defines "surplus-pessimism," then, is the effect of a singular relation between an inside and an outside that is chaotic and formless. Thus, it makes more sense to speak of *contingency* rather than *impossibility*, a contingency that, first, defines the pessimist as irreducibly singular, and second, discloses their truth to be a lie. At this point we will encounter Shipley's "post-pessimism," but let's discuss the first two points before we get there.

While I think it makes sense to speak of a "pessimist" or a "pessimistic attitude," I'm not sure that we can approach pessimism as an "ism," as a distinctive philosophy, doctrine or system. Thacker acknowledges this. "The very term 'pessimism' suggests a school of thought, a movement, even a community. But pessimism always has a

Foreword

membership of one—maybe two (one of them imaginary)."[9] Given, as Thacker also states, that pessimism is as much about "mood" as meaning, I'm not sure that when someone says or writes that they are a pessimist, that they mean the same thing as their pessimistic neighbour trying to distract himself with his yapping dog, noisy music or mobile phone. Everyone is a pessimist in their own particular way. My pessimism has nothing to do with yours. In my pessimism, I am one-all-alone. Yet I am interpellated, as Marxists used to say, by the discourse of pessimism. What do they want from me? As Antonio Gramsci famously said: "Pessimism of the intellect, optimism of the will." Behind the intellect, then, there is still the *will* that drives the poor pessimistic subject to come up with more thought, more constructions of the truth that life is meaningless. What does the pessimist want? What does the pessimist desire? All that one can grasp and name of desire is life. Gramsci's formulation thus suggests that we are not only interpellated by the discourse of pessimism, but also by *life* qua locus of suffering and affect. As a *locus*, suffering is constituted by different intensities, some more or less pleasurable, more or less painful than others, as originally posited by Bentham of course. The pessimist wants life, as Shipley states time and again—even immortal life. But since no one knows what life is, the question defaults to *a* life, a history in which past contingencies are given the sense of necessities to come, the implacable laws that condemn it to futility. It is a form of rationalisation in which the truth discloses itself as a lie. It is a construction; a rational one, but a construction nevertheless. The pessimist complaint is true, but it has the structure of a fiction. This construction is driven by a "will" or desire for life (as a locus of affect) that can only be approached by the device of such a fiction. But the point of this fiction is not to produce truth as an end in itself, but for truth to disclose itself as the semblance of the singular *affect* that articulates the relation the pessimist has to his suffering.

Thus, as Shipley maintains, such a fiction is an apparatus for the production of life, or rather a certain mode of life. Art, writing, language generally is a device of and for life and thus for a "post-pessimistic" attitude that combines the pessimism of the intellect with the monstrous "optimism" of the "will-to-life." It is post-pessimistic even though all it may think, feel and speak about is its will-to-suffering. All-alone, this will is silent, but it is the implacable force

---

[9] Thacker, *Infinite Resignation*, 8.

behind a noise that is neither the sound of the grumbling contentment of (non)meaning, nor the whining anxiety of extra-discursive horror, but rather a resonance of thinking-feeling. This is the phrase that Shipley posits, following Lispector and Pessoa, as the characteristic feature of post-pessimism. And accordingly, as Lispector contends in her novel *The Passion According to G.H.*, this thinking-feeling occurs in a register of pure tonality or attunement: a "mood," or indeed a drone.

III. The unbearable moodiness of the Drone Gods

"If pessimism had a sound," Shipley proposes, it would not be a down note or minor chord, it would be "the harsh interior noise of tinnitus—the way that every person would hear themselves if they refused their distractions long enough to listen: a lungless scream from the extrasolar nothing of the self." It is out of tune with itself, in disharmony, its "tinnitustic needles sew back shadow" (Scott Walker, "Tar," 2013). The shadow, that life serves no purpose and that it ends in death, gives definition to the will that demands that it sustain itself, demanding that it go on and on, more and more, even to the point of immortality. This is Shipley's quasi-Nietzschean challenge, the gage that he throws down to his readers, that they will immortality even as a "pestilential drone," "the drone of [a] hypothesised forever [that] comes from within, and . . . will either destroy us (in some hideous yet non-fatal destruction) or else turn us into gods."

These are immortal "junkie" Gods, however, who manage to turn the excess of surplus pessimism into post-pessimism through the practice of "an exalted form of addiction" that manages to sustain a superior homeostasis in the routinised form of the drone. A drone addict becoming drone, the very substance to which they are addicted, "wherein the returns do not wane but instead accentuate": the noise of ourselves mutating in excess. With the arrival of the Drone-Gods we move from the homeostatic status of pleasure-pessimism and its disruption in the surplus that exceeds the limits of its gloomy well-being, to the status of post-pessimism which restores homeostasis through the routinisation of the excess in the infinite resonance of the drone. The point of the drone, I believe, is that within the same immediately apparent tone—that Shipley insists should be assumed to be painful, even "excruciating"—there are infinite variations that

Foreword

sustain an enthusiasm and a satisfying level of aesthetic pleasure (one thinks of the French noise-artist Vomir who blasts static at a captive audience required to wear black bags over their heads). The art of post-pessimism that turns suffering into aesthetic pleasure is consistent with a shift in significance or value from an idea of meaning grounded in semantics to a somatic dimension that aims at sense and sensations that are sensitive to the regularities and variations of a sonic environment, thereby achieving a certain level of satisfaction. Thinking-feeling flows into a form of "*reasonation*" that vibrates endlessly in variation with itself.

To return to Lispector, in "thousands of years from now," she writes, "we are finally no longer what we feel and think: we shall have something that more closely resembles a 'mood' than an idea. . . . And I shall not wander 'from thought to thought,' but from mood to mood. We shall be inhuman—as the loftiest conquest of man."[10]

No longer man, just a flickering vibration of "thought-feeling," a bad mood ill-adapted to an ocean of hostile magnetic radiation, reasonating in a wild and raging mixture of different wavelengths.

Scott Wilson

---

[10] Clarice Lispector, *The Passion According to G.H.* (Harmondsworth: Penguin, 2012), 182.

ON THE VERGE OF NOTHING

Introduction

Pessimism's Impossible Beyond, Or the Junkies of Futility

> A nihilist wants to live in the world as is,
> and yet gaze the everlasting hills to rubble.
> —Robert Lowell

For some of us, a conspicuously select few, the intrigue of philosophical pessimism is not concerned with whether or not we can reason our way around its unpalatable conclusions,[1] but whether there is any legitimate way to exist that does not fall prey to the opposing inanities of optimism, where the idea is not to orchestrate an escape from pessimism but a pessimistic escape, an escape without new hope or destination. My intention here, then, is not to further augment in any substantial way the main premises and conclusions of pessimism, or to debate their validity in any great depth, but to instead assume their truth[2] and see where this leaves us, to delineate the pessimistic state as a given, and from there attempt a survey of post-pessimism's ineludibly nebulous terrain. And while the concept of post-pessimism is paradoxical—what does pessimism insist upon if not the claim that there is nothing beyond pessimism, which is, after all, the primary reason its conclusions are so hard to stomach—it will be this very implausibility that, while at first seeming an obstacle, will turn out to

---

[1] There is forever the nagging suspicion that the primary reason philosophy has always been, and continues to be, so hostile to pessimism is because philosophy's (secret) function is to perpetuate intricacies and conundrums, and not to obviate or resolve them.

[2] In short: as long as humans exist you will have the problem of human suffering; and given this, nonexistence is always preferable to existence, in that the former precludes the possibility of harm while the latter in practice necessitates it.

provide the only cogent way beyond or through pessimism's ostensible dead end.

From the time we are born, conceived even, it is too late: there is no choice left to us but to drown, for even when our internal life has all but corroded we continue to struggle to breathe: "A man in chains who was being dragged down—the muscles still moved but only at the command of a soul already decomposed. They followed in the wake of putrefaction."[3] It's not that the floods are coming, but that they're already here. Only, most of us can't see them. We have learnt to breathe underwater, and have forgotten how to miss the fresh air: "[O]ne is never as happy as one thinks."[4] We must unlearn how to struggle. We must learn how to float. The icecaps are melting, there's no going back, and the only climate emergency is how long it is taking to finish us off.

NON-PRESCRIPTIVE SUICIDE

It is important from the start to try to get a fix on the pessimist that does not go insane, or suicide, or else seek refuge in some reformulated version of the very illusions they claim to have overcome, to get a fix, then, on the pessimist that endures, and just what could induce a stance so seemingly at odds with itself.

To the pessimist, these words by Silenus are uncontentious: "The very best thing is utterly beyond your reach: not to have been born, not to be, to be nothing. However, the second best thing for you is: to die soon."[5] And yet most pessimists do not choose this *second best thing*, but instead a much worse thing, choosing to live out their lives until such time as it is ended for them. They profess to believe one thing and then do the opposite, and from this arrives the suspicion that they do not believe their own theory, and that their espousal of it is insincere. Yet there is another more credible possibility, for while it might clearly be better if you'd never existed, the conditions that comprise that existence make it extremely difficult to voluntarily undo it. To die soon

---

[3] Hans Henny Jahnn, *The Ship* (London: Peter Owen, 1970), 145.
[4] Marcel Proust, *Remembrance of Things Past: 1*, trans. C.K. Scott Moncrieff and Terence Kilmartin (London: Penguin Books, 1989), 386.
[5] Silenus quoted in Friedrich Nietzsche, *The Birth of Tragedy And Other Writings*, trans. Ronald Speirs (Cambridge: Cambridge University Press, 1999), 23.

might be better, but that does not mean we then have the motivational resources to override our biology in order to get it done. Despite what some guileless detractors might think, pessimism contains no obligatory prescription to suicide, for to regard being born as an unequivocal misfortune does not logically entail that you must then extirpate yourself at the first opportunity, at the risk of being found guilty of dissembling. As Thomas Ligotti, after Arthur Schopenhauer, states:

> Naturally there are pessimists who kill themselves, but nothing obliges them to kill themselves or live with the mark of the hypocrite on their brow. Voluntary death might seem a thoroughly negative course of action, but it is not as simple as that. Every negation is adulterated or stealthily launched by an affirmative spirit. An unequivocal "no" cannot be uttered or acted upon.[6]

With no rational requirement to suicide, the pessimist can still legitimately live out a life that they'd nevertheless prefer had never been imposed on them in the first place. Alternatively, it could be that your pessimism stretches beyond death, and so not even suicide would bring about the desired escape from existence. In this case, like Julius Bahnsen, who held just such a view, you would despair to the brink of suicide, but stripped of all motivation for enacting it would go no further.[7] Of course, the world will always attempt to appropriate any such pessimist suicide—to account for it in other terms, to absorb it into a narrative still utterly in thrall to the perceived sanctity of living— but the concern is to make sure that the world hasn't already appropriated it long before you manage to enact it. Or in less prosaic terms, as Frederick Seidel puts it: "[H]ow many other men / Had smelled the rose in the bud vase / [. . .] And put the shotgun in their mouth, / And noticed that their hunting dog was pointing."[8]

---

[6] Thomas Ligotti, *The Conspiracy Against the Human Race* (New York: Hippocampus Press, 2010), 50.
[7] Julius Bahnsen, "Zur Verständigung über den heutigen Pessimismus," (1881).
[8] Frederick Seidel, *Ooga-Booga* (New York: Farrar, Straus and Giroux, 2006), 14.

On the Verge of Nothing

Many of us do not only fear the process of dying, but irrationally fear our own nonexistence. We fear the latter for the same reason we fear the most effective creatures in horror fiction: that is, we fear it because we cannot properly conceptualise it. Its formlessness corrupts our rational faculties. Thus we cannot, it seems, live by the incontrovertible Epicurean logic which points out that where our death is we are absent and where we are it is not, for our inevitable death permeates everything with an absence that, although it will not be felt when it occurs, is nevertheless felt prematurely through some misguided imaginative projection. And so to suppose that the pessimist has some unique cerebral process with which to inoculate themselves against this inbuilt visceral illogic is perversely out of proportion in its demands. And no easy consolation is to be found in immortality either, where once again we find similar conceptual impasses—as we fail to imagine what a never-ending life worth living might amount to. So much so, in fact, that any remedies we come up with no longer directly involve us, but rather involve some improved, remotely connected versions of us, beings made somehow worthy of immortality through immortality itself: distant creatures, speculative descendants, Drone Gods.

In his novel *Guernica Night*, Barry N. Malzberg imagines our future as one of isolated communities in which suicide (the "Final Trip") is offered to all under-25s. Due to the uptake rate being exceedingly high, the main character, Sid, is sent to investigate the case of one such individual, Jag, who has expressed his intention to die, saying how "he is disgusted with his life and is disgusted with all of life as he knows it and that he cannot put up with it any longer."[9] Sid attempts to discover the reasons behind these high rates of suicide, but by the end of the book comes only to the conclusion that despite all life's stale dreams and luxuries—including a technological advancement that facilitates instantaneous transport to anywhere on the globe[10]—"there is no

---

[9] Barry N. Malzberg, *Guernica Night* (London: NEL Books, 1979), 23.
[10] Connected to this technology, that literally offers you the world, is the argument by Philipp Mainländer, which claims that only by procuring and experiencing every conceivable human good could we come to realise the inherent worthlessness of life and all its possibilities, because until we reach this stage we will forever hold out hope that something is missing and that it is that very something that will finally redeem our existence. While it is evident that the best way to shatter your illusions about the things you desire is to get

reason to stay, but there is none to go either; [that] life at whatever level is perversely interesting," and that he is therefore "doomed to live."[11] When we think of what else might be considered perversely interesting—the effects of a bomb-blast or an automotive accident on a human body, the behaviour of serial killers, certain debilitating genetic abnormalities, for instance—it's hard to think of this as necessarily being any kind of genuine endorsement for sticking around. What is clear, however, is that given the low expectations of the pessimist a corresponding apathy is most likely to prevail; and the apathetic suicide is, I contend, a rarity indeed, and much rarer in fact than the perennially disappointed optimists who, replete with passion and egregiously disavowed of their hopes, come to their senses with a resounding crash.

PESSIMISM, NIHILISM AND JUNKIEDOM

While the two theories are closely related, pessimism is not nihilism. For while the latter is a theory advocating a state voided of beliefs, values, purpose, desires and adherences, the former is vociferous in its condemnation of suffering, and in the defence of this belief. According to pessimism, suffering is a malignant condition that ought to be eradicated, an at first all too reasonable objective that quickly becomes unpalatable to most when conjoined with the premise that suffering is an inescapable and integral part of all sentient existence. In short, pessimism is an ethical theory, whereas nihilism denies the very legitimacy of ethics. And it is around this last vestige of human meaning that all post-pessimistic theorising must gravitate.

The pessimist concedes that being a pessimist is the more arduous course, that continuing to lie to yourself, wallowing in the

---

the things you desire, it is less obvious that there can ever be any such thing as peak-human-happiness, and that even if there could be, that it could in all credibility induce in us a "will-to-die," when a radically imperfect happiness is not up to the task, is counterintuitive in the extreme. If we manage to attain increased levels of happiness then, by definition, we will feel less disgruntled about our human lot. As Ligotti himself makes clear, if we were in a constant state of well-being any questions as to the meaning of our lives would never get asked, let alone pressure us for an answer.
[11] Malzberg, *Guernica Night*, 117–118.

zombification of self-deception—indulging in those four coping strategies identified by Peter Wessel Zapffe in "The Last Messiah": *isolation* (the defensive compartmentalisation of our minds), *anchoring* (how we root ourselves in various institutions), *distraction* (allowing trivial pleasures to take our minds off the equally trivial horror of our own existence), and *sublimation* (fleeing the truth through sham confrontations with it)—is by far the easier option. The pessimist also concedes that pessimism is ineffectual, that it is unlikely to be accepted by more than a very select few; and that even among those who do accept its truths, the chances that such acceptance will alter their behaviour in any dramatic way are extremely slim (biology or the will-to-life proving too powerful to overcome): like "religions that ask of their believers more than they can possibly make good on, pessimism is a set of ideals than none can follow to the letter."[12] For while Karl Popper's negative utilitarianism (which seeks to reduce or eliminate suffering rather than the classical utilitarian preoccupation with promoting happiness) can, as pointed out by R. N. Smart,[13] only ever advocate universal nonexistence, and while it is possible to find the logic of this anti-natalism compelling, and so concur with David Benatar "that zero population is the optimum size,"[14] it does not follow, by the pessimists' own admission, that any significant implementation of this theory will ever come about.[15] Given these admissions, an apparent paradox at the heart of pessimism reveals itself: why when pessimism is equated with increased suffering, not less, do pessimists seek to multiply its adherents? Why do they not instead accept their conclusions and give up, resolve themselves to the indelible human truth of escapist subterfuge, and advocate instead the improvement of all practicable means to mitigate suffering?

With the reality of this inevitable failure in mind—and the pessimist is after all the supreme realist, much less the unhinged radical, as they

---

[12] Ligotti, *The Conspiracy Against the Human Race*, 43.
[13] R. N. Smart, 'Negative Utilitarianism' *Mind*, vol. 67, no. 268 (Oct., 1958) 542–543.
[14] David Benatar, *Better Never to Have Been: The Harm of Coming Into Existence* (New York: Oxford University Press, 2006), 181.
[15] In the event, that is, that certain futurists, who either hope or fear some AI may one day be technically situated and logically impelled to implement biocide, are not accurate in their predictions.

Pessimism's Impossible Beyond

are often portrayed, and much more the forensic purist—wouldn't a consistent (a genuine) pessimist be the one who, rather than fatuously pursuing the annihilation of mankind (an annihilation they concede will not be consciously brought about by humans themselves), be the one who instead pursues the acceleration and accentuation of all and any available mechanisms of escape? How, when the pessimist sets themself up as the ultimate realist amidst a coterie of pretenders, can they still cling to the pipedream of the self-inflicted extinction of human kind? If a reduction in suffering was truly paramount, pessimism would advocate more abstraction, more artificiality, more creative delusions, not less. As Zapffe and others have pointed out, the strategies we employ to escape ourselves and the unpleasant truths of our existence are often not fit for purpose, sufficient, one could argue, only for children and idiots, but to imagine that they cannot be substantially improved, and elaborations made that might transform these tired mechanisms, is to ignore the tenacity and manifestly inexhaustible nature of human ingenuity when it comes to avoiding or subverting unpleasant truths. Once the chimera of mankind's autoextinction has been acknowledged as such, what else remains? If a "utopia in which we no longer deny the realities we presently must repress cannot be realistically hoped for,"[16] then neither can the collective self-annihilation of humanity.

Ligotti talks of the division between optimists and pessimists, and how the question of which of the two sides is right is ultimately irresolvable. For while it is clear which side Ligotti is on, it is, he claims, beyond him or anyone else to categorically settle the matter once and for all. Taking a lead from Derek Parfit,[17] we ought to regard this division itself as the resolution, and any question about which group is right as empty. Presuming we have all the facts in these two scenarios, we are not deciding between two different possibilities, but only our descriptions of them. Life may be impossible for me to defend in good faith, but life is what I have, life is what is here and now, and any desire I might have that it should not be has so far always fallen short of motivating any concrete plans to curtail it—in me and most others of a pessimist persuasion. This is a common predicament among pessimists and it lends weight to those on the opposing camp

---
[16] Ligotti, *The Conspiracy Against the Human Race*, 71.
[17] See Derek Parfit, *Reasons and Persons* (New York: Oxford University Press, 1984).

when they, with increasing pontifical disdain, criticise the pessimist for failing to accept and make the best of what they are manifestly powerless to change.

If optimism "is the default condition of our blood and cannot be effectively questioned by our minds or put in grave doubt by our pains,"[18] then by extension we are not only subject to the appalling conditions of life but are ourselves appalling, for as Schopenhauer claims, optimism is "not merely an absurd, but also a really *wicked*, way of thinking, a bitter mockery of the most unspeakable sufferings of mankind."[19] The onus, then, is not to simply escape life for the sake of ourselves, but to escape ourselves in order that life might consequently be avoided.

While the position I'll defend in response to these problems is not the so-called heroism of Friedrich Nietzsche, Albert Camus and others (who seek to mollify pessimism with hard-won pretences of optimism), it does share some surface similarities with that approach. However, proponents of my proposed position are not so much "absurd heroes," or heroes of futility, as they are *junkies of futility*, those who although they accept pessimism as true, and eschew all contrivances to undermine it, are still actively engaged in neutralising its negative effects though a creative program of lucid intoxication. The idea is not that we ought to live in spite of the truths of pessimism, but that our living ought to become some kind of aberrant testament to those truths, that we become ingenious celebrants of pessimism's sour medicine.

In *The Myth of Sisyphus*, Camus tells us that in order to transcend the cruel absurdity of Sisyphus's plight we must imagine him happy in his task, content to roll his boulder up and down the mountain for an eternity. But without accounting for this happiness in any credible way, it is difficult to take seriously. Countering this unfounded shift of perspective, we should instead imagine that Sisyphus isn't even there, but existing in some other dream-world of his own creation, in which the boulder and the mountain do not even feature, that he is like the undernourished and penurious heroin-user nupping in some filthy hovel, who in the midst of his buzz would not comprehend the pity

---

[18] Ligotti, *The Conspiracy Against the Human Race*, 64.
[19] Arthur Schopenhauer, *The World as Will and Representation Vol. 1*, trans. E. F. J. Payne (New York: Dover Publications, 1969), 326.

Pessimism's Impossible Beyond

you have for him—when after all, in that moment, chances are he feels better than you. In other words, there is no solution to be found in an imaginative flight from suffering that then fails to provide some detail to the mechanics of such a flight. And while the junkie is not the end of this crucial explanation, he is nevertheless an important and pragmatic starting point from which we might realistically extrapolate.

Once you take away the notion that a junkie is wasting their life—that there is anything of value there to waste, that there is a more meaningful existence a junkie could be living if they were free of their habit, that the drugs will shorten their life, etc.—then the problems of the junkie become a single problem: staying high. And this is pessimism confronted head on; this is pessimism confessing its own impotence in the face of nature. The junkie's solution is not to pretend there is no problem to begin with, but to nullify its negative effects as much as possible. We are all medicating, but only the junkie takes it seriously: existing as little more than their addiction, all the other petty concerns of life having gradually atrophied, leaving behind a "grey, junk-bound ghost. [. . .] El Hombre Invisible—the Invisible Man."[20] For what else can the pessimist hope for if not to disappear? And the crucial difference here, with the junkie of futility, is that they will never seek a cure because they know there is no cure. As long as they remain in their intoxicated state they will never again have to endure that "utter depression of soul which [Edgar Allan Poe could] compare to no earthly sensation more properly than to the after-dream of the reveller upon opium—the bitter lapse into everyday life—the hideous dropping off of the veil."[21]

In connection with this, it is worth considering Robert Nozick's "experience machine" thought experiment from *Anarchy, State and Utopia*: a device that offers all your desired experiences without the correlative real world impingements.[22] Should you chose to plug in, an option that is offered to you every two years, your life will be one of almost uninterrupted bliss, as opposed to the life you currently live, which most certainly is not similarly blissful. The problem, as Nozick sees it, is that it won't be you that *actually* does any of the things you experience doing because, of course, they won't *really* be happening. He

---

[20] William Burroughs, *Naked Lunch* (London: Flamingo, 1993), 63.
[21] Edgar Allan Poe, "The Fall of the House of Usher," in *Complete Stories and Poems of Edgar Allan Poe* (New York: Doubleday, 1966), 177.
[22] Robert Nozick, *Anarchy, State and Utopia* (New York: Basic Books, 1974).

concludes that we are not only concerned with how our time is spent, but also with what we are, and that the latter is not some dispensable part of the equation. However, even with this in mind, simply transforming us into the people we'd like to be before we plug into the experience machine, via some transformation machine, is also not enough to allay our concerns; for regardless of the increased personal utility, "what we desire is to live (an active verb) ourselves, in contact with reality. (And this, machines cannot do for us)."[23] While the conclusions that Nozick draws from his thought experiments are valid, they are only part of what is wrong here. However, before discussing these more nuanced discrepancies, it should already be evident that the pessimist would have no reason for refusing to plug in: Nozick's machine offers a life without suffering, and that this life might preclude you from some deeper meaning could not logically dissuade someone for whom this deeper meaning is a complete illusion, and for whom life (whether authentic or inauthentic) is utterly worthless.

Regarding those other potential issues, we ought to note that one significant concern that goes unmentioned in Nozick's experiment is that of the nagging disquiet that something has eluded us in the real world, an epistemic lacuna that fuels a genuine sense of mystery inseparable from our existence (whether we actively cultivate it as a defence mechanism or not), and that plugging into the machine will as a consequence always seem to be a renunciation of our role in that communal mystery, however misguided that role might be. This is what's so terrifying when contemporary physicists tell us we are most likely simulants living inside a simulation, a holographic universe, because whatever this epistemic lacuna might be, whatever its elusive configurations might entail, its details cannot, we think, be realised by a humanly possible world in which our proxy gods are either aliens or just more technologically advanced versions of ourselves. A second, methodological, difficulty with this thought experiment, and indeed for all cases theorised off the back of imagined and perfected states (which I will discuss in the following section), is our fundamental inability to conceptualise a state that is both alien to us and desirable.

The problem with how you might extend beyond a state of perpetual intoxication involves the broader complexities of human imagination, its effectiveness and its inadequacies. If, as William

---

[23] Nozick, *Anarchy, State and Utopia*, 45.

Pessimism's Impossible Beyond

Burroughs claimed, "there isn't a feeling you can get on drugs that you can't get without drugs," the issue is how to tap this supposed resource without the relevant narcotic stimulus. Whether or not imagination is itself part of the problem, a symptom of our doleful human state, a release valve for a creature otherwise ill-equipped to confront its existence, there is no escaping the fact that were it a more reliable and potent mental facility we might at least be able to conceptualise a salvationist outside, an hallucinatory deliverance, some far-fetched yet emancipatory other. According to Ligotti, imagination is "a misbegotten hatchling of consciousness, a birth defect of our species," and that although it "is often revered as a sign of vigor in our make-up . . . it is really just a psychic overcompensation for our impotence as beings."[24] But yet again this is to value reality for its own sake, and to consider any attempt to subvert its debilitating truths as an unforgiveable weakness. And yet pessimism, whose single guiding principle concerns the maximal diminution of suffering, does not have the evaluative apparatus with which to establish such a position. The world offers no way out, and it was after all not us that "create[d] an environment uncongenial to our species [but] nature,"[25] so why then this dogged allegiance to the barbarous trap that imprisons us? If it were the case that confronting these truths would achieve the gradual reduction of the human race to zero, then this would make sense, but no pessimist actually believes this will ever happen: "We are captured by illusions and there is no way out."[26] The problem, then, is not our imaginative excesses, but rather our imaginative deficiencies. If, given the truths of pessimism, we could radically minimalise suffering through whatever means, what other stipulations are there to impede us on this course? Where is the rationale for staying true to some fixed notion of the real, when reality itself is thought to be of no positive value? The problem with pessimism, therefore, is not so much its negativity but its continuing and unjustifiable reverence for and deference to reality.

While the hidden is not only a staple of horror fiction—whether what is hidden is obscured by our unwillingness to see it, or our inability to comprehend what it is that's (only superficially) seen—but also of pessimism, which invariably expounds a situation, the truth

---

[24] Ligotti, *The Conspiracy Against the Human Race*, 218.
[25] Ligotti, *The Conspiracy Against the Human Race*, 79.
[26] Ligotti, *The Conspiracy Against the Human Race*, 137.

about our existence no less, too nightmarish to behold or fathom, it also provides an opportunity for our imagination to reinvent that which is beyond our senses and our intellect. The failure of our imaginations to so far take us beyond these horrors, although problematic in its own right, is also, more crucially, itself an ingenious mechanism of escape: the realised unrealisable, the untouchable beyond, the impossible possibility that becomes a refuge through its very illusiveness. A lacuna opens up and because we cannot touch it, cannot think it, cannot imagine it beyond its unimaginability, we also cannot taint it with our humanness. The ineptitude of our imagination therefore gifts us what its proficiency never could: a beyond. And although this beyond is unavoidably and emphatically apophatic and alien, we need to ask ourselves just what other kind of beyond there could be. The apophatic process is essentially the construction of a hole, a tunnel, an escape route: through a series of laborious negations a cavity is formed in the otherwise solid ground of our claustrophobic human existence, and we continue digging, removing the hard soil that keeps us trapped in what we know and know to be accursed and futile.

THE PROBLEM OF CONCEPTION

Echoing what was gleaned from Nozick's experiment, *Invasion of the Body Snatchers*[27] is not a placatory tale for the perennially disillusioned, but a horror story all the more effective for having drilled down into the pernicious paradox of our human predicament. The Pod People (perfectly content in their erased state) have what we want, and yet we do not want to become them; and this is because we do not want to be rid of our sufferings but want instead to have them mean something. The pessimist will tell you that suffering cannot be redeemed, that it is only ever negative and, what's more, inseparable from all human existence. What nobody can satisfactorily answer is how suffering might mean something, a narrative at the end of which it is justified. And this is not us running up against the limits of reality, but us running up against the limits of imagination.

---

[27] Don Siegel (dir.), *Invasion of the Body Snatchers* (Los Angeles, CA, and New York, NY: Allied Artists Pictures Corporation, 1956).

Pessimism's Impossible Beyond

There is an epistemological canker at the core of human existence, and unless we dissect it carefully we will never be rid of its debilitating effects. Recall H. P. Lovecraft's bleak expository overview from "The Call of Cthulhu," in which he claims that the progress of scientific knowledge will reach a stage of completeness that will either send us mad or have us scurrying with even more fervour for the relative serenity of ignorance. And yet the problem is not merely with scientific knowledge, or just with knowledge, but with our own speculative capacities. For it is not only the unlikelihood of the world revealing any appeasements to our sickened condition, but that we are unable to imagine what any such appeasements might be. It is not, then, simply a case of what is missing and never likely to arrive, but our complete failure of pre-emptive recognition. Our thinking in this regard is so impoverished that we cannot even conceptualise what we would need to know in order to be redeemed; it's not just that an exhaustive knowledge of the universe will terrify us even more than what we already know, but that we cannot imagine what we might come to know, regardless of how unlikely these truths might be, that would have the opposite effect.

Lovecraft also details, in "The Colour Out of Space,"[28] for instance, the second horn of this epistemological dilemma: in short, how it is that the unknown and unknowable haunts us with a force equal to those horrors that we would come to know if we knew the universe as it is. If knowledge provides no refuge, then neither it seems does our inexorable ignorance. And again the problem is not just our horror at not being able to conceptualise some feature of the world, for it to remain resistant to human intelligence, but that we fail to imagine how any such epistemic lacuna can be a source of anything other than terror.

However, an important distinction needs to be made between epistemic lacunae per se and the circumstances in which we are thrown into uncomfortable proximity with them, because it is only the latter that terrorise. The former, as indicated in the first horn of the dilemma, are in fact responsible for actualising the possibility of that impossible knowledge and thus a narrow egress through which the mind can evade epistemological horror. When asked what we will "dream of

---

[28] See H. P. Lovecraft, "The Colour Out of Space," in *The Call of Cthulhu and Other Weird Stories*, ed. S. T. Joshi (London and New York: Penguin Books), 170–199.

when everything becomes visible," Paul Virilio answered, echoing Lovecraft, "[w]e will dream of being blind."[29] And while it is easy to see this manoeuvre as essentially cowering and retrogressive, the blindness we might come to dream needn't be a blindness of apprehension and tenebrosity, but of creative vigour and preternatural refulgence.

That we deceive ourselves about our existence in order to maintain our sanity and some flimsy sense of wellbeing is for Zapffe a tragedy. We cannot face what we are and what will happen to us so we distract ourselves with false narratives that allow us to ignore the fact that we are slowly decaying and will one day soon perish altogether. And while this seems somewhat incontrovertible (I say "somewhat" for aren't we also those self-same *things* that constantly construct and exist inside those escapist narratives?), whether we regard it as a tragedy is not. Like Camus and Samuel Beckett, we might instead see it as some absurdist comedy. Or maybe, like Miguel de Unamuno and Joshua Foa Dienstag, we might accept the challenge of existing as a creative exercise. If we were of a more optimistic bent we might even regard these practices as the fledgling stage of something that will become increasingly edifying as we learn to manipulate and expand our abstractions in ever more elaborate and gratifying ways. Positing how it is we manage our thought processes in order to circumnavigate the full blown suffering of being alive, Ligotti details our predicament as follows: "If we must think, it should be done only in circles, outside of which lies the unthinkable."[30] And yet it is this "unthinkable" itself that can be characterised not only in the sense of the horror which we dare not gaze upon, but also as the paradisiacal conditions that we cannot create or imaginatively access. For it is not only the extremity of horror that we cannot think, but any possible escape from it. Unthinkability, then, is both the receptacle of some ultimate annihilating horror and the source of our possible escape from it.

We are, almost by definition, ignorant of the details of heaven (or any paradisiacal realm or state), for there is an indelible foreignness there that we cannot resolve; that is, we cannot accommodate it in our

---

[29] Louise Wilson and Paul Virilio, in Louise Wilson's interview (Wilson and Virilio 1994), "Cyberwar, God and Television: Interview with Paul Virilio," on CTheory.org, published 1 December 1994 (http://www.ctheory.net/articles .aspx?id=62).
[30] Ligotti, *The Conspiracy Against the Human Race*, 30.

conceptual frameworks and so make its foreignness otherwise familiar. It is not that our conceptions of paradise do not sufficiently console us because they are obviously fictitious, but because we cannot imagine them sufficiently well. And yet it is precisely because we cannot imagine paradise that it consoles us at all. It is this incompleteness that saves, because it saves without saving, leaves us lost and (in the absence of universal bliss) suffering, but leaves us nonetheless. In short, once the details of how any eternity in paradise might be spent are provided, they all too quickly start to resemble gilded hells and us Pod People. As Ligotti puts it:

> Once you had made it through this life to an afterlife of eternal bliss, you would have no use for that afterlife. Its job would be done, and all you would have is an afterlife of eternal bliss—a paradise for reverent hedonists and pious libertines. What is the use in that?[31]

However, the prima facie appeal of this observation aside, once again we see that same old requirement that something external to the paradisiacal state be there to justify the state, whereas if we were truly pessimists there should be no need for this condition to be met. Ligotti asks what use heaven would be as if usefulness were some prerequisite for the eradication of suffering, which it is not. Life is useless, this has been accepted as fact, but why should our transcending the suffering that life induces be any less useless? Why can we not envisage a positive state in which life becomes benignly useless (like art, for instance)? Ultimately, it is this very failure that ends up pitting the pessimist against him or herself.

We want the infinite life as long as we don't have to look at it. We want to survive in the details and be spared the boundedness and the boundlessness of those same details—details as from a detail of something larger that is itself left alone. As Kōbō Abe put it: "When I look at small things, I think I shall go on living: drops of rain, leather gloves shrunk by being wet. . . . When I look at something too big, I want to die: the Diet Building, or a map of the world."[32] Or Blaise Pascal: "The eternal silence of these infinite spaces fills me with

---

[31] Ligotti, *The Conspiracy Against the Human Race*, 77.
[32] Kōbō Abe, *The Box Man* (New York: Vintage Books, 1991).

dread."[33] But there is also the danger of looking too closely, beyond the microscopic, where even the details degrade and come apart, expand into that world inside our world in which we will once again find ourselves giddy and adrift. As correlate to the infinity of the large is the infinity of the small, with the world of just-about-sufferable details somewhere in the middle (that Aristotelean median). As Zapffe and other prominent pessimists have iterated many times, it is consciousness itself that is the problem, and our survival relies on our facility for restricting (or at least manipulating) its contents. Although, quite obviously, without consciousness there would be no issue in the first place: no self-consciousness, no suffering, no need or capacity to have a view on existence one way or the other.

IMAGINING THE IMPOSSIBLE: THE ART OF PESSIMISM

Though we might, by force of reason, conclude that free will and selves are nothing but illusions, and that one's existence and existence in general is incontrovertibly useless and without meaning, it almost invariably proves impossible to implement these ideas. I cannot, through rational thought alone, *feel* what it is for determinism to be true, or what it is like to exist as anything other than me, or experience a world utterly devoid of meaning. I might experience approximations of these things, but they are fleeting and inchoate at best. (Although, it's not clear that in the case of selves this inescapable feeling that you are such a thing isn't itself what it is to be/have one, and that maybe instead of attempting to eradicate this self or sense of self as a means of liberation, as Buddhism teaches, we could instead follow a technique of proliferation—in the mode of Fernando Pessoa—to the same ends: "I can imagine I'm everything, because I'm nothing.")[34]

That we are able to sublimate our terror of existence by reprocessing it as various forms of art and literature—as comedy, as media, as video games—and so entertain ourselves, even with the very worst aspects of human life, displays an ingenuity and flair for invention that we have no good reason to think is exhausted by the

---

[33] Blaise Pascal, *Pensées* (London: Penguin Books, 1995), 66.
[34] Fernando Pessoa, *The Book of Disquiet*, trans. Richard Zenith (London: Penguin, 2002), 154.

products so far realised. That we so often choose to exist in fabricated worlds, that either because of their being safely removed from the realities they depict, or else being idealised versions of those worlds, manage to deliver us from less favourable realities, is not unequivocally a source of disgust or lamentation—although the overly generic nature of a vast majority of such creative distractions might well be. Given this, when asked to provide a description of the human, what is stopping us from saying something like the following: *A creature that finds its unfiltered conscious existence on planet Earth to be disagreeable, and so exists instead in a plethora of self-fabricated realities which it finds more amenable to its tastes.* In other words, why all this concentration on the importance of a reality that we successfully usurp at every available opportunity? It is like berating the man who has successfully built a house on stilts above a festering and putrid swamp, who from his terrace can observe (and even enjoy) the swamp, while no longer suffering its noxious substances, for refusing to continue to live inside it. And that his stilted residence will inevitably collapse back into the swamp is in itself no reason to precipitate that collapse. After all, what's the justification for this prescriptive stance when it comes to confronting reality head-on, when the notion that such a stance has any deeper meaning has already been dispensed with? With this in mind, maybe the optimists aren't fanciful dreamers at all; maybe they are the genuine realists. And to continue along this admittedly contentious line of thought, perhaps they know that pessimism is incontrovertible, but seeing the paradox of its dead end (nowhere to go but impossible to stop) they instead embrace the reality of distraction. And maybe this too is at the heart of their call for the pessimist to somehow just get over it, that accepting a fate that you have no choice but to accept, and doing what you can to minimise suffering, is the only rational and considered approach.

There is also a problematic assumption made by pessimists (present in the works of Carlo Michelstaedter, Zapffe, Ligotti, and others) that it is only through limiting our conscious experience that we evade the reality we cannot face, when this seems a misrepresentation of what is actually going on. For it seems evident that what the pessimist disapproves of is a diversionary expansion of our conscious experience rather than a diversionary narrowing of it. We experience worlds that don't exist as a solution to this world. And so while it is clearly true that humans restrict the content of their thoughts, refusing to contemplate any number of distressing subjects, it is equally patent that those distressing subjects are eluded just as effectively by expanding our conscious experiences beyond the rather restricted arenas of our unmediated day-to-day lives. The ways in which we evade the world are (at least) in equal parts constriction *and* expansion.

The problem, after all, is not just that suffering exists but that it is pointless, utterly useless, as is life (the two being virtually indistinguishable). With this as our underpinning, why not embrace that uselessness and transcend purpose altogether? Thus the true answer to pessimism is not (and never was) optimism, but instead a thoroughgoing pessimism (an exalted nihilism, if you will), the best answer to pessimism being to truly accept pessimism's conclusions, to be truly pessimistic. For only then can we neutralise the vestiges of our spurious hopes and self-deceptions, and instead realise our very human stake in the impossible.

In *Too Loud a Solitude*, Bohumil Hrabal's alcoholic wastepaper compacter, Haňt'a, is in many ways a reimagining of the trial of Sisyphus. Time and again he fills the machine and presses the red and green buttons, and yet somehow he finds diversions, difference where he might only see tedium and sameness. From the opening line we see that from this drudgery he has created a comprehensive and deeply idiosyncratic haven: "For thirty-five years now I've been in wastepaper, and it's my love story."[35] (And as we will see, as Pessoa will show us [Chapter 3], there is no better theoretical facilitator for a post-pessimistic egress than love.) For while the fact that Haňt'a spends his waking hours inebriated is not to be ignored, neither is the rich internal world of ideas and literary landscapes into which he escapes every day. And despite the fact that by the end of the book, reality, in the form of socialist "progress," with its new, more efficient compacting machine and bales of "inhumanly" clean, white, wordless paper, arrives to destroy the palimpsestic sanctuary of his workplace, Haňt'a still refuses to succumb to the vagaries of other men, to reduce (to compact) the immensity of his meticulously invented world in order to accommodate this change of circumstance. His isolation over the years has become indistinguishable from his freedom, indistinguishable from the boundlessness of his imaginative experiences; he has, as he puts it, occupied a "heavily populated solitude, a harum-scarum of infinity and

---

[35] Bohumil Hrabal, *Too Loud a Solitude*, trans. Michael Henry Heim (London: Abacus, 1993), 1.

Pessimism's Impossible Beyond

eternity, and Infinity and Eternity seem to take a liking to the likes of [him]."[36] To claim that Haňt'a is not confronting the reality of his situation is to miss the point, and neither is it altogether accurate: it misses the point because his regimen of bibliophilic dreamscapes *is* his experiential reality; and is inaccurate because he knows exactly what he is doing, and knows all too well the place his thoughts are transcending. In other words, he knows what is at stake. So much so that in the concluding pages he opts to emulate other likeminded literary suicides, and sacrifices his terrestrial biological life for the sake of the dream he's created, to enter his beloved compactor and submit once and for all to its overwhelming and transformative force:

> Instead of compacting clean paper in the Melantrich cellar I will follow Seneca, I will follow Socrates, and here, in my press, in my cellar, choose my own fall, which is ascension, and even as the walls press my legs up to my chin and beyond, I refuse to be driven from my Paradise.[37]

The point, then, is not that Haňt'a isn't deploying various methods to make his life more bearable, but that he is doing so self-consciously. He is not some deluded drone sucking up the tawdry and easily digestible morsels of the world around him in blind allegiance to some prescribed set of escapist norms, but is instead forging an alternative consciousness through which the world and its palliative offerings are emphatically rejected in favour of a bizarre assemblage of his own making. To take Zapffe's four points in turn: his *isolation* while defensive is also combative; his *anchorings* are not the fatuous givens of state or church or morality etc., but a collage of astute and often scathing human responses to such institutions; and while he *distracts* himself with trivialities, as anyone who does anything must, he does so in a way that does not shirk the horror of existence but constructs something else from it. However, when it comes to *sublimation*, the final symptom, he does indeed appear to fall prey; for his confrontations with the true awfulness of existence are by no means as pure and unequivocal as they might be, his obsession with elaborate baling practices a mere pastiche of the cold, hard stare of the exemplary pessimist. But, as already noted, the supposed virtue of this ascetic act

---

[36] Hrabal, *Too Loud a Solitude*, 9.
[37] Hrabal, *Too Loud a Solitude*, 97.

of perspectival endurance is out of kilter with an enlightened pessimism that not only must acknowledge the inhuman task of this inert gaze, but also the untenably prescriptive precedent it sets for a theory whose only substantive goal is the practical diminishment of suffering.

In line with Schopenhauer, who thought life "an unprofitable episode, disturbing the blessed calm of non-existence,"[38] Ligotti argues that we should replace the word "worthless" with "useless" when explaining pessimism, so as to concentrate our minds on the real scourge of existence, for only by doing this can we set aside issues of relative value and desirability, and so emphatically conclude that "any kind of existence is useless."[39] And it is precisely a failure to realise this that is so distasteful and wrongheaded about thinkers, like Dienstag[40] and Nietzsche before him, who are determined to find pessimism useful, to redeem it in the eyes of the world, to put its clarities and its tenacious rigour to good use—the ultimate affront.

If anything, pessimism is a branch of art not philosophy (or politics). According to Schopenhauer, art provides us with a fleeting respite from the tortuous carousel of desire, frustration and transient satisfaction. This is possible because aesthetic experience is abstracted from the world of representation, the world of petty satiation and suffering, and is thus divested of will, if only temporarily, and as a consequence disinterested, objective and true. Art in this sense is a means to circumvent the illusions of worldly interest that otherwise obscure the truth. Here Schopenhauer puts art to work in the service of pessimism, whereas what I'm contesting is that they have in certain key respects become the same thing: both useless, both posturing, both autophagic to the point of vanishing altogether.

---

[38] Arthur Schopenhauer, "On the Sufferings of the World," in *Complete Essays of Schopenhauer*, trans. T. Bailey Saunders (New York: Willey Book Company, 1942), 4.
[39] Ligotti, *The Conspiracy Against the Human Race*, 77.
[40] See Joshua Foa Dienstag, *Pessimism, Ethic, Spirit* (New Jersey: Princeton University Press, 2006).

Pessimism's Impossible Beyond

POST-PESSIMISM: PESSOA, LISPECTOR AND THINKING-FEELING

Nietzsche's response to pessimism is nuanced and conflicted, for while he ostensibly accepts the metaphysical reality of pessimism, he nevertheless refuses to follow the litany of negations all the way down, instead advocating a proactive regimen of artistic affirmation. This approach can be seen in *The Birth of Tragedy*, in which he argues that the perfect alignment of the Dionysiac and Appoline worldviews can through the medium of tragedy transmute the otherwise enervating effects of pessimism into something that, while not blandly optimistic, is nonetheless more life-affirming and robust. Nietzsche claims tragedy provides a vicarious proximity to the underlying horror of existence, and that coming out the other side, for the performers and audience alike, invigorates and enhances those individuals that are up to the task. On the face of it, this stance is no longer recognisably pessimistic, but rather a watered down variation of pessimism that blatantly shirks its most uncomfortable and destructive implications. Indeed, this affirmation of the negative looks like little more than philosophical posturing, "a sadomasochistic joyride."[41] As counterpoint to what he sees as Schopenhauer's pessimism of weakness, Nietzsche asks:

> Is there a pessimism of strength? An intellectual preference for the hard, gruesome, malevolent and problematic aspects of existence which comes from a feeling of well-being, from overflowing health, from an abundance of existence? Is there perhaps such a thing as suffering from superabundance itself? Is there a tempting bravery in the sharpest eye which demands the terrifying as its foe, as a worthy foe against which it can test its strength and from which it intends to learn the meaning of fear?[42]

The appealing rhetorical zeal of such passages aside, given what we know of the human propensity to evade the annihilating truths of pessimism at all costs, Nietzsche's pessimism of strength suspiciously resembles nothing more than a cleverly disguised pessimism of weakness. When Nietzsche talks of the "higher men" or *übermenschen*,

---

[41] Ligotti, *The Conspiracy Against the Human Race*, 120.
[42] Nietzsche, *The Birth of Tragedy And Other Writings*, 4.

who instead of trying to eradicate pain put it to use, we once again see someone determined to find utility in what is essentially useless. For although his observations on how suffering has in "lower men" (the *maggot men*) given rise to many institutionalised manifestations of madness, from morality to church to state, and how "too long the earth has been a madhouse,"[43] claims that are themselves perfectly in keeping with a pessimistic outlook, his proposed solution, whereby suffering is employed in the service of cultivating human excellence at the expense of mere happiness (those squirming and guileless capitulations that seek pleasure as the remedy of pain), while conceding the integrality of suffering, nevertheless still seeks to mitigate pessimism's effects through a revaluation of values: "I doubt that such pain makes us 'better'—but I know it makes us *deeper*,"[44] or more profound. The question here is whether instead of favouring aesthetics over ethics, as Nietzsche does, we can't instead unite them, and in doing so have our elaborate and lucid escapes *from* pain, and not the pain itself, achieve those selfsame depths and profundities.

Because Pessoa, it's fair to imagine, took some small solace from his coterie of persons (his heteronyms), shoring them up somehow against the void of himself, it comes as no surprise when he voices concern over the destructive impact of genuine physical danger, outside of one's everyday suffering: "I abhor running real risks, but it's not because I'm afraid of feeling too intensely. It's because they break my perfect focus on my sensations, and this disturbs and depersonalizes me."[45] Like Nietzsche, Pessoa recognised the essentially fabricated nature of persons, and yet rather than pursue some sustained attempt to further destabilise them in the vain hope of achieving their eradication, or focus his attentions on the unity of a single character as we see with Nietzsche, he chose instead to engage in their proliferation, to test the limits of many persons at once, to play a lifelong aesthetic game with the very concept of personhood. Pessoa goes beyond Nietzsche, and in many respects represents the next stage of his post-pessimistic project, his propagation of characters

---

[43] Friedrich Nietzsche, *On the Genealogy of Morals and Ecce Homo*, trans. Walter Kaufmann (New York: Vintage, 1969), 93.
[44] Friedrich Nietzsche, *The Gay Science*, trans. Josefine Nauckhoff and Adrian del Caro (Cambridge: Cambridge University Press, 2001), 6–7, original emphasis.
[45] Pessoa, *The Book of Disquiet*, 73.

Pessimism's Impossible Beyond

reinforcing their status as abstracta while at the same time further aestheticising their reality as creative individuals; for Pessoa's characters are not only literary in construction, but literary in the sense that they themselves generate literature. He diversifies the plethora of connections and continuities that go to make up a single person, to reveal on the one hand the malleability and unrestricted nature of these relations, and on the other the unutterable abyss behind each person thus formed.

If the self is a dream that has progressively begun to resemble a nightmare, it is one that we cannot wake from, for to what would the "we" that wakes refer? Nothing wakes from the nightmare, and yet still there is this postulated waking, this solution of vacated consciousness that itself amounts to the eradication of that for which we sought a cure. Although the post-pessimist tends to eschew this abdication of their person or persons, it is not through some naïve belief in their importance, some desperate attachment to their stabilising reality, but because as realists they have looked and found no way out that is not a debilitating lack destined to be filled once more, and so instead decide to perform the curse of themselves as they themselves have been performed. In line with this, we might even think of Pessoa's heteronyms as perfected persons, or in other words the idea of persons, persons no longer desecrated by the foul ignominy of having to exist: "The one who committed beautiful, lavish, fruitful crimes was our dream of Borgia, the idea we have of Borgia. I'm certain that the Cesare Borgia who existed was banal and stupid. He must have been, because to exist is always stupid and banal."[46] This is not to say that they are any less persons than you or me, for we too are no more than the idea of ourselves, but only that no additional suffering is incurred through their production.

Nietzsche's primary motivation with his repurposing of pessimism (from an ethical theory concerned only with the elimination of suffering to an aesthetic theory concerned only with redeeming the human experience) is to prevent pessimism from cascading into nihilism, a refuge of the powerless, the pathetic, the unhealthy miserabilists he so despised. Even his notion of Eternal Recurrence can be interpreted as little more than testing ground for his higher men, for only they are able to gladly welcome this doctrine, to truly qualify as *yes-sayers*, they who can be as positive about their sorrow as

---

[46] Pessoa, *The Book of Disquiet*, 395.

they can their joy. But, in one important respect, his attempt to move beyond pessimism is scarcely different from those moralists about whom he is so scathing and critical, engaging as it does in that same "'endless struggle' to think well of ourselves."[47]

According to Ligotti, although the hero of futility may appear importantly distinct from the average self-deceiving dupe, the difference is strictly trivial: "[B]oth are spoiling for survival in a MALIGNANTLY USELESS world. And survival is for the pigs."[48] However, it is not survival that Nietzsche is primarily concerned with here but style. And although survival is patently a necessary prerequisite to establishing this style, without which his idealised persons, those coherent and self-created individuals, couldn't possibly exist, survival is no more than a backdrop for this exercise in extra-literary character building.[49] It is not that Nietzsche values survival (or indeed the associated malignancies of reproduction or pleasure), but rather that we should aspire to more than mere survival, that life if it must be anything should be an exercise in style, in vigorous aesthetic abundance. The main problem with Nietzsche's reformulated pessimism is its refusal to embrace nihilism, for only once you have ceded ground to the manifest uselessness of human existence can you then begin to play in good faith. The recreation of life-as-art or some self-governed imaginative episode should take place only in the context of an objective devaluation of human existence, rather than some strained and desperate revaluation. As Pessoa states:

> The useless is beautiful because it's less real than the useful, which continues and extends, whereas the marvellously futile and the gloriously miniscule stay where and as they are, living freely and independently. The useless and the futile open up humbly aesthetic interludes in our real lives.[50]

To live is to live in denial. There's no way round it. That you are decaying and will one day die, that you will suffer your future as you've

---

[47] Philippa Foot, "Nietzsche's Immoralism," in *Nietzsche, Genealogy, Morality* (California: University of California Press, 1994), 11.
[48] Ligotti, *The Conspiracy Against the Human Race*, 181.
[49] See Alexander Nehamas, *Nietzsche: Life as Literature* (Massachusetts: Harvard University Press, 1985).
[50] Pessoa, *The Book of Disquiet*, 436.

suffered your past, that nothing you have done or will do or can do will ever alter the course of this hopeless and futile episode are things you know without actually knowing them: "[C]ourage isn't being alive, knowing that you're alive is courage."[51] This knowing that nevertheless fails (or refuses) to know is what it means to think without feeling, to separate the two and so never experience the explicit elucidations of their combination. This *feeling-thinking* or *thinking-feeling* is a perspectival state that runs through the work of both Pessoa and Lispector, each not only making repeatedly clear that the one without the other is inadequate, but also that this inadequacy represents a genuine impoverishment for the individual in question, who while managing to evade the combined burden of thought-feeling will consequently reap none of its reward. For example, Pessoa argues that "[w]e all know that we die; we all feel that we won't die," and it is only the "visceral logic"[52] of the two combined, the thought-feeling, that makes us truly confront the essential paradoxes of our existence. If this were the extent of what can be achieved through thinking-feeling, we might well think that we were better off without such an amalgamation, that each kept in isolation from the other would diminish the suffering sustained by really knowing and thereby really feeling the horror of our predicament. However, both Pessoa and Lispector go on to utilise this state as a kind of medicament for that very angst, claiming that it opens up the imaginary and with it new realities that through their obscurity offer clarity on what an interior life that escapes itself might become.

The importance of felt-thought, especially its ability to wake us from the dream of life, if only momentarily, is by no means exclusive to Pessoa and Lispector—although they ought to be credited with both making the combination explicit and scrupulously exploring just where it might take us once its initial shock has been absorbed—and a clear example of it can be found at the heart of Sartrean existentialism, for example in the "nausea" of Antoine Roquentin, as the filters of meaning fall away while sat in a municipal park looking at the root of a chestnut tree:

> I no longer remembered that it was a root. Words had disappeared, and with them the meanings of things, the methods

---

[51] Clarice Lispector, *The Passion According to G.H.*, trans. Idra Novey (London: Penguin Books, 2014), 16.
[52] Pessoa, *The Book of Disquiet*, 388.

of using them, the feeble landmarks which men have traced on their surface. . . . It took my breath away. Never, until these last few days, had I suspected what it meant to "exist"; . . . usually existence hides itself. It is there, around us, in us, it is *us*, you can't say a couple of words without speaking of it, but finally you can't touch it. . . . It had lost its harmless appearance as an abstract category: it was the very stuff of things, that root was steeped in existence. Or rather the root, the park gates, the bench, the sparse grass on the lawn, all that had vanished; the diversity of things, their individuality, was only an appearance, a veneer. This veneer had melted, leaving soft, monstrous masses, in disorder—naked, with a frightening, obscene nakedness.[53]

In Heideggerian terms, the objects around him are suddenly stripped of their "readiness-to-hand," their assumed contextual utility, and instead are there, like Descartes' ball of wax, resting in his palm "present-at-hand" during his Second Meditation, available to speculative examination but devoid of human setting and all associated practical application: "[T]ake away everything which does not belong to the wax, and see what is left: merely something extended, flexible and changeable."[54] However, unlike Descartes' detached, contemplative perspective (uniting intellect and sensory perception), the experience Pessoa, Lispector, Roquentin and others describe is both abstract *and* visceral, something felt to their core as a threat, an unanswerable challenge, a theoretical skewer. Unless the thinking is blended with feeling in this way nothing happens outside of the observations themselves, outside of the recognition that we can intellectually dissect objects in ways that momentarily divest them of human consequence before we then go back to seeing them as they were before. But when that intellection is felt, and what's more felt as something itself hostile in its indifference to our very existence, then it is that much harder to slip back inside the world-as-it-is-for-you and prioritise that immersive validity over the other. In fact, without this mutual immersion (of

---

[53] Jean-Paul Sartre, *Nausea*, trans. Robert Baldick (London: Penguin Books, 1965), 182–183, original emphasis.
[54] Descartes, *The Philosophical Writings of Descartes Vol II*, trans. John Cottingham, Robert Stoothoff, and Dugald Murdoch (Cambridge: Cambridge University Press, 1994), 20.

human and world) our very sense of ourselves is put into question, as Pessoa puts it: "To be lucid is to be out of sorts with oneself."[55]

Whether or not such thought-felt experiences reinforce an existing proclivity towards pessimism, or whether they in part establish that outlook, is unclear—and while pessimism is by no means coextensive with depression (although the two are not unrelated and often conflate in telling ways), it is worth noting that depressives often report experiencing the world around them on similar terms—but what is evident, in the writings of Pessoa and Lispector, is that for all their abundant poetic renderings of emancipatory dream-states (albeit states that are nebulous, frustrating and inconclusive), they clearly emanate from a substratum of profound and almost[56] unambiguous pessimism. Here, by means of illustration, is first Pessoa then Lispector:

> To live strikes me as a metaphysical mistake of matter, a dereliction of inaction. I refuse to look at the day to find out what it can offer that might distract me and that, being recorded here in writing, might cover up the empty cup of my not wanting myself.[57]

> Ah if I had known I wouldn't have been born. Madness borders the cruellest good sense.... I swallow the madness that is no madness—it's something else. Do you understand me? But I'll

---

[55] Pessoa, *The Book of Disquiet*, 429.

[56] I include this qualification because Pessoa states emphatically that he is not a pessimist, asserting it four times in *The Book of Disquiet*. This somewhat curious disavowal emanates from his refusal to speak for others, to build systems based solely on his own experience—a deplorable habit that he considers a mere "primary stage of suffering" (Pessoa, *The Book of Disquiet*, 341). He will not allow himself the indulgence of shaping the world in his image, to make from it a home where everyone is similarly afflicted. Unwilling to say more than he knows, he chooses to remain alone in his suffering, and thereby enhance it. However, aside from this refusal to generalise, his writings are often undeniably pessimistic, and it is only his epistemological reserve and his investment in his own unique strain of sadness (the record of which will usurp "*Alone* as the saddest book in Portugal") that prevent him from extending the horror beyond the confines of his own life.

[57] Pessoa, *The Book of Disquiet*, 96.

have to stop because I'm so and so tired that only dying would release me from this fatigue.[58]

Whatever may be concluded about the success or otherwise of their proposed solution to human life, it is beyond contention that they originate in a probing and gimlet-eyed view of just what it means to be alive, and not in some purely theoretical abstraction or indeed some delusional, sanguine haze.[59]

Pessoa writes: "Hush and, unless it's to think, don't feel."[60] And, as if in in direct response, Lispector stipulates that "thought needs to be a feeling."[61] In both their bodies of work, the state of thought-feeling develops more distinctly into a thinking that feels almost to the detriment of thinking, with the emphasis on the felt taking precedence as the credibility of this state being readily recognisable as thought becomes harder to establish. According to Lispector, the "imaginary doesn't happen through actions but through the feeling-thinking that is actually a dream."[62] And in order to leave the dream intact it is necessary that we feel our way through the thoughts it induces as opposed to thinking our way through them—and so distancing ourselves from it. Thought, then, is not eradicated through this process, but brought closer to us as it is gradually integrated into our internal sensibilities. As she puts it: "The oblique life is very intimate. I shall say no more about this intimacy so as not to harm thinking-

---

[58] Clarice Lispector, *Água Viva*, trans. Stefan Tobler (London: Penguin Books, 2014), 76.

[59] Also, apropos of the connection that exists between thinking-feeling and pessimism and to what extent it can be established, it is important to be aware that Ligotti's account of the uncanny, which constitutes an integral part of his explication of pessimism, is completely indistinguishable from the experience so far associated with visceral abstraction. For example, about how the uncanny can enter our lives in any number of pedestrian ways, he has this to say: "One day those shoes on the floor of your clothes closet may attract your eye in a way they never have before. Somehow they become abstracted from your world, appearances you can't place, lumps of matter without a fixed quality or meaning" (Ligotti, *The Conspiracy Against the Human Race*, 86).

[60] Fernando Pessoa, "Glosses," in *A Little Less Than the Entire Universe: Selected Poems*, trans. Richard Zenith (London: Penguin Books, 2006), 301.

[61] Clarice Lispector, *A Breath of Life*, trans. Johnny Lorenz (London: Penguin Books, 2014), 74.

[62] Lispector, *A Breath of Life*, 67.

feeling with dry words. To leave the obliqueness in its own uninhabited independence."[63] Thus, while thinking-feeling simpliciter is thought to give us a truer sense of knowing, a knowing that is also felt, a visceral recognition, this appears to want to occupy some penumbral area in which we might avoid the destructive elements of knowing, while at the same time not falling prey to a state in which we cannot recognise ourselves as thinking beings, for "to know is to kill, in happiness as in everything else. Not to know, on the other hand, is not to exist."[64]

At the final stage of this process, language and thought break down altogether: "I'm stealthily entering into contact with a reality that is new to me and still doesn't have corresponding thoughts, and much less any word that signifies it. It's more of a feeling beyond thought."[65] All that remains is feeling, but a feeling transformed, a feeling now unrecognisable to our faculties of thought and language, a feeling without a feeler, some anomalous intimacy. In the end, it seems, there is no escape without escaping ourselves. And wary as we ought to remain of any proposed transcendence into uncharted realities, we should not mistake this intellectual delirium for Lispector's character somehow thinking-feeling the possible meaningfulness of existence, but rather as someone thinking-feeling the possible meaningfulness of our (as yet impossible) subversion of that state.

The trajectory through pessimism to post-pessimism (however that latter state is portrayed) consistently involves someone going through an agonising and disturbing (and it is always gruelling in this way) confrontation with and subsequent acceptance of some undistorted reality that they then cultivate embellishments in order to overcome, to exist in spite of, or to otherwise transform, thereby neutralising (to some degree) its negative impact. The decision whether to move through or beyond, to retreat to the standardised illusions, or else stay put and endure the raw, unclad spectacle of your existence (that nauseating existential overtness), remains equivocal, barely a decision, more a reaction to a prolonged state of indecision in fact—more a patient waiting for that inevitable moment when the oscillations finally break their medium. As Lispector herself vacillated, "the naked thing is

---

[63] Lispector, *Água Viva*, 62.
[64] Pessoa, *The Book of Disquiet*, 336.
[65] Lispector, *Água Viva*, 61.

so tedious. / Ah, so that was why I had always had a kind of love for tedium. And a continual hatred of it."[66]

While, *pace* Camus,[67] there is no post-nihilistic phase, no breach inside nihilism from which to establish some beyond of nihilism (at least no beyond that has not first passed through pessimism), the phenomenon of suffering and its desired eradication offers just such a lacuna for a pessimistic beyond, a post-pessimism. For although suffering itself offers no redemptive meaning, the ethical position that it be eliminated itself becomes meaning's last stand: a pessimism of genuine indifference, an enlightened junkiedom, the dreamscape of the perpetually impossible. For Pessoa, the one path left is clear: "To create at least a new pessimism, a new negativity, so that we can have the illusion that something of us—albeit something bad—will remain!"[68] And this remainder will be "something bad" because pessimism has not been undone, the "new negativity" has not erased the old negativity, post-pessimistic life is not suddenly worth living. All that will have happened is that, as Pessoa points out, *something of us* will persist, something quintessentially us, and so something absurd, ridiculous, human and bad, but, the claim goes, it will at least be *us*, at least *that*. But us as opposed to what, we might ask. And, of course, the answer has been given already: either the timorous creature in denial of its own nature, or else that same creature no longer in denial but completely stymied as to where to go from there, and so ineffectual in its misery. It is the wakeful dreamer who continues at the expense of both the delusional weakling, who lives in denial of pessimism, and the enlightened weakling, who though he accepts pessimism nevertheless for the most part persists with the old delusions for want of anything to replace them. The post-pessimist has no more need for delusions, for they have been replaced with self-conscious dreams, with lucid illusions, with impossible escapes; and their state is not a deluded one, for the simple reason that while they might indulge in subverted realities they do not believe in them, or more precisely believe in them only as dreams, as illusions, as impossibilities.

---

[66] Lispector, *The Passion According to G.H.*, 147.
[67] In the preface to *The Myth of Sisyphus*, Camus writes: "[T]his book declares that even within the limits of nihilism it is possible to find the means to proceed beyond nihilism," in Albert Camus, *The Myth of Sisyphus*, trans. Justin O'Brien (New York: Vintage Books, 2018), 6.
[68] Pessoa, *The Book of Disquiet*, 388.

Pessimism's Impossible Beyond

Although the pessimist should feel under no pressure to expedite their own death, as already discussed, there is an argument for why pessimistic thinking should emphatically embrace the thinking of death, for why their mode of thought should emulate the very open-endedness of his inevitable expiration. As Maurice Blanchot explains in *The Writing of the Disaster*:

> Dying to no end: thus (through this movement of immobility) would thought fall outside all teleology and perhaps outside its site. To think endlessly, the way one dies—this is the thinking that patience in its innocent perseverance seems to impose. And this endlessness implies not gratuity but responsibility. Whence the repeated, motionless step of the speechless unknown, there at our door, on the threshold.
>
> To think the way one dies: without purpose, without power, without unity, and precisely without "the way." Whence the effacement of this formulation as soon as it is thought—as soon as it is thought, that is, both on the side of thinking and of dying, in dis-equilibrium, in an excess of meaning and in excess of meaning. No sooner is it thought than it has departed; it is gone, outside.[69]

In a post-pessimistic condition there are no more conclusions, no more resolutions, no more principal objectives, no more revered constraints: the conclusions are behind us (as pessimism), and we carry on only in the sparkling fog of the endlessly indeterminate, the unresolved panoramas of a perspective that shouldn't be but is, a directionless direction, wandering for the sake of wandering, arriving nowhere, leaving nowhere, suffering only our less than complete indifference to the old, now defunct, possibilities of suffering, suffering only the impossibility of impossibility. Also, it is worth paying particular attention to how thinking-dying (like thinking-feeling) is bombarded by a glut of meaning at the same time as being beyond its scope, outside its false prosperity, its hyperinflation, its worthless promise.

When you imagine the idyll, the impossibility of the place is the place. When you build the escape tunnel, the tunnel *is* the escape: a tunnel's exit nullifies the possibility of exodus, so all there is in the end

---

[69] Maurice Blanchot, *The Writing of the Disaster*, trans. Ann Smock (Lincoln: University of Nebraska Press, 1995), 39.

is the warren and the impossibility of a way out that is not the way out of impossibility, that is not the endless branching of the tunnel itself. And if post-pessimism on this model is absurd, so be it. Absurdity is what's left. Absurdity is sense becoming senseless. "Absurdity is divine."[70] (But terrestrially divine, like Dostoyevsky's Kirilov committing suicide in order to become God.)[71] The route through suffering and beyond is routeless and unrooted, as any joy not so fleeting so as to go unrecognised must be. To go beyond suffering is always to become absurd; after all, what is more absurd than a joyful life? There is no other way, no course between them, for as Camus observed: "Happiness and the absurd are two sons of the same earth. They are inseparable."[72]

It is not life, therefore, that is absurd, despite all supposed evidence to the contrary, but our flight from life while still inside it; which is not, however, something to lament or take action to correct, but something to own as uniquely human, which though still worthless is at least a curiosity we might exploit in good faith: "[A]bsurdity is one of the most human things about us; a manifestation of our most advanced and interesting characteristics."[73] Although the optimum state of affairs remains never to have been born, for those denied this possibility there is, by way of (not quite) the next best thing, a life devoid of living, a life dreamt under the noumenal auspices of the impossibility of that very dream:

> Living isn't worth our while. Only seeing is. To be able to see without living would bring happiness, but this is impossible, like virtually everything we dream. How great would be the ecstasy that didn't include life![74]

Further to this, and as if to augment his claims for thinking-feeling, Pessoa writes: "To live is to not think."[75] And from this we get the

---

[70] Pessoa, *The Book of Disquiet*, 27.
[71] See Fyodor Dostoyevsky, *The Devils*, trans. David Magarshack (London: Penguin Books, 1953).
[72] Camus, *The Myth of Sisyphus*, 121.
[73] Thomas Nagel, *Mortal Questions* (Cambridge: Cambridge University Press, 1996), 23.
[74] Pessoa, *The Book of Disquiet*, 388.
[75] Pessoa, *The Book of Disquiet*, 105.

corresponding claim: to think is to not live. But, the question arises, what way out does this leave, when to think is to suffer and to live is to avoid thinking only at the expense of living itself? To which the answer is already at hand, for is this not just another reason why thinking must be turned into something else, something more akin to feeling: a feeling incongruous with suffering and inseparable from the realisation that life ought to go unlived within the very impossibility of doing so, inside the thinking-death that survives, inside the dream of disappearing inside the absurd impossibility of dreaming such a dream.

In order to get a better fix on what's being proposed here, it is worth considering these words from E. M. Cioran: "There's no salvation without the immediate. But man is a being who no longer knows the immediate. He is an indirect animal."[76] And yet there is a solution to this apparent stalemate, and it is precisely the solution proposed here as post-pessimism; for in order to achieve that lost immediacy, that sense of the present routinely obfuscated by our projections into the past and into the future, and with it some semblance of salvation, it is with man's own essential indirectness that we must become intimate and coextensive. Only by embracing our diversionary strategies themselves as the timeless now of our experiential reality will we ever rescue ourselves from the temporal discomfort of our waiting to be saved.

Pessoa, as Soares, unaware it seems of the elucidations he will repeatedly provide, writes of how his beloved district "the Rua dos Douradores contains the meaning of everything and the answer to all riddles, except for the riddle of why riddles exist, which can never be answered."[77] And yet, as it stands, the riddle of why riddles exist is one of the few things that Pessoa does answer, and keeps on answering, performing his solution in innumerable interactions and phrasings. For the answer, in all its iterations, is that the existence of the riddle is all that remains of what we are. The riddle of why riddles exist is us.

---

[76] E. M. Cioran, *On the Heights of Despair*, trans. Ilinca Zarifopol-Johnston (Chicago: University of Chicago Press, 1996), 111.
[77] Pessoa, *The Book of Disquiet*, 19.

Chapter 1

On Cosmic Pessimism: Some Preliminary Comments and Aphorisms

Pessimism is the refusal to seek distraction, the refusal to remodel failure into a platform for further (doomed) possibilities, the refusal of comfort, the acceptance of the sickness of healthy bodies, the cup of life overflowing with cold vomit. If, as we see in *Invasion of the Body Snatchers*, humans prefer the anxieties of their familiar human lives to the contentment of an alien one, then the pessimist, we could argue, represents some perverted combination of the two, preferring (presuming there is a choice) the defamiliarisation of human life to the contentment of its unquestioned mundanity.

The quasi-religious state of mind that Wittgenstein would mention on occasion, that of "feeling *absolutely* safe,"[1] is a state the pessimist could only imagine being approximated by death, or perhaps some annihilative opiate-induced stupor. This Wittgensteinian comingling of certainty and faith looks every bit the futile gesture, a mere rephrasing of collapse or partial collapse. The only certainty open to the pessimist is that of the toxic formula of life itself—a formula known and lacuna-free. Certainty, far from being the gateway to deliverance, becomes the definitive impediment, while the possibility of salvation, as long as it remains, becomes crucially reliant on postulations of ignorance, epistemic gaps, a perennial incompleteness: "[T]he perfect safety of wooed death . . . the warm bath of physical dissolution, the universal unknown engulfing the miniscule unknown."[2]

---

[1] Ludwig Wittgenstein, "A Lecture on Ethics," *Philosophical Review*, vol. 74, no. 1 (January 1965), 8, original emphasis.
[2] Vladimir Nabokov, *Pale Fire* (New York: Vintage, 1989), 221.

On the Verge of Nothing

The height of Leibniz's Panglossian insanity nurtured the idea that our knowing everything—via the universal calculus—could be accurately described as a triumph, as opposed to a nightmare in which our every futility is laid bare. Stagnancy and boredom are perhaps two of the greatest ills of Western civilisation, and the most potent pessimism tells you that you're stuck with both. The most we can hope for, by way of salvation, is to throw open our despair to the unknown.

The fact that Schopenhauer's pessimism stopped short of morality and allowed him to play the flute, as Nietzsche complained, highlights the predicament of a man who despite having adorned nothingness with a smiling face still found himself alive. The demand here is that it be felt: a cross-contamination of intellect and emotion. The safety net of numerous parentheses makes for a failed philosophy, rather than a philosophy of failure.

Depressives make bad pessimists; for unless they choose to die, living will always infect them with necessities of hope, forcing them to find something, anything (all the various "as ifs") to make existence tolerable. As Cioran observed, while "[d]epressions pay attention to life, they are the eyes of the devil, poisoned arrows which wound mortally any zest and love of life. Without them we know little, but with them, we cannot live."[3] And even when cured of our depressions we'll find ourselves consumed, eaten alive by the hyper-clinical (borderline autistic) mania that replaces them: a predicament captured all too clearly in the microscriptual fictions of Robert Walser, where spectral men and women stifle their depressive madness with protective comas of detail, their failed assimilations buried beneath thick crusts of remote data. Like Beckett's Malone, their stories may have ended but cruelly their lives have not.

Pessimism is an extraneous burden (a purposeless weight) that makes everything else harder to carry, while at the same time scooping it out and making it lighter.

---

[3] E. M. Cioran, from *The Book of Delusions*, trans. Camelia Elias, in *Hyperion*, vol. v, issue 1 (May 2010), 75.

On Cosmic Pessimism

If pessimism had a sound it would be the harsh interior noise of tinnitus—the way that every person would hear themselves if they refused their distractions long enough to listen: a lungless scream from the extrasolar nothing of the self. The music of pessimism—if indeed we can imagine such a thing—is the reverberating echo of the world's last sound, conjectured but never heard, audible only in its being listened for. The one consolation of this hollow paradox of audibility being, that "he will be least afraid of becoming nothing in death who has recognized that he is already nothing now."[4] The pessimist suffers an unfiltered derangement of the real, a labyrinthitis at the nucleus of their being: always the stumbling ghost relentlessly surprised that others can see them.

If Cioran's refusal is manifested in sleep (when even saying "no" is too much of a commitment), then Pessoa's resides in the dreams inside that sleep. Pessoa chooses to exploit the fact that he's being "lived by some murmuring non-entity both shadowed and muddy"[5] by growing more voids to live him. His is a Gnostic breed of sleep, "sleeping as if the universe were a mistake,"[6] a sleep that dreams through Thacker's cosmic pessimism ("a pessimism of the world-without-us," "the unhuman orientation of deep space and deep time"[7]), through the critical error of there being anything at all when there could be nothing.

Pessimism is a paradox of age, being simultaneously young and old: its youth residing in a refusal to accept the authority of existence (its rich history, its inherent beneficence), a refusal to "get over" the horror of what it sees with its perpetually fresh eyes, and its maturity in the unceremonious disposal of the philosophical playthings (those futile architectures) of adolescence. As Thacker remarks: "Pessimism abjures all pretenses towards system—towards the purity of analysis and the dignity of critique."[8] A sentiment shared with Pessoa, who duly

---

[4] Arthur Schopenhauer, *The World as Will and Representation Vol. 2*, trans. E. F. J. Payne (New York: Dover Publications, 1969), 609.
[5] Eugene Thacker, "Cosmic Pessimism," *Continent* 2.2 (2012): 2.
[6] Pessoa, *The Book of Disquiet*, 35.
[7] Thacker, "Cosmic Pessimism," 3.
[8] Thacker, "Cosmic Pessimism," 8.

categorises those who choose to enact this futile struggle as being "in the primary stage of suffering."[9]

If the pessimist has shared a womb with anyone, it's with the mystic and not the philosopher. As Schopenhauer tells us: "The mystic is opposed to the philosopher by the fact that he begins from within, whereas the philosopher begins from without. . . . But nothing of this is communicable except the assertions that we have to accept on his word; consequently he is unable to convince."[10] The crucial difference between the mystic and the pessimist is not the latter's impassivity and defeatism, but his unwillingness/inability to contain in any way the spread of his voracious analyticity, his denial of incompleteness, his exhaustive devotion to failure.

The truth of our predicament, though heard, is destined to remain unprocessed. Like the revelations of B. S. Johnson's Haakon ("We rot and there's nothing that can stop it / Can't you feel the shaking horror of that?")[11] the pessimist's truths are somehow too obvious to listen to, as if something inside us were saying, "Of course, but haven't we found a way round that?"

Pessimism is simple and ugly, and has no desire and no incentive to make itself more complex or more attractive.

The true moral pessimist knows that the utilitarian's accounts will always be in the red. They can see that for all their computational containments, the only honest path is a negative one, and that such a path has but one logical destination: that of wholesale human oblivion.

Thacker notes how at the core of pessimism lies the notion of "the worst," through which death is demoted by the all-pervasive suffering of a life that easily eclipses its threat. And so with doom made preferable to gloom, death begins to glint with promise, "like beauty passing through a nightmare."[12] But even among pessimists suicide is,

---

[9] Pessoa, *The Book of Disquiet*, 341.
[10] Schopenhauer, *The World as Will and Representation Vol. 2*, 610–611.
[11] B. S. Johnson, "You're Human Like the Rest of Them," in Jonathan Coe, *Like a Fiery Elephant: the story of B. S. Johnson* (London: Picador, 2004), 177.
[12] Pessoa, *The Book of Disquiet*, 415.

for the most part, considered to be an error of judgement. Schopenhauer, for instance, regarded suicide a mistake grounded in some fundamentally naïve disappointment or other. Pessoa too thought suicide an onerous escape tactic: "To die is to become completely other. That's why suicide is a cowardice: it's to surrender ourselves completely to life."[13] There is a call here to be accepting of and creative with the puppetry of your being, an insistence that it's somehow a blunder to attempt to hide in death from the horrors you find in life.[14] Tied up with this perseverance is the slippery notion of the good death, for maybe, as Blanchot warns, suicide is rarely something we can hope to get right, for the simple reason that "you cannot make of death an object of the will."[15]

"Even in cases where the entire corpus of an author is pessimistic, the project always seems incomplete,"[16] and this is not simply because the project itself belies something yet to be disclosed, but because the project itself is a thing waiting. It waits on a cure it knows will not come, but for which it cannot do anything (as long as it continues to do anything) but wait.

Pessimism as an absolutist position is inherently romantic, something we relish only because we can never see it clearly enough. We sip it like a fine cognac, but we never finish the bottle. It makes connoisseurs of us, purveyors of shit and nothingness, of life's emptiness that as a taunt never quite empties: by his own admission, Cioran wrote the same book over and over again. Once the rot has been truly acknowledged, there are no other topics. Cioran realised this and lived up to its demands. The truths of depression are the only truths, the only challenge that remains is keeping hold of them. But given the open-ended complexities of our value systems, we are denied even the luxury of pessimism in its pure state—it has become intellectually incoherent, and emotionally unliveable. Such is the state of the truth.

---

[13] Pessoa, *The Book of Disquiet*, 199.
[14] "Suicide is, after all, the opposite of the poem" (Anne Sexton, *No Evil Star: Selected Essays, Interviews and Prose* [Ann Arbor: University of Michigan Press, 1985], 92).
[15] Maurice Blanchot, *The Space of Literature*, trans. Ann Smock (Lincoln: University of Nebraska Press, 1989), 105.
[16] Thacker, "Cosmic Pessimism," 10.

On the Verge of Nothing

The pessimist must do their best to hide the limits of what we can know, for like Kant, for whom moral and metaphysical transparency are necessarily denied to us (our reasoning transcendental not transcendent) in order that we not depose God, the mystery or incompleteness left by the pessimist's epistemic shortfalls will itself provide the very meaning they claim to have overcome, that is, meaning as the unexplained, or that which must remain untouched by the work of pessimism.

As David Hume noted, melancholy and incomprehensibility are the cornerstones of religion. The cornerstones of pessimism are melancholy and complete transparency. It is religion without the gaps, without space for hope to grow and fester.

We've been so busy thinking about what could save us from hell that we've neglected to consider what might save us from paradise.

Plutarch mourns birth and celebrates death. The pessimist celebrates only their own cleverness and resolve, as one who has seen through the dupe of meaningful existence. They mourn nothing but everybody else's gullibility.

Is the fact that we are decaying and will die an impetus to embrace life while we can, or an impetus to snarl and spit and vomit? The problem is not that the pessimist cannot engage in the former so ends up doing the latter, but that the former inevitably leads to the latter. For the pessimist has made the mistake of waking up, of seeing and smelling what it is we're clinging to.

The optimist will at most wake from a nightmare only once a day, but the pessimist must endure it at least twice in that time: once when they wake up and once again when they fall asleep. For if they have learnt anything at all, they have learnt that the nightmare does not go away just because they are momentarily distracted from it.

It is not the pessimist who is the friend of misery but the optimist. Schopenhauer asks, "who could bear even the mere thought of death, if life were a pleasure."[17] Can we answer with examples? Can we cite all those self-confessed lovers-of-life peacefully resigned to their own deaths? We could, but to be believed we would first have to be believed: we would have to be believed without having said anything, which is what this amounts to. We have a statement and its contradiction. Somewhere in the middle there is the same essential misery ingratiating itself with varying degrees of success. Whoever concedes the need for a conciliatory tone and yields to the misery trying to insinuate itself makes and maintains a friendship the same way everyone makes and maintains friends: in necessary ignorance of the befriended being's reality.

"The whole presents nothing but the idea of a blind nature, impregnated by a great vivifying principle, and pouring forth from her lap, without discernment or parental care, her maimed and abortive children."[18] This is why there are wonders of nature but not the wonder of nature. Although the pessimist acknowledges neither, for the pessimist's burden (their gift) is that they can never just see the parts in isolation from the whole. For the pessimist there are no more parts, no more small things.

The optimist sees nothing at the expense of what is seen. The pessimist sees everything at the expense of what is not seen.

The irrevocable curse: to have the disdain of a god and the ineluctable tendencies of an insect.

To be lucid without a cause is to withstand everything for the sake of nothing. And no thoroughgoing lucidity admits a cause.

How pessimism differs from the religions of the world, many of which are relentless and forthright in disparaging this human life, is that pessimism has nowhere else to go. Only the pessimist spends their days smearing shit over every inch of their house without even the dream of an exit. For death is not the discovery of a door to somewhere else, but the house collapsing in on us, or else suddenly expanding without end.

---

[17] Schopenhauer, *The World as Will and Representation Vol. 2*, 578.
[18] David Hume, *Dialogues Concerning Natural Religion* (London: Penguin, 1990), 121.

On the Verge of Nothing

It is possible to treat depression: that treatment is called pessimism. And while it may not cure you, it will cure you of your belief that a cure may be found.

Everyone fails and is a failure. It just depends how many people acknowledge that failure, and are compelled to cover it up. Why else is praise heaped on anything?

I am so sick I have forgotten I am sick. That I can remember this forgetting, but not what was forgotten, means that any final cure, should it ever come, will arrive not from the future but the past.

While pessimism can often seem like little more than an exercise in petulance, it's important to recognise that petulance serves nothing and no one.

The proof of burden supplants the burden of proof.

What is there left to do when everything has been done—not by us but to us?

Pessoa tells us that "[w]e weary of thinking to arrive at a conclusion."[19] And as usual he is right. And as usual the pessimist creates their own arrangement, as one who never concludes thinking because their thinking is weariness.

"The creators of metaphysical systems and of psychological explanations are still in the primary stage of suffering."[20] The pessimist often postures like they are in the final stage, but that can't be the case, for suffering can always get worse. And is this realisation not also a very secret indulgence of theirs, because that the pessimist's current stage of suffering is only at most penultimate leaves open the possibility of a completing stage—wherein suffering redeems.

It's no wonder that anguish and illness tire us out: we have been woken

---

[19] Pessoa, *The Book of Disquiet*, 206.
[20] Pessoa, *The Book of Disquiet*, 341.

On Cosmic Pessimism

up from an all-consuming sleep, and are out of the habit of being awake.

It is commonplace for the pessimist to be considered childish. The thought is that grown-ups are aware of their arguments but have moved on—have accepted what couldn't be denied and reinterpreted the rest, inoculated themselves against it—and that the pessimist should similarly grow up. They even claim to be amused by this recalcitrant doom: "They must be doing this for comic effect. How else can we make sense of them?" But although the laughter wants desperately to express a hardened condescension, it is instead forced and hysterical. For these people haven't so much grown up as prematurely embraced the comforts of senility. After all, they are already institutionalised. In sum, they mistake a passive verb for an active one. They are grown up like a garden cane is grown up.

Each of us carries our own secret: nobody else knows what it's like to be me. Thomas Nagel famously asked what it is like to be a bat, and concluded that we couldn't know. The mistake in our case is to imagine that we are as experientially different from each other as bats are from humans. The mistake is to imagine there can be a secret without the power to disclose it to someone—and that includes you.

If modernism is characterised by disillusionment and post-modernism by playfulness, what movement might be characterised by the pessimist's pathological boredom? Perhaps a movement that refused to move: inactivism. Or else a movement that moved without wanting to: the persistent (and persistently dull) inseparability, then, of life and art reclaimed.

Suffering is pointless, but pointlessness is where the art is at.

The sound of the universe is not a sigh, but the silence that immediately follows a sigh.

The Christian submits to being eaten by God, the pessimist to being regurgitated—by their own mouth.

On the Verge of Nothing

"Life would be unbearable if it were real."[21] It's an interesting metaphysical stance when your disgust has more reality than that which provokes it. It's akin to the atheist who abhors not the (manifest) belief in God but God himself.

The only thing worth mourning is your own life, as you live it, and as it mourns you.

The depressed person knows how every life is acted, knows the erased space behind a life. To be cured they act their return, acting whatever character will allow them to forget they are acting.

Only in a profoundly hideous world would clarity seek a cure.

Life can be endured, or embraced, only when we become much cleverer with words and concepts. Only when the word "immortality" ceases to suck the air from us in a panic can we hope to become a match for it.

The middle course: Nietzsche says "Yes," Schopenhauer says "No," Pessoa says, "Perhaps."

What we are is the point at which we wake up. Consequently, most of us aren't anything.

It's too late to write a philosophy that doesn't cast a spell.[22] But the philosophies we like best are still the ones no one has ever lived inside—not even the philosophers who wrote them.

Cioran said that it was the complete absence of melancholy in Kant's work that turned him from philosophy for good. While Kant doesn't touch on melancholy as a subject, I have always considered his entire oeuvre as a work of melancholy: the convoluted sadness of a man desperately trying to dissolve himself in the acid bath of logic.

---

[21] E. M. Cioran, *Tears and Saints*, trans. Ilinca Zarifopol-Johnston (Chicago and London: The University of Chicago Press, 1995), 102.
[22] Hasn't it always felt too late?

On Cosmic Pessimism

One possible reason the pessimist does not commit suicide is that death is their one remaining hope and they want to keep hold of it. They need it to keep themselves warm. And the threat is there: what if they should use it only to find it has been a cruel hoax all along?

Humanise the abstract or vice versa.

Make of the world a more efficient hospice.

Time's up: there's no more room in the abyss.

Chapter 2

Dreaming Death: The Onanistic and Self-Annihilative Principles of Love in Pessoa's *The Book of Disquiet*

A BAPTISMAL SLEW

Pessoa had many heads, seventy or more, but was essentially just an empty space behind a diverse drama of literary men: poets, essayists, prose writers, translators, philosophers, critics, etc. Pessoa's orthonymic head—itself shredded into various personalities and roles—together with the predominant heteronymic Ghidorah of Alberto Caeiro (philosopher shepherd), Ricardo Reis (doctor and classicist) and Álvaro de Campos (naval engineer and excursionist) formed the drama's core poetic Svetovid. The fictional actors working Pessoa's unique literary universe ranged from mere characters and pseudonyms through to a nucleus of fully-fledged heteronyms, a status derived from the expansion of pseudonyms into autonomous human perspectives, each with its own distinctive literary style and personal history. It is for this reason that Bernando Soares, so clearly confluent with Pessoa himself, did not have a head of his own,[1] and why Pessoa ("person" in Portuguese, a fact which acted like a goad to the endlessly partible referent, who continually failed to reveal the unity that such a term implies) had no choice but to label him a semi-heteronym, for the two were not merely anent but overlapping. It was possible, and proved no real wrench, for Pessoa to have a hand in the deaths of Caeiro and the Baron of Teive, to see their deaths from a safe distance—the first from TB, the second from suicide. But this was not the case with Soares, for he, unlike the Baron, was made for the

---

[1] Even his vocation and place of residence is appropriated from the vacated heteronym Vicente Guedes.

inherent incompleteness and open-endedness of *The Book of Disquiet*, and so would be there till the end, slowly accumulating himself in a trunk. In order to kill Soares, Pessoa would have had to commit a partial suicide. Partial, for there were differences and lacunae, or "mutilations" as Pessoa liked to call them—mutilations that make Pessoa's fragmentary and displaced autobiography a portrait of the troubled emergence of the author who was to eventually write it. Soares, by far the more sombre of the two, has a personality that, while constructed in part from Pessoa's life (and those convoluted mechanisms for contextualising the various subtleties and inscrutabilities of his literary existence), is far more prone to indulge in the far reaches of societal disengagement, and it is this increased detachment that allows Soares to restyle Pessoa's heteronymic territories into the elaborate displacements of some root futility. The book's slow conception was itself entropic: a rag-bag personage becoming increasingly disorganised the more inclusive it became; for Soares, like Pessoa, is not a single voice but many, a proto-person essentially erased by his own diversity, a stand-in for the undermined multitude, the many-headed void, the entity both made and unmade by its own (un)self-induced polycephaly. It could be argued, then, that rather than being a mutilation of Pessoa, Soares is in many ways a true reflection of the distortion Pessoa had undergone, more a reflected distortion than a distorted reflection, a reflection of what Pessoa had done to himself in order to exist at all, to exist in Soares. Soares is the mirror-image of the reality of the book he's to author—another false face for the many, a mangled perpetrator of a mangled creation, a mutilation of collectivity, a rimose fabrication. The book is the whole of two disunities: a struggle for concord where none exists, a whole where there can be only parts. Pessoa teaches by example, and his lesson is that every person is many, and the psychological adhesives we employ to hold the various together under one name, one "I," are all of them dishonesties and limitations; and being that all alterations are also deaths, he chose to honour those nonreducible roles with names and identities—tagging the involute fragments as he fell apart.

With this in mind, and before proceeding any further with this lovesick commentary, the following abjuration is most likely requisite: Pessoa's central undertaking in the book he eventually entrusted to Soares was no less than that of detailing the veracities (in all their slipperiness, and such as he could locate them), the intellectual and emotional substance that resides in incompleteness, of multiplicity, contradiction, disorder and penumbra; and so to falsely pin him/it/them down beyond this, to territorialise the drifting and merging waters of his/its/their thought, would amount to an assault, a betrothal not of adoration but of violence. The distortion and the conflict found in and between the four core Pessoan themes—of identity, dreams, death, and impossibility—gathered and ventured into here will not be served by a process that unsnarls and harmonises, for such a process would exemplify no kind of love. And so we arrive at the following exhortation: "Every effort is a crime, because every gesture is a dead dream."[2] The cogency of this sentence is difficult to ignore and, as Soares himself realised, equally difficult to follow through on. The following efforts are, then, criminal in inception, and can be redeemed only by their preservative (loving) properties. The hope (that accursed and futile accompaniment to all non-accidental creation—our disillusion waiting in the wings) is that Soares' *dead dream* can here be resurrected—its hawking, bug-eyed corpse no doubt every bit as disconsolate as Schopenhauer's grave-dwellers stirred spitting from their slumber—and then once again dispatched with no grimace added to its twice-dead lineaments.

SELF: LOVE AS AUTOPHAGY

To love is to leave untouched: untouched as both expression of intangibility and withdrawal from alteration. Love cannot change its object without destroying it. But one cannot change what cannot first be captured, and love's true object always eludes our every grasping facility, for it is impervious, and its seeming destruction (over various instantiations) only ever love's own implosion. Love's true object is a "placid abyss,"[3] the uncertain variant colouration of a moon's insoluble light. Love and love's objects are unseen and unknown: we see/know only the manifestations of our inability to see/know, and it is not worthwhile to construct complaint or remorse from this, for we may see and know its "outskirts,"[4] and just as virgins who stifle their inclinations to put love into action may see love clearer than love's

---

[2] Pessoa, *The Book of Disquiet*, 263.
[3] Pessoa, *The Book of Disquiet*, 136.
[4] Pessoa, *The Book of Disquiet*, 235.

most rampant purveyor, we too might find love's essence residing in the very condition of its veiled disincarnation. The subtractions are not exhausted outside the person; they are as virulent internally as they are externally, a curtailment of self being considered a prerequisite to any hope of preserving love's purity. A comparable devouring of prurient selfhood can be found in M. K. Gandhi. Explaining the divestment of the person required by ahimsa, he expresses these requirements without equivocation: "[T]o rise above the opposing currents of love and hatred, attachment and repulsion . . . I must reduce myself to zero."[5] In order to avoid doing violence to love's objects, one must do violence to oneself instead.

To be removed from love, to pretend it truthfully at a safe distance, is not to dream of love—and such is Soares' predilection for caution that he issues an emphatic warning: "Let's not even love in our minds"[6]—but to dream a mind dreaming of love, and to dream that mind static, chaste, lamenting and unreal, to dream a mind imprisoned eternally in the inanimate imaginings of love. By avoiding the inherent precariousness of love in this way we might expect such a lover, preserved by their rationale of timidity,[7] to be capable of successfully maintaining a self that would otherwise have been surrendered. After all, it is "running real risks . . . [that] disturbs and depersonalises,"[8] not dreaming the dreamt risks of fictions. But love, it seems, cannot so easily be extricated from its terminal appointment, for love in its purest state is death, and these layers of distance and conjecture are themselves tools of purification. The impossibility and falsity of love's objects are perfectly suited to the unrealisable desire which love names—that of desiring to possess the sensation of possession—and while this desire, such as it is, may be free of the perils of humiliation associated with more worldly manifestations, it is nevertheless itself an acquiescence, a relinquishing of self to non-existence. To renounce the self in this way—as votive offering to the abstract other of love as dreamt dreaming—is to ordain one's own death, is to sacrifice the self to a state of possession (a possession that possesses in turn its

---

[5] M. K. Gandhi, "Truth and Ahimsa," in *Ethics*, ed. Peter Singer (New York: Oxford University Press, 1994), 220.
[6] Pessoa, *The Book of Disquiet*, 244.
[7] Preserved in something resembling a Cioranian state of "enthusiasm." See Cioran's *On the Heights of Despair*, 77–78.
[8] Pessoa, *The Book of Disquiet*, 73.

possessor) in which there is nothing possessed and no possessor, and by so doing cease to be.

What, then, of this love that risks nothing? We might be tempted to conceive of Soares' layered firmaments of dreaming as little more than the high-minded and pusillanimous mewling of one who is all too aware that anyone who takes their pursuit of love into the world "will, in so far as he conceives it to be missing, feel pain."[9] A love in which there is never anything to go missing can never make threat of absence. But this is not to be thought of as a situation structured in degrees: the retreat is not, for instance, the one we find in the soma-saturated society of *Brave New World*, where "the greatest care is taken to prevent you from loving anyone too much."[10] It is not a timorous recoil from the harrowing consequences of love's physicality, but simply a rejection of the inherent contradiction in love having any kind of genuine physicality. There are times when Soares is hard to distinguish from Rimbaud's "very young man" from the beginning of "Deserts of Love," a young man of terminal reticence who had not "loved women—although passionate!—[for] his soul and his heart and all his strength were trained in strange, sad errors."[11] Similarly, Soares' own explorations of love are symptomatic of a wider epistemological affliction: how in finding the truth of things as they are accessible to him he finds only himself (as an accessed means of distortion), while those things that are always sought after, the concrete abstractions which by their very nature defy life, inevitably presage a state of death, a state in which the forfeiture of the self is enacted to preserve the sincerity of the incommunicable, and the sad sanctity of the perpetually erroneous. Thus evidencing how a commentary on love is just one of several ongoing and unresolved (qua unresolvable) epistemological and ontological commentaries, which regardless of their object always lead Soares to (and sometimes even progress from) some form of self-annihilation.

To understand love is to at once realise that nothing is, or can ever be, worthy of it. For love's true object is itself a nothing. It is as crass and misguided to love a cup as it is a person, so if one is to love at all,

---

[9] Benedict de Spinoza, *Works of Spinoza Vol. II*, trans. R. H. M. Elwes (New York: Dover Publications, 1955), 154–155.
[10] Aldous Huxley, *Brave New World* (Grafton Books, 1977), 190.
[11] Rimbaud, *Rimbaud: Complete Works, Selected Letters*, trans. Wallace Fowlie (Chicago: University of Chicago Press, 1966), 287.

one would be advised to love what is at hand, what can be relied upon, what serves the purposes of one's dreams. Mutuality is not necessary; in fact it's a scourge, as is life itself.[12] Love's purity (as objectless and impredicative) demands that one first dispose of life and other. Such maximal essentialism is not, of course, the preserve of Soares alone. The tradition is rich, the mythology its own keepsake. In his essay on *The Lady of the Camellias*, Roland Barthes pinpoints this "bourgeois" isolationism in Armand, whose concept of love is "segregative . . . that of the owner who carries off his prey; an internalised love, which acknowledges the existence of the world only intermittently and always with a feeling of frustration, as if the world were never anything but the threat of some theft."[13] But here the feared theft is not a removal, an extraction, but an addition, a poisoning, or a branding as one might steal cattle. The world can only steal what's inside if what's inside is nothing and what's there to be stolen is that very emptiness: the world, then, steals by occupying, a squatter in a house left deliberately and vitally empty. Armand's love, like Soares', without flesh to perish, is immutable and without end; both vampires draining the invisible blood of essence, their desire, with the world's objects as mere oblation, will always be "by definition a murder of the other."[14]

You can love only the pictures of love, its imagery, its phrases, the bloodless trinkets of its mythology. To know love is to sanctify it with impossibility and absurdity, to know that even that veiled contact is foreign and begets a foreign self: "We do not possess our sensations, and through them we cannot possess ourselves."[15] Although love is possession, such possession is impossible. The approximations of possession are ludicrous and abject, eating without digesting, digesting without first eating: the awkward nestling of magnets, the chronic bulimia of the soul, the autophagic compromise of love's ideal.

Only love allows us to see (or plant, our fingers caked in our own mud) the self that resides within others.

---

[12] "Friendship" is the term that we might most readily associate with love soured by life and mutuality: "[O]f the love of lifeless objects we do not use the word 'friendship'; for it is not mutual love," in Aristotle, "Nicomachean Ethics," in *The Complete Works of Aristotle Vol 2*, ed. Jonathan Barnes (New Jersey: Princeton University Press, 1984), 1826.
[13] Roland Barthes, *Mythologies* (New York: Vintage Books, 1993), 103.
[14] Barthes, *Mythologies*, 104.
[15] Pessoa, *The Book of Disquiet*, 301.

Dreaming Death

Love is torment, its devices cast in oblivion. Love is a craving for something that even the imagination cannot deliver. It is the purity of longing, the perfect chastity of the eternally unconsummated (the words "chaste" and "chastity" both deriving from the Latin adjective *castus* meaning "pure"), the dream of some unencounterable other.[16] From the mouth of Diotima via Socrates via Aristodemus, we are told how Love (as spirit not god) truly is: "[A]s the son of Resource and Need, it has been his fate to be always needy; nor is he delicate and lovely as most of us believe, but harsh and arid, barefoot and homeless."[17]

The impersonality that Soares envisages for his refinement of love is, in certain respects, not so far removed from love's carnal origins, the perpetuation of which he so thoroughly admonishes. A reminder, in case we needed one, of his impeccable realism, for Soares' dreams are not the dreams of a blinkered romantic, but the dreams of a realist who at once recognises his bloodless reconstructions as being both insignificant and unsatisfactory, while also realising that the alternative demands that we sleep so that the world may live. Soares knows that freedom, beauty, and the impossible are not in the world, but in how one escapes it. He claims that "love is a sexual instinct," but is quick to qualify this by pointing out that "it's not with sexual instinct that we love but with the conjecture of some other feeling. And that conjecture is already some other feeling."[18] Love's genesis is in impersonality, for instincts are always impersonal, and it is in impersonality that it culminates. The transitory state is, however, speculative, and so no longer entirely impersonal, the emotional import of love being a creative extrapolation. But once created Soares no longer finds himself there. The construction excludes self. He experiences love most intensely as an awareness of a feeling of love, rather than as one who

---

[16] "Unlike love in possession of that which was / To be possessed and is. But this cannot / Possess. It is desire, set deep in the eye, / Behind all actual seeing, in the actual scene, / In the street, in a room, on a carpet or a wall, / Always in emptiness that would be filled, / In denial that cannot contain its blood / A porcelain, as yet in the bats thereof" (Wallace Stevens, "An Ordinary Evening in New Haven," in *The Collected Poems of Wallace Stevens* [New York: Alfred A. Knopf, 1971], 467).
[17] Plato, "Symposium," in *Plato: The Collected Dialogues*, ed. Edith Hamilton and Huntington Cairns (New Jersey: Princeton University Press, 1989), 555.
[18] Pessoa, *The Book of Disquiet*, 66.

merely feels it, thereby dissolving any clear notion of the personal entity that loves. In order to feel, feelings must be disowned; only this way can they remain honest—an honesty precluding all moral encumbrance.[19] He loses himself "not like the river flowing into the sea for which it was secretly born, but like the puddle left on the beach by the high tide," a locus of impassive awareness extruded from the flow through an imagined analysis[20] of sensations from which it has successfully disembarked, "its stranded water never returning to the ocean but merely sinking into the sand."[21]

The perfect objects of love are, like those staples of Soares' trance-like animatism—those stained-glass figures or Chinese women painted on porcelain—made not born, and made, ordinarily, as receptacles of intimacy, exemplars of the purist devotional spirit. It comes as no surprise, then, that Soares should make the following disclosure: "Like Shelley,[22] I loved Antigone before time was; temporal loves were flat to my taste, all reminding me of what I'd lost."[23] But this feat, this dismissal of flesh, is not enough. To love a fiction made to be loved is not to stretch for the impossible. Soares, like some poet-lover of the Middle Ages for whom, as Bertrand Russell points out, "it had become impossible to feel any poetic sentiment towards a lady unless she was regarded as unattainable,"[24] is all too comfortable with this aseptic

---

[19] The dangers of which Kant extolled at length: "For love out of inclination cannot be commanded; but kindness done from duty—although no inclination impels us, and even although natural and unconquerable disinclination stands in our way—is practical, and not pathological, love, residing in the will and not in the propensions of feeling, in principles of action and not of melting compassion; and it is this practical love alone which can be an object of command" (Immanuel Kant, *Groundwork of the Metaphysic of Morals*, in *The Moral Law*, trans. H. J. Paton [London: Routledge, 1991], 65).
[20] "Only the eyes we use for dreaming truly see" (Pessoa, *The Book of Disquiet*, 111).
[21] Pessoa, *The Book of Disquiet*, 137.
[22] Referencing a letter to John Gisborne, in which Shelley writes: "Some of us have in a prior existence been in love with an Antigone, and that makes us find no full content in any mortal tie" (Percy Bysshe Shelley, *Essays, Letters from Abroad, Translations and Fragments* [London: Edward Moxon, 1845], 335).
[23] Pessoa, *The Book of Disquiet*, 141.
[24] Bertrand Russell, *Marriage and Morals* (London: Routledge, 1991), 49. Russell goes on to explain how "nobler spirits of the Middle Ages thought ill of this terrestrial life; . . . [and of how] pure joy was to them only possible in ecstatic

connection, finding its rewards all too possible. His solution, it turns out, lies in establishing love for the most despicable of fictional female characters: "No greater romantic adventure exists than to have loved Lady Macbeth with true and directly felt love. After a love like that, what can one do but take a rest, not loving anyone in the real world?"[25] A more venal and murderous repository for love could not easily be found, so to love such a fiction, a fiction created to incite loathing, is an emotional exploit undoubtedly worthy of his talents as dreamer and purveyor of disembodied eroticism. But as Soares makes clear, there is no love that is not love for self and is not also pity for that same self[26]—a sandwiching of self that epitomises wisdom, whether our focus is the external world or the world of oneiric objects—and so Soares' passionate entanglement with Lady Macbeth is, to delineate in more detail, ardour attached to his successful conceptualisation of impossible love and the self-sympathy requisite to it.[27] In perfect accordance with the template laid down by Plato, she becomes "a

---

contemplation of a kind that seemed to them free from all sexual alloy" (Russell, *Marriage and Morals*, 50).

[25] Pessoa, *The Book of Disquiet*, 290–291.

[26] "Swann felt a very cordial sympathy with the sultan Mahomet II whose portrait by Bellini he admired, who, on finding that he had fallen madly in love with one of his wives, stabbed her to death in order, as his Venetian biographer artlessly relates, to recover his peace of mind" (Proust, *Remembrance of Things Past: 1*, 386).

[27] The self-serving core to this anfractuous and insulated artifice can be seen here as a way in which to dissolve the boundaries of selves and the divisive conditions in which they're realised, a detail brought to the fore in the following passage by Gilles Deleuze and Felix Guattari: "[I]t would be an error to interpret courtly love in terms of a law of lack or an ideal of transcendence. The renunciation of external pleasure, or its delay, its infinite regress, testifies on the contrary to an achieved state in which desire no longer lacks anything but fills itself and constructs its own field of immanence. Pleasure is an affection of a person or a subject; it is the only way for persons to 'find themselves' in the process of desire that exceeds them; pleasures, even the most artificial, are reterritorializations. . . . The field of immanence is not internal to the self, but neither does it come from an external self or a nonself. Rather, it is like the absolute Outside that knows no Selves because interior and exterior are equally a part of the immanence in which they have fused" (Gilles Deleuze and Felix Guattari, *A Thousand Plateaus: Capitalism and Schizophrenia* [University of Minnesota Press, 1987], 156).

mirror in which he beholds himself":[28] his condition, his failure, and the ascendancy he forges from that failure.

Because the dreamer is invisible to others, despite them taking the dreamer's skin to be their own, they will often, in return, see those others as internally barren, clockwork aggregations of flesh alive to the world and all its clumsy impositions while dead to their own—now atrophied—selves. The true (long-subjugated) self of the dreamer, although rarely encountered even by the most skilled practitioner of dreams, is instantly recognised as both genuine and unsustainable. It is a void. The dreamer encounters reality from within, feeling in a state of revelation that their "soul is a real entity."[29] Waking from life into the reality and the lacuna of his soul, the world is made instantaneously remote, an alien land inhospitable to real persons. This is the self that can be everything because it is nothing, simultaneously everything and nothing, the non-relational entity indifferent to the world and the dreamer's lesser selves, the dreamer's true being, the empty variable, the placeholder, the transcendental self, the self-spark. Soares tells of his revelation: "To know nothing about yourself is to live. To know yourself badly is to think. To know yourself in a flash, as I did in this moment, is to have a fleeting notion of the intimate monad, the soul's magic word."[30] After the flash has abated, the dreamer returns to being (embodying) the dreams of that real self, that nothing that can be all things (*The Thing*), and that dreamt self in turn, once the flash is over, finds anchor in the fictitious non-existence of a worldly sleeping self, the self that knows no other home but the unconsciousness of the world.[31] The deepest self comes to us like a vacant apparition, like another person's emptiness, derailing thought, intelligence, speech, inducing inertia and sleep: "And now I'm sleepy, because I think—I don't know why—that the meaning of it all is to sleep."[32] But, as it turns out, the meaning of it all is also the return, because the meaning becomes the failure to understand it or to sustain it. All its subsequent sense is encapsulated by this impotence, and one sleeps in one's enthrallment of it. If indeed great men exist in this state their whole

---

[28] Plato, "Phaedrus," in *Plato: The Collected Dialogues*, 501.
[29] Pessoa, *The Book of Disquiet*, 40.
[30] Pessoa, *The Book of Disquiet*, 40.
[31] Heidegger's *Being and Time* must then qualify as the world's longest treatise on slumber.
[32] Pessoa, *The Book of Disquiet*, 41.

lives, as Soares tells us, then there can be no real mystery surrounding why he neglects to give their names. Soares' fleeting ekstasis haunts him, and experiencing the ghost of himself—his true self—leaves him with an irresistible desire for a time when "our deepest selves will somehow cease participating in being and non-being."[33] According to Sartre's phenomenological systemisations surrounding the void at the centre of our being, "[w]e find ourselves . . . in the presence of two human ekstases: the ekstasis which throws us into being-in-itself and the ekstasis which engages us in non-being."[34] But Soares, in the face of being and non-being, wants for neither, concocting instead a third path: the self existing outside of both. In short, he has the self that eludes him reflect the absurd incomprehensibility of the experience.[35] Once again he is thinking with his feelings,[36] and whereas for thinkers such as Schopenhauer for

---

[33] Pessoa, *The Book of Disquiet*, 45.

[34] Jean-Paul Sartre, *Being and Nothingness: An Essay on Phenomenological Ontology*, Hazel E. Barnes (London: Methuen, 1984), 44.

[35] Here we have not so much a Humean honest bewilderment (as we see expressed in the appendix to A *Treatise of Human Nature*) as a bewilderment of honesty. Soares writes in earnest: "I'm never where I feel I am, and if I seek myself, I don't know who's seeking me" (Pessoa, *The Book of Disquiet*, 161). This is none other than the metaphysical subject revealing its nothingness, the Wittgensteinian eye that does not see itself (see Ludwig Wittgenstein, *Tractatus Logico-Philosophicus*, trans. D. F. Pears and B. F. McGuinness [London: Routledge, 1974], 57), and to be distinguished from the self that eats into his outwardly-directed consciousness, the scourge of any (sublimely futile) attempt to aestheticise the world: "I see the way I saw, but from behind my eyes I see myself seeing, and that is enough to darken the sun, to make the green of the trees old, and to wilt the flowers before they open" (Pessoa, *The Book of Disquiet*, 329).

[36] It is important to note that this homogeneity of thought and feeling is among the most prominent points of contact between Soares and Pessoa-as-himself, expressed most clearly by the latter in the lines: "In me what feels is always / Thinking" (Pessoa, *A Little Larger than the Entire Universe*, 284). This proximity led Pessoa to the realisation that Soares was not truly autarchic, and so only a "semi-heteronym," a maimed and depleted version of that most adhesive of selves. Pessoa's inability to cleave Soares from his derivation is connected to this inability to separate thought and feeling: what Soares "thinks depends on what he feels" (Pessoa, *The Book of Disquiet*, 475), and what he feels depends on Pessoa, and whatever Pessoa feels is, he confesses, felt solely in order that he may write (in a style he shares with Soares) that he felt it,

whom heart and head make the person but it is always the latter that is "secondary" or "derived," with Soares (especially in the work that is closest to Pessoa himself) they invariably merge. Again, comparisons with Sartre will help codify Soares' poetic musings, the eloquence of Soares' lyrical philosophy coming alive in the contrarieties. For it is possible to attribute a tripartite theory of the self to Soares, comprising the unconscious worldly self of life, meditating on its detail, the self that is dreamt and itself dreams a world for itself, and the self that is missing, absent from the world and impervious to it; and these demarcations fit more or less neatly with Sartre's three ekstases (three stances on the for-itself, as the inevitable dispersion of human being-in-itself). The first ekstasis involves the realisation of existence, the "leaping out" of grounded (worldly) consciousness, the realisation of nothingness as the reason for the found disparity between worldly consciousness (living), and awareness of existence as brute human fact (knowing);[37] the second involves the failure of justification, a further fracturing as that which seeks to know and actualise the initial awareness encounters its own difference; while the third has the Other emerging as subject, but one that cannot be known as subject, as a subject would know itself. But Soares, with no interest in uniting these perspectives (subjects), turns away from synthesis, from the one *transcendent ego*, and instead accepts (welcomes) the proliferation of such egos that arrive in their wake. For Soares, modes of awareness invariably spawn selves, or levels of dreaming each with a dreamer. Like Sartre, he does not posit the reality of selves,[38] but instead sees selves as imaginary devices through which we can transcend reality, the reality in which the self is a nothing.

Our adjectives mostly fail to touch the world as it is; they do not chart the skin, but dress it. And this is not a mistake, an error to be corrected, but a freedom, a playground replete with bountiful spawning materials. It is for this reason that the deepest self must be an impredicative, unanalysable gap—the something of nothing—"no more than the ray of sunlight that shines and isolates from the soil the

---

making any separation one that would have Pessoa existing as his own amputee.

[37] Soares tells of how his "normal, everyday self-awareness had intermingled with the abyss" (Pessoa, *The Book of Disquiet*, 95).

[38] In Sartre's 1936 essay, "The Transcendence of the Ego," we see him set upon Husserl's positing of the transcendental reality of the ego.

pile of dung that's the body."[39] Instead of a reductionist or eliminativist reading of the self, we get an exploitative one, a rigorous celebration of the diverse possibilities of consciousness. Soares nurtures the internal remoteness achieved when consciousness turns in on itself; he nourishes the phenomenological state of being somehow host to your own self, as opposed to embodying it, and from this groundwork he starts to build.

At times Soares feels himself becoming that abyssal eye staring out from nowhere and acknowledging the knotted materials of the self, as one might acknowledge the presence of a tumour, or some foreign growth squirming in the rat-infested back alleys of a tale once told about your life and your role inside it. He sees the human soul's unconscious filth, sees it "is a madhouse of the grotesque, . . . a well, but a sinister well full of murky echoes and inhabited by abhorrent creatures, slimy non-beings, lifeless slugs, the snot of subjectivity."[40] So what does he do with these grotesqueries of the soul once they've been disinterred? He takes them on holiday: they are transformed into "huge heads of non-existent monsters," "Oriental dragons from the abyss,"[41] and finally the hollow stratagems of the city, resignation, and Destiny.

In the *Tractatus*, Wittgenstein claims that "[w]hat brings the self into philosophy is the fact that 'the world is my world'. / The philosophical self is not the human being, not the human body, or the human soul, with which psychology deals, but rather the metaphysical subject, the limit of the world—not a part of it."[42] Soares captures the exact same revelation, saying: "We possess nothing, for we don't even possess ourselves. We have nothing because we are nothing. . . . The universe isn't mine: it's me."[43] And then even more succinctly: "I'm lost if I find myself."[44] This constitutes the birth of Soares as dreamer, for this unity of world-self and world is a convening of two nothings: the self that cannot be mine (cannot be anything for me) and the world itself abyssal in constituting the everything of the absentee world-self. The

---

[39] Pessoa, *The Book of Disquiet*, 58.
[40] Pessoa, *The Book of Disquiet*, 208.
[41] Pessoa, *The Book of Disquiet*, 209–210.
[42] Wittgenstein, *Tractatus Logico-Philosophicus*, 58.
[43] Pessoa, *The Book of Disquiet*, 112.
[44] Pessoa, *The Book of Disquiet*, 209.

challenge is laid out thus: "Everything is us, and we are everything, but what good is this, if everything is nothing."[45]

That "*[t]he limits of my language* mean the limits of my world"[46] is something that Soares accepts—he is, after all, the "selfsame prose" he writes—but when he accepts this, it is not merely as some rationally punitive stricture, but as a provocation, an ontological ultimatum.

According to Soares, the psychological self is a fiction: "It's only the self who no longer believes and is now an adult, with a soul that remembers and weeps—only this self is fiction and confusion, anguish and the grave."[47] This self (this objectified person)[48] is the fiction that the world configures, the self lived into obscurity by the blind processes of its own brute reflexivity. Oh to realise that there is no destination, that where we've been is as unknown and distant as where we're going. The dreamer's prescription is to have as much expectation for, and make as much demand on, the past as on the future, to be deliberately aimless—time's own magniloquent vagrant—not to simply become one of the world's clumsy fictions, devoid of identity and "so scattered,"[49] but to found one's being in the very impossibility of being anything other than yourself, that is, to found your being in what you cannot be, forging an escape from materials that confine (and define) you. Evidence that this experiment is even in operation is scant and fragile and pervaded with logical perversity, as when Soares happens on the "absurd remembrance of [his] future death."[50] The real world demands artifice of its sleepwalkers, revealing itself most fruitfully when bent out of shape. Bending to fit the world we mimic how the world sees us, not how the world is.

If we consider the exposition of Zeus' bisection of man found in Plato's "Symposium," of how those eight-limbed, two-headed men, women and hermaphrodites of myth were cleaved like pieces of fruit, we can begin to see how it is that love came to be regarded as some corrective for lost unity, naming the condition which leaves "each half

---

[45] Pessoa, *The Book of Disquiet*, 149.
[46] Wittgenstein, *Tractatus Logico-Philosophicus*, 56, original emphasis.
[47] Pessoa, *The Book of Disquiet*, 129.
[48] This is the person of the psychological theorist, the indeterminate aggregate of psychological properties to which the self is reduced by John Locke, David Hume, Derek Parfit, Sydney Shoemaker, et al.
[49] Pessoa, *The Book of Disquiet*, 55.
[50] Pessoa, *The Book of Disquiet*, 68.

with a desperate yearning for the other, [wanting] for nothing better than to be rolled into one."[51] Soares internalises this myth, describing a state which seeks to both exploit and salve division within the self, to mitigate the distance not between human beings but between estranged segments of the same self, those "Siamese twins that aren't attached."[52]

UNREALITY: LOVE AS DREAMING

The world is a dead reality, a weightless husk, its dreamable resources sucked out like the guts of some plundered insect.

Consciousness forces a state of being: act one's dreams and dream one's acts. But therein lies a danger: to dream the life that others merely live is to invest yourself in your surroundings, both the animate and the inanimate, having them exist only partially on your terms, leaving the way clear that they may walk away at any time and take parts of you with them. (What's more, the inevitable disclosures of falsity become a source of disgust, as "those which have no relation to reality nor even any point of contact with it," for only pure dreams can enchant.)[53] The consequence of dreaming life is this: "Everything that happens where we live happens in us. Everything that ceases in what we see ceases in us."[54] Every loss, however insignificant to our state of active dreaming, or to our intellect in which it might barely register, becomes a mortification, a partial amputation of the soul. For else why would Soares cry, "My God, my God, the office boy left today"?[55]

You can no more own the objects of love than you can own your dreams. To be skilled at dreaming is to realise a state in which your dreams can own you. And to be owned by a dream is to submit to the plot-less presence of the dead man. Similarly, to submit to the ownership of love is to avoid all of its narrative manifestations, in which its objects possess nothing but love's ephemera (sensations of the perpetually thwarted possession of its objects), relinquishing all love's worldly accoutrements, so that there may be something left to act as possessor. Love is the unpossessable possessor of its own

---

[51] Plato, "Symposium," in *Plato: The Collected Dialogues*, 543.
[52] Pessoa, *The Book of Disquiet*, 20.
[53] Pessoa, *The Book of Disquiet*, 460.
[54] Pessoa, *The Book of Disquiet*, 241.
[55] Pessoa, *The Book of Disquiet*, 241.

potentiality. By transcending the boundaries of the internal self, love realises its own dilution, for as it is lived (exteriorised) into something else it becomes estranged from the pretence on which its existence depends, an imagining both estranged and depleted—a lesser dream, tangible and lost.

If sex is the "accident"[56] of love, then the masturbator expresses, in their very abjectness,[57] the unfortunate truth (as disclosure of essential pretence) of this aleatoric conjunction. "Let us remain eternally like a male figure in one stained-glass window opposite a female figure in another stained-glass window,"[58] for there is no other way for us to non-destructively realise (from *réaliser* to "make real") love's immanent potential as self-sustained dream. These selfsame conditions for love's realisation, as being necessarily static and outside of time, are revealed to Jorge Luis Borges' Javier Otárola at the close of "Ulrikke": "Like sand, time sifted away. Ancient in the dimness flowed love, and for the first and last time, I possessed the image of Ulrikke."[59]

Understanding is inimical to love and to self. In something resembling an extreme take on Stendhal's aphorism on happiness, in which description becomes diminishment, we see that to understand one must first butcher oneself and then that which one seeks to understand. Love, in contradistinction, leaves no fingerprint, its aristocratic non-touch a hovering hand doubly displaced in dream.

To suffer in love is to want it to be more than it is, to be all at once flesh and idea. Worldly (undreamed) love is a template for suffering. Love is so important to us, enjoys such exalted preeminence in human life, because we imagine it to be all that we want from it. This is how it is able to transcend and enslave us. Having reconstructed our meaningfulness as human beings from an impossible desire, we set about trying to find its objects, and that all objects fall short is no detriment to the love that attaches itself to them, quite the opposite—their loss is love's gain: "Perfection never materializes. The saint weeps,

---

[56] Pessoa, *A Little Less Than the Entire Universe*, 351.
[57] The plight of those nine grinding bachelors ("malic molds") in Marcel Duchamp's *The Large Glass*, all of them with the "same useless expression" (Pessoa, *The Book of Disquiet*, 289).
[58] Pessoa, *The Book of Disquiet*, 289.
[59] Jorge Luis Borges, *Collected Fictions*, trans. Andrew Hurley (London: Penguin Press, 1999), 422.

and is human. God is silent. That is why we can love the saint but cannot love God."⁶⁰ Although, we can safely love the idea of God.

Love demands distance and intangibility from its objects, so a wise deployment reserves attention for one's dreams of love or, more precisely, one's dreaming of the dreamt love of fictional lovers. Only in this way can we hope to dissect the emotion of the idea, without mistaking the idea for flesh. Goethe's Eduard was a precise enough lover to make this distinction when it came to Ottilie: "Sometimes she does something that offends the pure idea I have of her, and it is only then I know how much I love her, because I am then distressed beyond all power of description."⁶¹ Love cannot survive our knowing it or its objects, the latter of which do not really exist: it is the dream of a dream, the dream of a dream that can't be dreamt. Or as Soares would put it: " 'I want you only to dream of you.' "⁶² But even the imagination destroys (possibilities) as it builds, so the formula of the dream requires the perpetual immanence of the impossible; thus if "there's always at least one dimension missing in the inward space that harbours these hapless realities,"⁶³ then it's for good reason. The desire for this dimensional deficiency to be healed is to want for love to be nursed to death, to be fortified to the point of extirpation.⁶⁴ The reality we seek for those creatures of our dreams is, then, an empty and self-defeating vanity.⁶⁵ To want the substance of your dreams to mimic that of the world is to will the creation of essentially antithetical beings, a need grounded in the knowledge that "[t]he more a man differs from me, the more real he seems, for he depends that much less on my

---

[60] Pessoa, *The Book of Disquiet*, 65.
[61] Johann Wolfgang Von Goethe, *Elective Affinities*, trans. R. J. Hollingdale (London: Penguin Books, 1971), 146.
[62] Pessoa, *The Book of Disquiet*, 101.
[63] Pessoa, *The Book of Disquiet*, 90.
[64] Not unlike the sad accounts concerning those released from Nazi concentration camps who, on liberation, ate themselves to death. Love is a form of starvation, and so requires a thin gruel, the almost figmental substance of Bengal famine mix.
[65] A reality captured in exquisite detail by Wallace Stevens: *"This image, this love, I compose myself / Of these. In these, I come forth outwardly. / In these, I wear a vital cleanliness, / Not as in air, bright-blue-resembling air, / But as in the powerful mirror of my wish and will"* (Wallace Stevens, "Poem with Rhythms," in *The Collected Poems of Wallace Stevens* [New York: Alfred A. Knopf, 1971], 246, original emphasis.

subjectivity."[66] Here resides the dilemma of love: the desire to possess when possession is inimical to the desire. That which I love must be mine and not mine: mine so that love is not torture, and not mine so that we can share in the discursive pleasures of propriety, pleasures known to Beckett's Mr Hackett who, of certain seats, "knew they were not his, [though] he thought of them as his. He knew they were not his, because they pleased him."[67] We want for the absent dimensions of our dreams to be merely hidden, just as the machinations of self-awareness instinctively lead us to suppose that what seems like our own absence is really a mere instance of the search obscuring what it seeks to find. We want what we cannot see and what cannot be seen to be implied by what we can and do see, and yet this implication, should it come, would transform illusion into reality; whereas the goal for the dreamer is to realise that reality and illusion are co-dependents and that it is this very co-dependence that makes not only an internalisation of the universe possible, but an internalisation of every universe, including the infinite and incomplete universes whose internal contradictions imply something beyond reality, something transcendent rather than transcendental. However, the toll on the self, imposed by these Aleph-like internalisations, can be considerable: "How much I die if I feel for everything."[68]

Like the retired librarian in Borges' "The Book of Sand," a man slowly consumed by the infinite book that has come into his possession, Soares is acutely aware that those that live life do so unconsciously, that life is best lived unconscious of itself and reinforced with spurious limitations. Consciousness exists in defiance of life; to live consciously is to regard life as one would an alien costume tailored to our shape but lacking any safe points of entry. To be conscious is to know feeling (or feel knowing) at a distance, to always maintain a scholarly reserve and perplexity even towards that which would appear most intimate.

When the dreaming of our waking life (that life discernible from lived dreaming because it is peopled with tangible occupants) is disrupted by non-routine elements, it becomes critically compromised. For when dreaming this life, we live the hypotheses and imaginings of

---

[66] Pessoa, *The Book of Disquiet*, 70.
[67] Samuel Beckett, *Watt* (New York: Grove Press, 1953), 7.
[68] Pessoa, *The Book of Disquiet*, 93.

these real people—we regret their absence while they are still present, mourn their deaths while they still breathe, witness mutations of character while they remain unchanged—so that if such things should really happen, our pre-emptive dreams of them appear disfigured by comparative association. The futures we have constructed for the people around us, futures in which those people are placed, insulated by the dreamer's despotic enchantment, have a reality that lays claim to a certain level of solidity, as too do their present-day selves as visited from the dreamer's future reminiscences, a solidity which is impaired (desecrated even) by the crude and unexpected vacillations of reality. The dreamer demands that life obey a certain formulaic continuity, that those people that have been transmogrified into symbols remain unaltered, that one's future recollections of them are not falsified by reality. To live this way is to no longer be one self but two, ("two abysses"): the self that dreams, lost in its attentiveness to the world and the banality of its detail, and the dreamt self reporting back from the vantages of imagination. They are the remote exhibits of a bisected unity, an omphaloskepsis continually swallowed and disgorged by its umbilici.

To act in one's dreams is to maintain an internal state of flux, to move on before having found a place to settle—in short, to play out the futile insanity of real life to much greater effect. *Played out* because the anchor of the real is never truly lost, even if its impressions elude all recollection, and to *greater effect* because the range is inexhaustible, and the self which lives it infinite (bearing the marks of its extrication), the pattern of its weave all "intervals," all "nothing," the purest possibilities of the absurd (of its divinity), the confused—a finely delineated oblivion. To attempt (even on a minimal scale) to mimic these conditions externally is to suffocate the infinite self, its lungs ill-formed to breathe the oppressive air of finitude: "The only way to be in agreement with life is to disagree with ourselves."[69]

The internal contradictions that starve the dreamer (of satisfaction) are the same contradictions that have them grow fat (on the nobility of disappointment). The dreamer cannot believe in success; the boundless possibilities consume all sense of it. Everywhere is nowhere. But therein lies an approximation of success, for to know your defeat intimately is to be victorious. Soares moves amongst "the flagless army

---

[69] Pessoa, *The Book of Disquiet*, 27.

fighting a hopeless war,"[70] and while he and this unaffiliated martial horde share the same vanquishment, he has other wars to continue losing, and losing gloriously, and with the necessity of his defeat providing fanfare. To know that you're what's left of something that's never been anything more is to be spared the vision of the pernicious and phantom-like augmentations of desire. The dreamer doesn't try to reach the end (the completion, or use) of anything, their own self most of all. Here lies meaning, sense, dignity: "Since we can't extract beauty from life, let's at least try to extract beauty from not being able to extract beauty from life."[71] The only perfection open to us lies in our failure to attain it.

The post-pessimist, a consummate dreamer, never loses sight of the phenomenon of dreaming, or through how many conduits their reverie is being filtered. They dream "without illusions,"[72] for they are aware that their entire consciousness bears the mark of the dream, be it the internal dream of others' internal dreams, or the dream of the world, soured by its proximity to claims of truth. It is for this reason that "[e]very dream is the same dream, for they're all dreams,"[73] just as every unconsciousness is the same unconsciousness "diversified among different faces and bodies."[74]

Soares has no desire to socialise the self (such as we see in late Sartre, for example), to meld ego with man; for man is a fetid potion, "a monstrous and vile animal created in the chaos of dreams, out of desires' soggy crusts, out of sensations' chewed-up leftovers."[75] The paganistic "cult of humanity" is grounded in the misguided premise that man is a legitimate replacement for God. Though makers of reality, we do not, as individuals, choose the manner in which it is made. If our dreams were to be made real—by which we mean encounterable in the way the world is encounterable, to be inside it as much as it is inside us—they would be made fact, and the facts would then overwhelm both dream and dreamer. If realities were to become Realities, then the dreamer would be altered as a result, altered into a god. This extra dimension, if added, would render the dream external

---

[70] Pessoa, *The Book of Disquiet*, 59.
[71] Pessoa, *The Book of Disquiet*, 261.
[72] Pessoa, *The Book of Disquiet*, 61.
[73] Pessoa, *The Book of Disquiet*, 60.
[74] Pessoa, *The Book of Disquiet*, 70.
[75] Pessoa, *The Book of Disquiet*, 63.

Dreaming Death

(for the supplementary dimension must come from outside these realities), see it subsumed into the world, and the dreamer would start to dream realities as they dream the world—that is, unconsciously. You would live (worldly) in your dream and thereby destroy the dreaming self. For these realities to gain this extra dimension the dreamer would have to disappear, all distance (that distance that creates nearness) lost. The reality would be yours in a way that the world never is, its independence (for there must be independence, or how else could you meet the friends you've dreamed of as distinct from dreaming such a meeting?) additional rather than inherent, but it would amount to a fundamental limitation of possibilities, namely one's presence as absentee. As when the dreamer returns to the world, and the focus inevitably shifts from acting one's dreams to dreaming one's acts.

Love is not for living but observing, as a form of self-awareness: the self that dies daily to the world and the dreaming self each watch the other fail—the former in disillusionment, the latter in artificiality. But the latter, at least, need never lose the object of its love, for it realises that it has created the object, and should it become threadbare can make it again.

To reform reality in the intellect, to tell of the images of one's dreams in a voice nobody will hear: this is how to survive the world and its dismal ministry. For once the world has colonised all internal space, there'll be nothing else left to dream and no one left to dream it.

The (post-pessimist) dreamer does not sacrifice their intelligence, their reason, for the sake of the dream. They unite them; they make dreaming a response to truth and not its replacement. They accept, like Wittgenstein, that there are no genuine problems of existence—"When the answer cannot be put into words, neither can the question be put into words. / *The riddle* does not exist. / If a question can be framed at all, it is also *possible* to answer it"[76]—and that a logical approach to the world rids us of the necessity of answers, for the world itself poses no questions, but yet they remain speculative, choosing to detail this non-existent riddle and set up home in its absence. The dreamer's riddle (the riddle that sustains them, for "[h]ow everything wearies when it is defined")[77] is the very lacuna left by the riddle of existence which does not exist. The task, then, is not the framing of answers to impossible questions, or even, for the most part, framing impossible questions,

---

[76] Wittgenstein, *Tractatus Logico-Philosophicus*, 73, original emphasis.
[77] Pessoa, *The Book of Disquiet*, 138.

but rather framing the very impossibility of certain questions, maddening in their ghostliness, their vague specificity, their uncertain certainty. The post-pessimist dreamer senses the questions, and senses their non-existence, as one would sense the missing. Their words construct the impossibility of construction; they are the blueprints not for impossible buildings, but the impossibility of building, thereby constructing a template for impossibility itself, for the necessity of nothingness.

And once again Soares' comments on the comingling of thought and feeling provide illustration, for it is as a consequence of their fusion that one can be aware of the strictures of logic while at the same time breaking them. The first task is to overcome *what is* instead of *what can be*. This is the initial flight of the dreamer, in which they anatomise "the metaphysics of autonomous shadows, the poetry of the twilight of disillusion."[78] The second, more fundamental, flight turns its attention on the necessary limitations of that first flight, that is, the substance of the nothing of undreamability. Even loves manufactured in dreams must pass. How else could we dream their allotted nostalgia? Love is an exercise; why else would we willfully replace its objects? "I can change my sweetheart and she'll always be the same":[79] to love this way is to love indifferently, to experience a paradox of feeling that is the apex of thought-feeling.

In real life we trail behind ourselves, all the while imagining that we are the ones with their heads over their shoulders. In the life of dreams the straggler and the vanguard are indistinguishable, united by the dream. Each must surrender to the other in order for the dreamer to be formed. Division, when clumsily executed, implies navigation, but the true dreamer does not navigate their dream, but instead becomes the dream, each performing the other. *Pace* Paul Valéry, knowing oneself is not foreseeing oneself and so playing the part of oneself, but foreseeing nothing and thereby locating oneself in the pathless landscape of the dream.

Love provides but one service to the dreamer: the increased fondness for what is absent. This fondness drives imagination, animating the dreamer, which when succumbed to without reservation can absent reality itself.

---

[78] Pessoa, *The Book of Disquiet*, 133.
[79] Pessoa, *The Book of Disquiet*, 403.

Dreaming Death

MELTING: LOVE AS DEATH

The deceased man of action was always "what Death would make of him."[80] The deceased man of dreams was always what he would make of Death. The idea of love, like the idea of death, is frozen, eternal and unoccupied, sensation without the ephemeral trappings of its cause, or its even needing a cause. There is nothing you can construct in the exterior world which does not first involve you destroying an element of yourself, and the exterior world contains nothing (no cause, no love, no discovery) worthy of our internal annihilation—not that there is especial calamity in the latter. To exteriorise is to submit to cowardice, to submit to the reassuring untruth of reality's concrete independence. But Soares gives us a way out, a way of protecting the internal from the external:

> The truly wise man is the one who can keep external events from changing him in any way. To do this, he covers himself with an armour of realities closer to him than the world's facts and through which the facts, modified accordingly, reach him.[81]

This carapace is the actualisation of a consciousness, a protective filter maintaining verisimilitude to nothing but awareness itself, and thereby constituting a retreat from the numerous "metaphysical mistake[s] of matter,"[82] internalising them. This is Soares tiring of truth, as weary from conflict with the world's persistence he eradicates all factful concerns, reducing them to an absent-minded dereliction of self.[83] And yet he claims to "remember only external things"[84] and to furnish his dreams, thus upping their intensity, with the rewards of a scrutiny

---

[80] Pessoa, *The Book of Disquiet*, 407.
[81] Pessoa, *The Book of Disquiet*, 94.
[82] Pessoa, *The Book of Disquiet*, 96.
[83] Soares' burden is that of the philosopher, for as Nietzsche observes, the "philosopher recuperates differently and with different means: he recuperates, e.g., with nihilism. Belief that there is no truth at all, the nihilistic belief, is a great relaxation for one who, as a warrior of knowledge, is ceaselessly fighting ugly truths. For truth is ugly" (Friedrich Nietzsche, *The Will to Power*, ed. and trans. Walter Kauffman and R. J. Hollingdale [New York: Vintage Books, 1967], 325).
[84] Pessoa, *The Book of Disquiet*, 183.

turned outward, with things prose-filtered and yet inescapably visual and spatially ordered. Externalising impressions is a way to locate them, to have them exist, to establish them as encounterable and so too ourselves as that which encounters, and much rather that than a false name fixed to the collected fragments of an unowned dream.

Love makes but one demand for incarnation: that its promise remain a threat. Seeking love's fulfilment among the objects of the world, seeking therein its vertex and conclusion, is a betrayal of the inherent chastity of loving-as-possession. There is no possession but the dream, a dream itself devoid of possessing. The loving dream, the idea of that loved, is the limit of the lover's claim to ownership, as one who does not even own their dreams. Meticulous attention to the outside should always be a prerequisite for a subsequent act of internalisation: the sexual impulse is a reversal of this. The sexualisation of love is a relinquishment of possibility, and a debasement of the dreamer's singularity, an immolation that Schopenhauer tells us "is the life of the species, asserting its precedence over that of individuals."[85] When Soares declares that "[l]ife should be a dream that spurns confrontations,"[86] it is this kind of banal skirmish to which he is referring, the anguished duelling that occurs when the narrator (of dreams) is narrated (by life). To place love in the world importunes an adjectival prefix, such as we see in the phrases, *sexual* love and *motherly* love, and also in Hegel's somewhat pleonastic clarification: "*Active* love—for love that does not act has no existence."[87] Soares would say that active love, by existing, is not love, but rather what is fashioned from love's residual scraps once it's been obliterated by activity. Action is never other than a destructive force, "a disease of thought, a cancer of the imagination. [And just as] God, becoming man, cannot help but end in martyrdom,"[88] love's descent into the meat of unclaimed bodies cannot help but end in surrender and eventual death,[89] consciousness abandoned to the inert flesh of the other. And yet there is no escape in

---

[85] Schopenhauer, *The World as Will and Representation Vol. 2*, 602.
[86] Pessoa, *The Book of Disquiet*, 145.
[87] G. W. F. Hegel, *Phenomenology of Spirit*, trans. A. V. Miller (New York: Oxford University Press, 1977), 255, my emphasis.
[88] Pessoa, *The Book of Disquiet*, 272.
[89] The fate of Strindberg's Miss Julie, whose post-coital subjugation and suicide provides perfect illustration of the annihilative vigour of corporeal passion.

essentialism either (the post-pessimistic condition is, after all, a precarious rope-walk), for love's fastigium is not free of death but riddled with a brand of abstract necrosis, a state in which we are "chaste like dead lips, pure like dreamed bodies, and resigned to being this way, like mad nuns."[90] And it does not end with love, for all interaction with others is a corruption of possibilities, a truncation of internal infinitudes: "To associate is to die."[91] Social existence involves crediting others with a level of reality that immediately confines and marginalises the self, and that part of us that extends into this realm becomes necrotised tissue.[92]

If love is to be suffered, then it should be suffered only as a possibility for sensation—a sensation of possibility. It is this nympholeptic sterility that conveys permanence, a sterility that while frequently associated with the moral implications of chastity is concerned with neither the virtue of oneself or others:[93] "Women are a good source of dreams. Don't ever touch them."[94] Not even with the prosthetic hands used to touch life. In summation, Soares' dictum can be seen as a reversal of one half of the Schopenhauerian distinction that couples life with permanence: where for Schopenhauer, "it is his *immortal* part [the will to life] that longs for her,"[95] for Soares it is his

---

[90] Pessoa, *The Book of Disquiet*, 289.
[91] Pessoa, *The Book of Disquiet*, 184.
[92] Mark Seltzer details the potential destructiveness of socialisation in his study on serial killers, in which he painstakingly explores "the manner in which serial violence is bound up with what might be described as the quickening of an experience of generality within: a psychasthenic yielding to generality, to affections with something stereotypical about them, to something statistical in our loves. Serial violence, in short, cannot be separated from experiences of a radical failure in self-difference" (Mark Seltzer, *Serial Killers: Death and Life in America's Wound Culture* [London: Routledge, 1998], 144).
[93] Like Pausanias' divine lover (as relayed by Aristodemus), Soares advocates a state in which we may "become one with what will never fade" (Plato, *The Collected Dialogues*, 537). But unlike Pausanias, he has no interest in this lover's moral status, or the viciousness or otherwise of his counterpart, the earthly lover, who lusts only after gratifications of the flesh.
[94] Pessoa, *The Book of Disquiet*, 351.
[95] Schopenhauer, *The World as Will and Representation Vol. 2*, 559.

immortal (or permanent/infinite)[96] part as the rejection of life (the will to anti-life) that longs (or ideally provides witness to such longing) for her (as a representation). This sense of there being an underlying aim is also present in Alfred North Whitehead, who saw love for one's child or one's spouse as the exemplification of a feeling concerned with a desired consonance somehow made manifest in loved objects. This love, he claimed, "involves deep feeling of an aim in the Universe, winning such triumph as is possible to it."[97] Soares would be unable to see any triumphs worth winning. This is the vulgarity of purpose infiltrating the sublime uselessness of love, as if the search and the silence were wanting, weren't themselves everything. Where Whitehead finds an implication of discord and division, Soares finds the opportunity for synthesis.[98] The conflict lies with "the principles of the generality of harmony, and of the importance of the individual. The first means 'order,' and the second means 'love.' Between the two there is a suggestion of opposition. For 'order' is impersonal; and 'love,' above all things, is personal."[99] The trick is to experience the personal from a distance, and thereby establish order. There is an inescapable universality to the personal, and it is this that can be observed dispassionately. It is that aspect of the personal that we consider peculiar to ourselves that allows us to relish the structures of love on a level considered intimate. In this way love and harmony become inseparable. It is only by surrendering love to particular objects that the ideal is forfeited.[100] This proposed experience of love is objectless, and so fraught with none of the deleterious consequences so often associated with love's worldly actualisation. But although free of the

---

[96] Although Soares is clear that nothing about human life is infinite, the dream, though it may be only momentarily embodied, is not itself asphyxiated by limitations of time.
[97] Alfred North Whitehead, *Adventures of Ideas* (Cambridge: Cambridge University Press, 1939), 373.
[98] Something we also find in Cioran: "Irrationality resides over the birth of love. The sensation of melting is also present, for love is a form of intimate communion and nothing expresses it better than the subjective impression of melting, the falling away of all barriers of individuation. Isn't love specificity and universality all at once?" (Cioran, *On the Heights of Despair*, 84).
[99] Whitehead, *Adventures of Ideas*, 376.
[100] Like Platonic, forms the objects of love must remain "free from all alloy" (Plato, *The Collected Dialogues*, 497).

raw anxieties of love's frontline, the death of the self remains inevitable. For by turning love into an anti-prosopopoeial conglomerate of abstractions, ideally experienced as a uniquely concerted sensation, Soares makes a simulacrum of the self at every level. There is no room for the self when sensation has been purified to this degree. It's the Cartesian corrective applied to sensation: *there is sensation*. Bataille, recognising the deep connection between the physical entrapment of love and the abdication of self, writes: "I said that I regarded eroticism as the disequilibrium in which the being consciously calls his own existence in question. In one sense, the being loses himself deliberately, but then the subject is identified with the object losing his identity."[101] In Soares' idealised picture of love, free of the disequilibrium of eroticism, the subject makes a quandary of their existence not through identification with the body, but through having no available repository for identification whatsoever.

If Soares ever managed to encapsulate his—and so Pessoa's—entire project in a single sentence, then he does so here: "I've externalized myself on the inside."[102] What we see with Schopenhauer's and Whitehead's picture of love—which is to name but two, for those with like-minded approaches are legion—is the exact opposite, for they understand the lover as someone who internalises themself on the outside.

The spiritualised transfiguration of two bodies into one, brought on by an individual's craven rapport with another, in Soares' hands becomes a mechanism of intimate self-viewing, the sensation of love facilitating a (Cioranian) "melting" of self-watched and self-watching. But to fuse is to annihilate by contamination. To love is to seek destruction and impurity. To desire the effects of love is to desire a distinctly Empedoclean[103] integration. Identity, or at the least one's

---

[101] Georges Bataille, *Eroticism*, trans. Mary Dalwood (London: Penguin Books, 2001), 31.
[102] Pessoa, *The Book of Disquiet*, 254.
[103] According to Empedocles, Love was the amalgam of the cosmic cycle—the agency that brought about the coalescence of the four roots (earth, air, fire and water) into a uniform sphere—and Strife the agency that sowed discord through that love-formed sphere, once again estranging its elements. But Love cannot retain the integrity of each root, as running "through one another, they become different in aspect" (Jonathan Barnes, *The Presocratic Philosophers*

sense of being a something that dreams, a something in dreams, a something that some disclosure of scientific truth could possibly make nothing, always comes at the expense of others. To relate to others on any level is to have them partake in the composition of your existence, to have their remote fingers help put you together. All action assumes company, a necroid promiscuity of the soul making the one who acts porous. To act is to recoil from the self, diluting it with alterity, entombing the freedom of nothingness inside the dirt of the world.

Physical love is a contagion (for Bataille "an impersonal growth") and sterility a partial containment. Soares asks us to pray that his hypothetical wife be sterile and never more than hypothetical. Sexual reproduction is the forging (knocking up) of violent materials, the manufacture of weaponry for a war that your children will fight for you, a war you can no longer see a point in winning, a war that exists only so that there may be soldiers to fight it, war as a reason for parturition. The self-annihilations of love do not mimic suicide, they mimic life; present even in the midst of sterility, they involve the destruction of what cannot be found, the mutilation of uninhabitable bodies: "Only to kill what never was is lofty, perverse and absurd."[104] If, as Bataille tells us, the human corpse is a "tormenting object," the object a prophecy of the viewer's own violent destiny, then human offspring, delivered into the world or pre-empted by infertility, represent the death of a dream, the snuffing out of possibility, of all opportunity for perfect surrender or love as death—a corpse-less death. A love in which both parties surrender completely to the other is not possible, but if it were each would lay their personality out on the mortuary slab: "The greatest love is therefore death."[105] All attempts to act out this surrender are failures that work towards death[106] only to document its impossibility, so that if, as Bataille also realised, "the urge towards love, pushed to its limit, is an urge toward

---

[London: Routledge, 1993], 309). The natural world is formed in this way, via the integrative betrayal of each of its constituent parts.
[104] Pessoa, *The Book of Disquiet*, 288.
[105] Pessoa, *The Book of Disquiet*, 449.
[106] "I FAINT, I perish with my love! I grow / Frail as a cloud whose [splendours] pale / Under the evening's ever-changing glow: / I die like mist upon the gale, / And like a wave under the calm I fail" (Percy Bysshe Shelley, "Fragment XXXIII," in *The Poetical Works of Percy Bysshe Shelley* [London: Edward Moxon, 1870], 577, original emphasis).

death,"[107] then it is the urge toward a dream of death, a death made our own now fading, a death found impossible, leaving us staring down at the vacated corpse of ourselves as it ridicules our dreams for it.

VOID: LOVE AS IMPOSSIBILITY

If all our words are marginalia on blank sheets of paper, then all we can do is make or unmake the suppositions of our existence.[108] There can be no true path for that which exists only by hypothesis. The only way for such a contrivance to live according to its (unnatural) nature is through an escalation of such pathways, ignoring the constraints of possibility forged, through misadventures in identification, along the way. Only recognition of the necessity of failure can go towards redeeming the efforts made, wherein failure once again makes its mark. The success of mystery comes at the expense of a solid footing from which to dream, so expediting the collapse of abstraction as possible recourse. From what do we abstract? The universality of Soares' self-professed ignorance is rewarded with the wisdom of his awareness of it; with the dejection of one who'd temporarily submitted to a hope he knew to be false, he writes: "I'll never write a page that sheds light on me or that sheds light on anything."[109] If we can speak of Soares having a moment of triumph, this is it. For what better way to nurture absurdity than by constructing the most elaborate strategies of illumination for that which no darkness could ever hide? (This is what it means to be "spiritualized in Night.")[110] It is within these strategies, those endless and sightless compositions, that he discovers the possibility for integrity: "I've always felt that virtue lay in obtaining what was out of one's reach . . . in achieving something impossible, something absurd, in overcoming—like an obstacle—the world's very

---

[107] Bataille, *Eroticism*, 42.
[108] One way of approaching this partitioning of our control is to see it in terms of Wilfred Sellars' distinction between our *manifest* self-image and our *scientific* self-image: only the former can be made or unmade, the latter if it is not to unmake the former must remain (to the persons it threatens) a blank page. See Wilfred Sellars, *Empiricism and the Philosophy of Mind* (Cambridge, MA: Harvard University Press, 1997).
[109] Pessoa, *The Book of Disquiet*, 134.
[110] Pessoa, *The Book of Disquiet*, 192.

reality."[111] (His Realist credentials are once again in evidence: to consider such a project of overcoming to be impossible and absurd one must first have accepted the concrete independence of that which one seeks to overcome, thereby accepting the limitations—only to then discard them in the service of the impossible—that such an acceptance implies.)[112] Whitehead states that "[i]n the extreme of love . . . all personal desire is transferred to the thing loved, as a desire for its perfection."[113] The thing loved, that whose perfection is desired, is, for Soares, none other than the incarnate love's impossible telos—which is itself transformed by the abstract telos found in that very impossibility.

Soares, despite his deep-rooted suspicion of persons of this type, is often almost indistinguishable from the ascetics and mystics of Christianity and Buddhism, those that "long for what they don't know."[114] The blank page is the unyielding human nothing of the scientifically-present world. The mystics "have emptied themselves of the world's nothingness,"[115] and so too has Soares. How could he fail to admire those who shun the world in favour of mystery and meditative voyage? However, what he cannot embrace about this mystic life is its prescribed loss of whim. He cannot couch his project in quagmires of belief, nor can he regiment his feelings with theoretical manacles. Instead he chooses to create a monasticism of faithless dreams.

The text must not simply remain open, something some slim aperture of inexplicitness would realise, but must be splayed to the

---

[111] Pessoa, *The Book of Disquiet*, 130.

[112] A stance comparable to that which Nick Land finds in the relation between fiction and theory in Bataille: "One might say that at the level of writing theory is a constricted species of fiction, in the same way that the actual constricts possibility (but what matters is the *impossible*)" (Nick Land, *The Thirst for Annihilation: Georges Bataille and Virulent Nihilism* [London: Routledge, 1992], 131, original emphasis). There's also a striking resemblance to the nameless man (the "somebody," the "you") in Borges' "A weary Man's Utopia," who sounds as if he was schooled by Soares himself: "No one cares about facts anymore. They are mere points of departure for speculation and exercises in creativity. In school we are taught Doubt, and the Art of Forgetting—especially forgetting all that is personal and local" (Jorge Luis Borges, *Collected Fictions* [London: Penguin Press, 1999], 462).

[113] Whitehead, *Adventures of Ideas*, 372.

[114] Pessoa, *The Book of Disquiet*, 147.

[115] Pessoa, *The Book of Disquiet*, 147.

point where it cannot even contain itself. This is what it means to be alert to one's willed self-ignorance, mindful of our turning as we turn away, as we strive "[t]o consciously not know ourselves—that's the way."[116] To rewrite what was never written, to give presence to absence and absence to presence, to cultivate the ludic solemnity of a child, to pummel solid rock to the very form of indeterminacy, these are the things required of the fertile dreamer of selves. "We weary of thinking to arrive at a conclusion,"[117] and we weary of our emptiness to arrive at ourselves. Close and sustained scrutiny always reveals an illusion, and in the end even the possibility of illusion reveals itself as illusory. Clarity: that impossibility of all impossibilities, and one dreamt possible so that we may have a reason to fail.

Soares returns to himself after months spent happy and erased in the dead sleep of life, and embarks upon a bout of nerve-philosophy in which he synthesises with a blowfly. The experiment is almost Cronenbergian in conception, and the full horror of his altered embodiment felt with an excruciatingly carnal detail. In a revelation worthy of Gregor Samsa, he finds himself present to the hideous fusion: "I was a fly when I compared myself to one. And I felt I had a flyish soul, slept flyishly and was flyishly withdrawn. And what's more horrifying is that I felt, at the same time, like myself."[118] All of a sudden becoming reacquainted with the futility of his former absence in life, he transmogrifies his recaptured presence into an imagined presence known, but not felt, to be impossible.[119]

The nothing (a vacuum) with one view: one's own self spread like tar across the possibility of seeing. Nothing remains for me to see, because I've seen the way I see and the way I will see. Anything I could see has been seen by my seeing that transparency of seeing.

When the sensation of love is at its purest it is possible for one to love excrement; but to translate this love into an impetus, to absorb and be absorbed by excrement, is to forget that the service of love is to create the distance from which such things can be loved. Only a madman can love the shit he's drowning in.

---

[116] Pessoa, *The Book of Disquiet*, 133.
[117] Pessoa, *The Book of Disquiet*, 206.
[118] Pessoa, *The Book of Disquiet*, 281.
[119] An impossibility that Thomas Nagel would later detail in his seminal paper, "What is it like to be a bat?," *Philosophical Review*, LXXXIII (October, 1974).

On the Verge of Nothing

Love is (and should remain) a prayer at the altar (the arse-end)[120] of the impossible.

---

[120] Of which, as Dolmancé informs us, there is none more divine. See the Marquis de Sade's *Philosophy in the Bedroom*, in Marquis de Sade, *Justine, Philosophy in the Bedroom, & Other Writings* (New York: Grove Press, 1994).

Chapter 3

Nonhuman Materialisations: The Horror in the Detail of the Cockroach

During an interview in 1965, Vladimir Nabokov gave the following response to a question concerning his pedagogic methodology:

> When studying Kafka's famous story ["The Metamorphosis"], my students had to know exactly what kind of insect Gregor turned into (it was a domed beetle, not the flat cockroach of sloppy translators) and they had to be able to describe exactly the arrangement of the rooms, with the position of doors and furniture, in the Samsa family's flat. They had to know the map of Dublin for *Ulysses*. I believe in stressing the specific detail; the general ideas can take care of themselves.[1]

This attention to the concrete, the readily ascertainable details, the factual structure of works of fiction, is a way not of avoiding or merely bolstering later attempts at interpretation, but is itself a form of interpretation—not a tool of demystification, but a tool used to extend any existent puzzlement. It is not, as it might seem, a means of tying the work to the real world, but rather a means of having the work unrealise the world, a method by which we take the book to the real in order to undo it with words, a retaliation for the fact that the world in its turn is busy undoing us. The very concreteness and accuracy of the descriptions of Dublin in *Ulysses*, while undeniably increasing the factual density of Joyce's novel, has more to do with an attempt to fictionalise the space referenced than it does with an attempt to have real world locations anchor the book's narrative meanderings to one

---

[1] Vladimir Nabokov, *Strong Opinions* (London: Penguin Books, 2011).

particular place. The seductive import of what is written is being pushed forward in place of the correlation. The same can be said of Pessoa's *The Book of Disquiet* and Lisbon, and Prague and the novels and short fictions of Kafka. The fictions transform the cities, the cities do not materialise the fictions: the evening sadness of the Rua do Arsenal/Rua da Alfândega, the tired, anchoring drudgery half-constructed in daydreams of an office on the Rua dos Douradores, and the fourth floor home of a partially escaped life on that same street, are none of them manifested by some earlier presence there or some presence to come. I do not live Pessoa's lines more successfully via the possibility of this acquaintance being actualised according to geographical specifics. Any street will do for this, imagined or real. The significant alteration occurs when you take the page to the world, when you feel Soares on the Rua dos Douradores, or some other place you've substituted for it in ignorance or knowledge of the original. The oneiric disconsolation that you may then attribute to streets and shops and offices and passing pedestrians, even individual bricks and windows and voices, is the superimposition of a placeless place (*topos outopos*) on a particularity of place, a ragbag of sensations and emotive triggers that is placed like an annotated slide over an existing screen of the counterfactual postulation of the what-is-without-you (i.e. that which in turn unrealises you), which is not to say that the world must ask your permission in order to exist, but that the way it exists at any given moment also constitutes what it is to be you.[2] The two exist inside one another, exchanging pressures and influences, each unmaking the other.

In "The Metamorphosis," the fact that Gregor has been transformed into a beetle with a domed back, and not a flat-backed cockroach, lends consistency and credibility to his being able to, for instance, "set about rocking the whole length of his body evenly out of bed."[3] But then a domed beetle does not become flat when dead, no matter how desiccated it becomes—the exoskeleton retains the same shape as it did when living—and yet Gregor's corpse is also described (in the same translation)[4] as being "completely flat and dried out."[5]

---

[2] At least as far as you remain in the world of definability, of knowledge.
[3] Franz Kafka, "The Metamorphosis," in *Stories 1904–1924*, trans. J. A. Underwood (London: Abacus, 1981), 96.
[4] A translation which opts, in place of either beetle or cockroach, for the more nondescript "giant bug."

Nonhuman Materialisations

The obvious casualty of this contradiction is our image of Gregor, how confident we can be in our visual imaginings. How it is we can continue to trust a world in which Gregor wakes to find himself transformed into a man-sized insect, with a hard dome-shaped back like a dung beetle, when a few weeks after his death he is supposedly flat. Maybe we can accept this by hypothesising that the apple that lodged in his back after an earlier assault somehow resulted in the exoskeleton's subsequent collapse post-mortem, and in this way make the tale consistent, so we can once again see Gregor scuttling up the walls and across the ceiling of his room, as we imagine Kafka intended. Alternatively, there might be more to discover if we consider this an instance of a second transmutation, of species, of turning cockroach, of a slyly suggested mutability of physicality in general. But then this is not a technique applicable only to fictions: consider how we might want to describe ourselves as immortal creatures, and how we might also hope to resolve the paradoxes that existence makes of us. For not only do we not have any answers for what might give our existence some sense of ultimate meaning, we do not even know the questions we should ask, for we cannot make any real sense of what we might mean by *ultimate meaning*, or what kind of creature could be unquestionably deserving of it. To evoke Bataille, we seek the answer to a question we are unable to formulate.[6] For as Jean Baudrillard states: "Modern Philosophy flatters itself, in a wholly self-satisfied manner, that it asks questions to which there are no answers, whereas what we have to accept is that there are no questions at all, in which case our responsibility becomes total, since we are the answer—and the enigma of the world also remains total, then, since the answer is there, and there is no question to that answer."[7] But then, after all, it is *this* very enigma that we need to preserve: it must remain "impossible to say just what I mean."[8]

How could we deliberately overreach our understanding, and still expect our semantics to behave? The need to formulate and think and speak comes up against the necessity of the unthought and the unspoken—you can't say it without breaking the spell. You've got to

---

[5] Kafka, "The Metamorphosis," 142.
[6] See Georges Bataille, "The Cruel Practice of Art," in *Médicine de France*, 1949.
[7] Jean Baudrillard, *Cool Memories II*, trans. Chris Turner (Polity Press, 1996), 20.
[8] T. S. Eliot, "The Love Song of J. Alfred Prufrock," in *T. S. Eliot: Collected Poems 1909–1962* (London: Faber and Faber, 1963), 16.

leave it unadorned: "It would shrink to the earth if you came in."[9] No end-state satisfies, not even our acceptance of this incompleteness, this state of answers without questions, this sense of the meaninglessness of meaning. The poet accepts but accepts in such a way that they are still able to write, accepts with every part except the act of writing, which becomes in itself the illusion of resistance, an illusion in which reality can again seem real. Where something is attainable there is no art. You must see and inhabit the cul-de-sac and, squirming, see more than a dead end and yet see the dead end as everything and everything as a dead end. Wittgenstein said of Georg Trakl's poems: "I do not understand them; but their tone pleases me. It is the tone of true genius." And while the tone he acknowledges exists against the advice he'd delivered at the close of the *Tractatus*—as does most of the rest of his own output—he can nevertheless soak in the quietude Trakl has been compelled not so much to undermine as describe. (As Gaston Bachelard tells us: "There is nothing like silence to suggest a sense of unlimited space,"[10] and the quieted head need not recall its own entrapment.) It's the tone of silence in a state of prolapse, startled by its own noise, playing at returning to its former state. In a conquest worthy of Sadean Man, the nauseating infinity of Nature is countered with endlessly recurring autumns and afternoons collapsing in on themselves around a human tongue, where time and the very air can be seen yellowing in the felt sickness of being alive.

Theorising does not reveal, but instead creates its own hollows; it clarifies nothing but its own confusion, and that confusion is its truth. In order for it to taste the cockroach (à la Lispector), it must first turn itself into one. And what all art becomes, what it had to become, is the post-pessimistic wasteland of an increasing desperation—licking at itself and tasting only its disgustingly human skin—the paradox that comes of accepting the now revisionist structures of incompleteness, the pointless endlessness of striving toward no end beyond openendedness itself, its striving for the encapsulation of antithesis: the unreadable novel, the unwatchable movie, the unviewable artwork, the unlistenable music—the unliveable life. As Bataille remarks:

---

[9] Alfred Tennyson, "The Poet's Mind," in *Poems of Tennyson* (London: SPCK, 1910), 32.
[10] Gaston Bachelard, *The Poetics of Space*, trans. Maria Jolas (Boston: Beacon Press, 1969), 43.

Nonhuman Materialisations

On one hand, this small, limited, and inexplicable existence, wherein we have felt like an exile, a butt both of jokes and of the immense absurdity that is the world, cannot resolve to give up the game; on the other hand, it heeds the urgent call to forget its limits. In a sense, this call is the trap itself, but only insofar as the victim of the joke insists—as is common, if not necessary—on remaining a victim.[11]

And yet, following Nagel, there is no option but to fall victim: the inherent incompatibility of the subjective and the objective views of ourselves keeping the cockroach in sight and within our grasp. Although, when our mouths close on it they taste only their own tasting. This dichotomy of self-awareness seems for the most part all but unbridgeable, and our structures of human meaning themselves dependent on it remaining so. We do not often get to the material of this world, this place of places, to the material we carry around with us as if we'd already accepted it as constituting our existence, and if there's any mercy to be found in our existing it is there in the fuzz of this obligatory lacuna, this uneasy embracing of unease, this noisy silence, when after all "[o]nly silence is able to express what we have to say."[12]

Foot-binding produces dainty, pretty feet. It is only their nakedness we find ugly. Whoever understands this altercation knows how friendless the impossible becomes, how its fidelity to morning exhausts all concentration. Supererogation is cadaverous. But we God more forest, the ill-measure goaded in the existence of the long age, the gloom of now a visitant at work, the unchilded unheard inside their enervated screams. Every vow is a pestilence of occasion, a fancy of dizziness, the head full of termination-earth disturbances of mind up a tulip-tree. I ate at the cockroach for 24 months, and died inside it as a way of living, and through that reversed consumption death became

---

[11] Georges Bataille, "L'art, exercice de cruauté," in *Œuvres complètes, t. XI, Articles I, 1944–1949* (Paris: Gallimard, 1988), 480–486; 485. In the original French: "Cet appel et un sens est le piège, mais il ne l'est que dans la mesure où la victime de la plaisanterie tient, comme il est banal—disons même nécessaire—à demeurer victime."

[12] Georges Bataille, *The Unfinished System of Nonknowledge*, trans. Michelle Kendall and Stuart Kendall (Minneapolis: University of Minnesota Press, 2001), 113.

something I lost. I chewed on the cockroach and swallowed it down and watched it eat its way back up again, climbing into my hand to be eaten again as if my body (with my mind trapped inside it) was an amusement park ride and my unhealthy stretch of embodiment was its repeat ticket.

This state (this inner-ear infection of the soul): that of someone walking on my grave, not over but up and down repeatedly, a faceless someone, a faceless me.

My sanity is a diorama done out in yellowed lapses in concentration.

What I'm working on, all I can see interest in working on, are the dreams I will bring to the end of the world.

With the cockroach between your teeth, you bite down and you know: (1) A lie is the ultimate investment of meaning. And it was a gift that could be taken away; (2) Knowledge is a way of making the corridor go somewhere, whereas nonknowledge is a way of making the corridor impossible, of nonreasoning through the corridor's dead end; (3) To seek is to unravel—and perish in the sought; (4) Even hopelessness is a form of hope: the hope that hope's absence means something; (5) God is the enigma of an etymology of the nameless; (6) Noncomprehension is a wound dressed with action, underneath which it festers and blackens—eventually only death saves man from ever having to remove the bandages and behold the thing he's cultivated with neglect; (7) That reason fails us—goes back on its promise—opens a schism (between means and ends) into which we can if it happens fall, and there struggle—but ultimately hide. Better still, though, to have the schism collapse—to make of it a creative act.

There are entire schools of thought conceived with the cockroach on the tongue. And it still lies there unmolested. Like the cleverest parasite, it has convinced them that all the time it is there their teeth are not. But its "shell must be cracked apart if what is in it is to come out . . . if you want to discover nature's nakedness, you must destroy its symbols and the farther you get in, the nearer you come to its essence."[13] And that essence is the horror, not of itself but of the shell, of the mask around it—the mask that must be pierced for what's beneath it to ooze out, when all suspicions suggest we'll see only

---

[13] Meister Eckhart, *Meister Eckhart*, trans. Raymond B. Blakney (New York: Harper Collins, 1942), 148.

Nonhuman Materialisations

ourselves behind it, but only for an instance before we disappear[14]—the seemingly unsurpassable horror of the very needfulness of masks, the loose goo that the exoskeleton hides, the fluid life inside the rigid death. A reversal is apparent: we've constructed life from the inflexible dead matter, and avoided the watery, pococurante substance of life at all costs, avoided it because we somehow sense there's nothing and nobody there—just life, when we've constructed ourselves from the dead. "I had reached the nothing, and the nothing was living and moist,"[15] at which point the found becomes the unfound and the unfounded. The contrivance and the immanence of horror lies in our having to be constantly forgetting how we are daily conscripted into this lie of form around the formless, and how residing at its core we imagine ourselves and find nothing. It is not the reality of death that we deny, but that we are alive in the first place, and how all our squirming is just a result of this affliction, this threat that like water seeping into a damaged boat must be constantly displaced back inside the body of itself. Horror does not get to us, get into us, because it threatens death, but because it reminds us that we are alive.

Like Galen, we have created life according to what we've learnt of the dead, and not from any life we've ever found for ourselves, and not even from the dead of the kind we are, but from the pigs and apes of what life via death might look like. Even in anchoring ourselves to Vesalius (approximating life through the bodies of our own dead) we'd only come marginally closer to that which we do not know, closer in the sense that we would at least bear better witness to the mortification we call human life, to the specificity of our own trends in rotting out this existence. For it isn't being alive that terrifies, but knowing it. Being alive is for the most part synonymous with solidity, fixity and death, whereas knowing it, and feeling that knowing, is to see the sanctuary of your living death peeled back as if it were the sky. In the warm gloop of the cockroach is your own self-witnessing, and biting into it you bite into a someone you cannot taste or feel or experience beyond the sense that from somewhere came the thought that this was you. All the comforts of your dead reflection obliterated in an instant—no such thing as past, or sense in hope, or belonging in the other—and for as long as it lasts there is life there before you without

---

[14] See Gilles Deleuze, *Nietzsche and Philosophy*, trans. Hugh Tomlinson (London: Continuum, 2006), 5.
[15] Lispector, *The Passion According to G.H.*, 55.

the mask of its dead trappings, the undiluted, unfiltered essence of the inhuman nucleus of everything your existence so far has provided protection against. And what is there, then, but the fraught scramble to reassemble the deceased materials of your home, your exoskeleton of sameness through time? But such unearthly stress on this most terrestrial of dispositions is not one, it seems, that remaining human can sustain. And yet what else is there to the *meaning of human existence* that is not encompassed in these brief episodes involving the complete eradication of both meaning and humanity? Because when we put the humanness back together, we create ourselves in light of this knowledge, equipped somehow to live a life we know we cannot live, and like this correct (or else fulfil) God's work.

This work of perfecting (of accommodating the nonhuman), of continuing what has become senseless to continue, is to become something else, to be "caught up into the likeness of God,"[16] to make meaning out of meaning's absence, to establish sense where there is none. But it is only through the unbearable knowing of this necessity, this burden of continuance, through the felt nonknowledge of the state to which we must return, that creation has heft. Only via the disinterested (nonhuman) excretion of unliveable life is anything ever done. Only what is conceived in spite of itself is ever conceived. There are similarities here to the existential concerns for authenticity we see reinvigorated by Kierkegaard, Heidegger, and Sartre, but they go only so far, for the authentic state awaiting recognition is not that of a forgotten or subdued humanness, but instead the repression of a core nonhumanness which any self-examined humanness will come to know as something felt. It is not merely a case of not getting lost in the They, but of no longer curling up fetus-like inside individuality either, as both of these inevitabilities are crucially extrinsic to something known (as a felt nonknowing) through this bilinear boundary's momentary absence:

> The perfectly operative unworkability of the interface, a unilateral duality of thought and life, exposes the terribly unending and inescapable suddenness of being trapped alive in

---

[16] Eckhart, *Meister Eckhart*, 76.

consciousness, of finding oneself (to be) something like an always improper sum of thought and being.[17]

For once let us stay faithful to the enigma of these moments, to the "hell of living matter,"[18] the disenfranchising of the human, the pale, twitching ugliness of life for once seen (and not seen-as). "All philosophers should end their days at Pythia's feet. There is only one philosophy, that of unique moments,"[19] and we come at it already knowing we are in error, how in merely preparing to recount we've contributed to their going—and suspect this as the very reason such preparation was instigated, to be free of instances which we cannot be said to have experienced, but which nevertheless substantiated an experience for which we feel the need to account. Hope is attached to what was without it, concern to what had repelled involvement, the adrenaline of mortality to what was the purest expression of life: "Being alive is a coarse radiating indifference. Being alive is unattainable by the finest sensitivity. Being alive is inhuman."[20]

Through our seeing the cockroach's dead mask as dead, through our recognising that this investment in human life is at all other times via something rotted out, we see life as something necessarily beyond our being what we are. We know then that we cannot share in it, but cannot either shrug off the sense that the continuance of the human corpse is inevitable and desirable and unfairly deathless for never having lived. The whole history of philosophy is the expansion of a single moment, repeated over—the style dependent on the proximity, on the degree to which it was felt, and the extent to which each voice needed distance from its origin—in keeping with the Oracle of Delphi, a moment unique in content but not in number. All prioritisation of the human body (as essentially human) signals a retreat, a return to that which was savagely cleansed, recourse to a lifeless life (words and structures used like paddles to its decayed heart), for "to obey the flesh is to die,"[21] and to obey it when you've already seen and smelt its long

---

[17] Nicola Masciandaro, *Sufficient Unto The Day: Sermones Contra Solicitudinem* (London: Schism Press, 2014), 186.
[18] Lispector, *The Passion According to G.H.*, 53.
[19] E. M. Cioran, *The Book of Delusions*, trans. Camelia Elias, in *Hyperion*, vol. 5, issue 1 (2010): 61.
[20] Lispector, *The Passion According to G.H.*, 181.
[21] Eckhart, *Meister Eckhart*, 75.

having left is to die wilfully as something only humanity could embody. But in contrast to this timorous retreat there is what might be seen as a refusal to leave, once found, this inhuman material, a more authentic and vigorous obeying of flesh, a courageous persistence with this formless and indifferent substance, thus facilitating a long overdue and fundamental reappraisal of our humanness.

Even when Kafka becomes beetle, or mole or dog or mouse or ape, he remains for the most part human, intellect and reasoning powers intact, occupying only the guise and physicality of the animal in question. Remaining so archetypally human, we need to ask what purpose the animal incarnations serve. While in "The Metamorphosis" Gregor's being a man finding himself made insect is central to the narrative, in his other transpositions of persons into animals no reference is made to them being anything other than nonhuman. We are being asked to accept that access is being given to us to the creature in question, with no reference to the means of that access originating anywhere else other than from the animal itself. If the "I" has remained constant throughout this act of imagination, what is it that escapes the human in any meaningful way? We "want to eat straight from the placenta,"[22] but there has been no rebirth, no complete surrender and so nothing encountered that can be regarded as previously unknown and inaccessible. (Without this surrender, it is surely more sincere to stay outside, as for instance Paul Auster does with Mr. Bones in *Timbuktu*.) Returning to the succession of priestesses that comprise the Delphic Oracle, there is more force to the account that tells of how learned men translated the glossolalia of these gassed priestesses than there is to the more recent corrective account establishing these Apollonian reports' initial lucidity. The connection being, that from the adyton of these animals we would not expect a human voice, but a voice instead that would require at the very least some exploratory and approximated translation.

When Kafka is a dog he is a dog amongst dogs, "dogs like you and me."[23] By addressing us in this way he confesses that we are as much dog, in reading him as a dog, as he is a dog in writing himself one, and that our consequent inculcation into dogdom is a self-conscious

---

[22] Lispector, *Água Viva*, 3.
[23] Franz Kafka, "Investigations of a Dog," in *Kafka: Metamorphosis & Other Stories*, trans. Willa Muir and Edwin Muir (London: Minerva, 1992), 89.

mockery of identifying as anything—something acknowledged, we imagine, with our heads firmly on their sides. But then becoming dog is after all just becoming human again (for there are no humans in this world of dogs): the uniquely human facility for music, having been stripped away, is quickly returned to us in order to assist this self-identifying as canine. However, perhaps in this performance, this performance of being something, something unrecognisable, we are not dogs at all, but instead humans wrongly mistaken for dogs—like our narrator's performing seven, suggestively naked and upright—because both beyond our own species and within it there is only silence, a poisoning silence posed as a question: "Whence does the earth procure this food?"[24] And what is this question of food but the realisation that the world itself is food without being nourishment and the food inside of dogs a toxin, both non-foods made to look like food (the former thought by others to be a substance to "stop [the] mouth"),[25] when no such food can bring the needed silence, the end of questions, can bring about the question that in answering itself will become music. Therefore, Kafka-as-dog (as would-be-dog-messiah) can be thought to exist under the guise of some resurgent yet atheistic *Inedia prodigiosa*, back to modernise and educate, to science-fictionalise this drooling present with the deathless future of the past, and, like Catherine of Siena and Angela of Foligno, to decline the food of the world and drink nothing but the putrescence of its sickness, to refuse himself as he does in "The Fasting Artist" not *merely* for show (for there must be some element of show if only to see oneself) but for purposes of research, research into the possible means of allaying a hunger inseparable from the one who hungers, for purposes of starving yourself alive. Sharing in the flesh of dogs is just the pre-made decision to exist, and to not feed on a food that is in fact a placebo poison, but instead on a poison fit for a god (for doesn't his refusal of life make him appear backward?):[26] the food of our canine marrow, our deepest core, a manifestation of an inside that no ordinary life can taste while remaining ordinary, while remaining anything that can be framed in shared questions. Kafka-as-dog needs to spread the sickness of his self-awareness of existence (like those spreaders of *ressentiment* Nietzsche abhorred), but not in order to shirk the burden of life but to

---

[24] Kafka, "Investigations of a Dog," 95.
[25] Kafka, "Investigations of a Dog," 96.
[26] The God in a pack of gods.

convert his anorexia to gluttony, to feast on what it is that starves him.[27] Animals are not victim to the idea that suffering redeems. An animal's suffering is just suffering, so it can and must be stopped at any cost—even if that means that someone must suffer for them, even if that means that that someone is not as unlike them as they might at first imagine.

Just as becoming a Red Indian first involves the gradual disappearance of inharmonious tack and then the horse itself that you've imagined yourself-as-Red-Indian riding, so too does becoming nonhuman involve the continued fading of the vehicle you assumed to get you to that point, thus finding yourself nonhuman in the midst of being human, as the façade of the animal you became drops away or is discarded. The animals of these tales likewise disintegrate on contact with the human, for although they come to us via language, they lose themselves in the process: "What I felt then as an ape I can of course only describe today with human words, and they falsify the description."[28] Their way out, as the ape in his report concedes, is always the human way. Only in talking to humans does a jackal know its own hatred and hopes for freedom; left wordless, it simply eats the dead camels its enemies provide. Only in action and material constitution can the animal remain animal. Whether it is the assumed position of animal leaching into the human to be heard, or the human leaching into the animal to be seen, it is always the non-species-specific wound of existence itself that is the focal point of both. For while it is always the human perspective that permits the regenerative abrasion of life to be witnessed at all,[29] it is not about being either human or

---

[27] "For I want to compel all dogs thus to assemble together, I want the bones to crack open under the pressure of this collective preparedness, and then I want to dismiss them to the ordinary life that they love, while all by myself, quite alone, I lap up the marrow. That sounds monstrous, almost as if I wanted to feed on the marrow, not merely of a bone, but of the whole canine race itself. But it is only a metaphor. The marrow that I am discussing here is no food; on the contrary, it is a poison" (Kafka, "Investigations of a Dog," 99.)
[28] Franz Kafka, "A report for an academy," 222.
[29] "Man differs from animal in that he is able to experience certain sensations that wound and melt him to the core" (Georges Bataille "Madame Edwarda," in *My Mother, Madame Edwarda, The Dead Man*, trans. Austryn Wainhouse [London: Marion Boyars, 2003], 140).

Nonhuman Materialisations

animal, although this habitation of the blurred ground between them is a crucial tool, but instead that "incurable wound"[30] that comes of knowing you are anything at all, even if you are not even yourself. Recall how the mole-like creature in Kafka's "The Burrow" becomes less and less distinct from its network of tunnels—its blood should it ever be spilled would not be lost in them—how the earth is imbued with sentience and how the creature that shapes it is little more than a source of noise within it, as are all things like it: that other anonymous digging beast itself nothing but noise in shifted soil.

Becoming animal or becoming human-as-animal is, then, a transitory measure to facilitate becoming neither. To imbibe the liquid corpus of a broken cockroach, to wake as a beetle, to feel the pangs of human mystery as a canine, to renounce being ape for the exit of being human, to start as mole and end as noise in soil: the common strain in all of it is to source the wound of the need to be anything, the given-up-on freedom that remains always hidden in a series of desperate ill-fated ways out that are actually just ways back in. Kafka knew this, and as a result his excursions into the non-human are always humanly confined, remaining only superficially species-transcendent, because the true inexpressibility he was after was never the animal, but instead what it is about thought that cannot escape itself, the place in which Kant's dove is not seen to soar ever easier, but in which it is no longer a dove at all, but rather the very vacuum that removes it from the sky. The animal is merely the reimagining of a limit, as it is for Nagel and his bat, a perspective that cannot exist—not even for the animal, once we've indulged ourselves in tasting its approximated flavour, for the process denies both the animal and the human in its search for something more fundamental than either.

The taste of cockroach hemolymph is the taste of your own act of tasting, the taste of what it means to eat just about anything, of what it means to have existed on this planet for hundreds of millions of years. The earth will not suffer fussy eaters for long. As if these scuttling elders had made us their students, we have learnt to consume the world around us like we'd been here long enough to unlearn any diet that is not everything, as if we too had emerged from an ootheca, hissing and chirping, drooling at the prospect of swallowing the

---

[30] "[H]e only will grasp me aright whose heart holds a wound that is an incurable wound, who never, for anything, in any way, would be cured of it" (Bataille, "Madame Edwarda," 155).

universe. And the appetite of capitalism, with its wake of grey goo, is nothing to the accumulated hours of colourless slop that our experiential rut churns forth every second of every day. The world is not here unless I'm shitting it out, or else watching some other victim of experience fecalise the content their being alive has made necessary. In the manufacture of processed meat you start with the animal and end with slices or various grades of mush, and this food we understand, for the animal always makes more sense to us in its processed form.

Extrapolating from Hegel's master-slave dialectic, to become animal is to become slave, for a slave is anyone or anything more afraid of the other than they are of themselves: the mouse and the mole being archetypal in this regard. It is also provides a vicarious experience of an otherwise defunct direction, for the master has the opportunity to know that for all there is there's nowhere to go. All directions are open to the master and yet they cannot desire any of them. The emptiness of this erroneous elevation is alleviated through temporary identifications with the slave, with those for whom direction sustains itself, those for whom direction has direction and a vertical as well as a horizontal plane. As for the self-confessed human-worm of Kafka, he does not have the animalistic descent of the master, with which he cannot identify, but the humanistic descent through animal to its lowliest form.

According to Bataille, the merging of the animal with the human is the merging of the sacred and the profane, as the sacred fuses and liquidates in an intimate oneness that the profane seeks to individualise. And it is this particularly human awareness of time and distinctiveness that lead to anxiety, to "the impotent horror"[31] involved in letting them go, for this relinquishment of individuality and discontinuity, this embracing of intimacy, is of course indistinguishable from our fear of death, itself nothing more than a fear of formlessness.[32] However, it is not that animal consciousness, "lost in the mists of continuity where nothing is distinct,"[33] represents what he means by sacred, but rather our human acceptance of such a state—that paradoxical condition of

---

[31] Georges Bataille, *Theory of Religion*, trans. Robert Hurley (New York: Zone Books, 1992), 36.
[32] The correlations here with Schopenhauer's account of salvation (*erlosung*) are striking.
[33] Bataille, *Theory of Religion*, 35.

transition, kept forever in self-sacrificing perpetuity, the human in limbo in animal. Nevertheless, we must remember that Bataille's world is not the world but the acrid hundred-or-so-million-year-old sludge oozing from the cockroach, and its inaccessibility the blur we manage to bring into focus at the cost of becoming something, something worldly.

On the surface, Kafka's exercises in becoming animal appear to be in direct opposition to a Bataillean aesthetic—which indulges in disfigurement and primitivistic renderings of distortion—seeming instead to perform some eerie yet palatable gentrification of what it means to become animal, a process made most explicit in "A Report for an Academy." Often we are left guessing as to the presence of real animals, or else must remind ourselves that a particular animal is being evoked in the words we are reading. For example, in "Josephine the Singer, or The Mouse People," aside from the title, there is very little to suggest mouseness at all, little that is except for the constant reiteration of "squeak"—the squeak that remains, as the memory it always was, even after Josephine has gone. And this squeak is worth pursuing further, as a means of unpacking these nonhuman excursions as more than mere literary contrivance, more than the anthropomorphic prettification of supposedly baser modes of existence. For although only the title provides direct access to the world of mice, as from there on in all that is left to contextualise this opening promise is the squeak, it is via this squeak that we are able to orientate one species in the space of another. And the squeak retains its non-semantic allure even for those for whom we'd imagine it language. It is abstracted from all content: it is pure noise, gradually indistinguishable from any other instance of noise, it is the voice removed from what is said. And of the audience's silence there is something of Levinas' transcendent self-awareness, in which "this breathlessness or holding back is [maybe] the extreme possibility of the spirit, bearing a sense of what is beyond the essence."[34] It remains as unsubstantiated as anything else that just occurs, so that what looks like some kind of taxonomical marker is instead something more germane to existence in general: the temporary undoing of silence, the to-be-forgotten announcement of some non-historicised incidental. Mouseness, then, is indeed a distortion, a disfigurement, a crude enactment of primitive grappling, not through

---

[34] Emmanuel Levinas, *Otherwise Than Being, Or Beyond Essence*, trans. Alphonso Lingis (Dordrecht: Kluwer, 1991), 5.

the humanised narrator, but through the squeak, the common squeak elevated to meaning by the silence that surrounds it, that becoming-art of what is otherwise habitual and mindless. If here we have the quietly insidious melancholy of us witnessing our contrived impositions of form, what of the full-blown horror of what remains for the most part hidden and formless (in us and in the world itself)?

If "affirming that the universe resembles nothing and is only formless amounts to saying that the universe is something like a spider or spit,"[35] what can we say of the cockroach? Can that too be considered formless in the same way as the spider? Firstly, we need to establish just how it is the spider lacks form, and the most immediately obvious indicator of this—like the earthworm with which Bataille makes the spider congruous—is its lack of an independently formed head,[36] as what would in other arthropods constitute two bodily segments are combined in the spider into a single tagmata: the cephalothorax. It is here that any possible assimilation with the cockroach would appear to come to an end, as the cockroach's head is clearly segmented from the rest of its body. And while there are those often-discussed instances in which cockroaches are found to exist acephalously, this depleted state is not implicit within the cockroach's taxonomy. And it is for this reason that the cockroach's outside must be breached, its insides revealed, the indeterminate spit of its most intimate machinery shown to be nothing other than some secreted nexus of horror, an unrecognised and unrecognisable terror hidden even from its bearer, in a violent extrusion of liquid debasing whatever form surrounds it, because it is the mystery of the connection between them that ultimately makes room for attachments to be made, for mergings of thought and physicality to have a realm of senselessness in which to establish meaning: "A dog devouring the stomach of a goose, a drunken vomiting woman, a sobbing accountant, a jar of mustard represent the confusion that serves as the vehicle of love."[37] The

---

[35] Georges Bataille, "Formless," in *Visions of Excess: Selected Writings, 1927–1939*, ed. Allan Stoekl, trans. Allan Stoekl with Carl R. Lovitt and Donald M. Leslie, Jr. (Minneapolis: University of Minnesota Press, 1985), 31.

[36] For more on heads, headlessness and the formless possibilities of arachnids, see Eugene Thacker, "Thing and No-Thing," in *And They Were Two in One and One in Two*, ed. Nicola Masciandaro and Eugene Thacker (London: Schism Press, 2014), 10–30.

[37] Georges Bataille, "The Solar Anus," in *Visions of Excess*, 6.

Nonhuman Materialisations

spider, the earthworm, the insides of the cockroach: all are instances of form's transparency (transparent and non-transcendental), and so its failure and its ultimate formlessness. This malfunction of form is a glitch that reveals glimpses of that which form is ordinarily so proficient at concealing: that which is not merely not-human, not merely animal, but antithetical to humanness, the nonhuman as the active unmaking of humanity, our narratives and imposed recreations unrealising the world, and the world's returning not as the reciprocal manifestation of our act of manipulation, but as form (made formless) laid like glass over formlessness. Us in the world and the world in us, and neither one with any discernible shape or substance or purpose: Pessoa becoming Lisbon and Lisbon becoming Pessoa, Joyce Dublin and Dublin Joyce, and both sides a slippery powder cascading through the fingers of each, fingers which cannot remain fingers long enough to feel the contents drain away. Our structures and the structures of the world existing for a moment in a state of unitive honesty, a state emptied of contrivance on both sides and so somehow exhuming the mutually unconditioned: a univocal drool.

When the world is not there for me, or rather persistently there and yet available only as the backdrop of some past involvement, I look to the unreality of it and then to the unreality of myself. For the loss of the world eventually requires the loss of self, and this corrective measure is no less distressing, no less fought over, despite its clearly being requisite. This compensatory or restorative mirroring is both defensive and combative: for instead of suffering the world's lack, making yourself the victim of this enhancement of the distance-from,[38] you instead go about removing the world residing within you that can no longer find its correlate. The unassailable logic being, that two ghosts are better than one. Resistance to this likewise becoming ghost will more often than not manifest itself in various clinically recognisable states—anxiety, depression, psychopathology—whereby the illusion of the independent substantiality of the self seeks reinforcement in contradistinction to the intangible flow of sensory experience that is the world as it is found and how it has come to find

---

[38] It might be thought that distance is always in some sense distance-from, and that this precisification is an empty and unnecessary embellishment. However, this logistical preposition serves to distinguish the corrosion of the world from distance experienced in the abstract, i.e. the distance that precludes full presence without any determinate sense of lack.

us. This intangibility, though (cruelly enough) not literally without the sensation of touch, is nevertheless something equally transformative, as it demands from haptic experience what was never there, while fully imagining that it was (which in some ways it actually was, that is, in the sense that its absence had not yet been noticed), and so while still experiencing that tactile interaction with the world, it becomes instead just the conditions of the sensation vacated of history. The world then still there, but as a simulacrum, a copy of what was never there, a dream of a journey somewhere else that, for lack of a point of departure, was never embarked upon.

Elias Canetti once wrote: "If you look attentively at an animal, you get the feeling that a man is hidden inside and is making fun of you."[39] Correlatively, when I look closely at a man, I get the distinct impression that something neither human nor animal is hidden inside and ridiculing the presumption that any such scrutiny might reveal its nature.

---

[39] Elias Canetti in Jean Baudrillard, *Fatal Strategies* (Los Angeles: Semiotext(e), 2008), 155.

Chapter 4

Non-Terminator: Rise of the Drone-Gods

The abyss of death is as unthinkable as the abyss of infinite life, for immortality is itself a form of death: inescapable, without end, the unmaking of what we recognise as this distinctly human life. It is our inability to conceive immortality as anything but an increasingly pestilential drone that provides some lukewarm comfort to our eventual deaths. The situation is analogous to the reflexive excruciations endured by those outstaying their welcome in anechoic chambers—where the sound is you and the sound is unbearable. The drone of this hypothesised forever comes from within, and it will either destroy us (in some hideous yet non-fatal destruction) or else turn us into gods. In order to be clear about precisely what's at stake, we must consider the following two options:

1) The offer of immortality with a get-out clause.
2) The offer of immortality with no get-out clause.[1]

If offered a choice between these two options we would, it's safe to suppose, almost universally be inclined to prefer option 1 to option 2, and make our choice accordingly. For while option 1 looks to have no obvious drawback, option 2 would in all likelihood strike most of us as conceptually revolting, not to mention terrifying. Option 1 allows us room to breathe, room to keep death at bay for as long as the positive aspects of life remain, whereas option 2 threatens to drown you in its ineludible monotony. But if, as Unamuno explains, "longing is not to

---

[1] If the majority of physicists are correct, then the fate of the universe may well offer its own get-out clause, but let us suppose that this cannot be taken for granted, or maybe less contentiously that it isn't coming soon enough to affect the points I wish to make.

be submerged in the vast All, in an infinite and eternal Matter or Energy, or in God; not to be possessed by God, but to possess Him, to become myself God, yet without ceasing to be I myself, [for] we crave the substance and not the shadow of immortality,"[2] then option 2 is imperative in order to enact such a transformation, a transformation that is indeed necessary if we are to withstand the demands of an immortality which is not a mere shadow of the real thing (an immortality*).

In his 1973 paper, "The Makropulos case: reflections on the tedium of immortality,"[3] Bernard Williams claims to be discussing a "state without death," but he isn't. For the Makropulos case is the story of a woman (Elina Makropulos) who can at any time, and who eventually does, refrain from imbibing the elixir of life that keeps her alive. Williams never deals with option 2—although he is by no means isolated in this respect—and doesn't seem aware of the problems involved with not doing so. Williams claims that we are lucky to have the chance to die, but then Elina also had the chance to die, and is she really to be considered unlucky just because she had the chance of postponing it indefinitely? This is the immortality of Dracula, which though progressively burdensome, we imagine, is still a choice, albeit one muddied with compulsion.

It could be argued that by not choosing option 2, by lacking the necessary attributes needed to make such a commitment, we would not be giving immortality its due observance. For by retaining the option of death you will never be able to commit to your extended life in a way that is comparable to that forced by option 2, as it is only via the complete excision of death from our lives that we will ever come to terms with the implications of living forever, and so successfully make the psychological adjustments necessary for such an event. If you can always bail out at any time, you are not even experiencing what it is to be immortal—at least not in the sense that option 2 makes you immortal (from now on immortal*). Choosing immortality over immortality* would, no doubt, allow you to bear the burdens of life-extension rather better than those who opted for immortality*—

---

[2] Miguel de Unamuno, *Tragic Sense of Life*, trans. J. E. Crawford Flitch (New York: Dover Publications, 1954), 47.
[3] Bernard Williams, *Problems of the Self* (Cambridge: Cambridge University Press, 1976), 82–100.

initially at least. The opt-out clause might, in fact, be the only thing that could make the prospect of a possibly endless future bearable.[4] However, those that chose immortality*, or had it thrust upon them, would have no choice but to bear it. They might do so in a perpetual state of panic and misery, but endure it they would, for the choice is not theirs to do anything else. To get to the root of what we really think about death we must talk in terms of immortality* (an endless life in which death is not possible) as opposed to Williams' immortality, where nothing more is implied than the mere potential for continued life extension. To be truly immortal is to be in a state free from death, not to walk in its shadow for as long as one chooses. This being the case, it makes little sense to ask whether immortality* would be bearable, as, in a sense, there would be no way in which one could avoid bearing it. Is it not, then, more constructive to ask whether or not it is likely to be a happy or rewarding existence? Perhaps, if this question weren't equally ridiculous, for it remains unanswerable for a life of any duration. And to add to this insolubility, how are we to know the lengths to which we might go in order to occupy ourselves, the full extent of the inventiveness that would surface in people threatened with an endless life of insanity and desolation, should they crumble under the weight of time? "If a human being were a beast or an angel, he could not be in anxiety,"[5] but which would we become?

In concurrence with Kafka's famous proclamation on the existential beneficence of cessation, Williams claims that "[i]mmortality, or a state without death, would be meaningless, . . . death gives meaning to life."[6] According to these assertions, immortal life would not be worth living, would be worthless in a way that ordinary finite life is not; worthless, then, because it will rapidly exhaust our potential for meaningful growth, our limitations making us suited only to a finite and rather brief existence. But can we ask, with a straight face, if we are necessarily limited in this way? And need immortality*, by necessity, be

---

[4] It would, however, make a difference just how frequently your death was made available to you (assuming suicide is somehow made impossible): day by day, week by week, month by month, year by year, etc., one might always be able to face the thought of one more day, but one more year might prove more of a challenge the longer one had existed.
[5] Søren Kierkegaard, *The Concept of Anxiety*, ed. and trans. Reidar Thomte (New Jersey: Princeton University Press, 1980), 155.
[6] Williams, *Problems of the Self*, 82.

a ridiculous and arduous prospect? With this apparent nonsensicality in mind, I'll ask it anyway, even if I must smirk a little as I do it.

That pessimism would have to recede even further into the stygian murk of our consciousness might seem reasonable to conclude, given that we are hard pushed to give these ideas headroom when our lives are, by comparison, extremely brief. With human life made sempiternal, the toxicity of such philosophies would, the thought goes, surely prove untenable. As a luxury of intellectual conjecture it would need to be eradicated, or at least inoculated against, perpetually and forever. And maybe there, already, you have a purpose, a reason to be that itself depends on discovering a reason to be: the search for meaning that is its own reward, a pathway of endless and impassioned inventiveness that, quite rightly, fears a faltering step more than anything else.

Quoting from Ernest Becker's *The Denial of Death*, Ligotti lays down our contrivances in the face of terror, of how we crawl away from the "outlawed truisms" and "taboo commonplaces" that tell of our essential meaninglessness and scant existence, and how in running from one madness we fabricate a different one, a liveable one: "I believe that those who speculate that a full apprehension of man's condition would drive him insane are right, quite literally right. [Man] literally drives himself into blind obliviousness with social games, psychological tricks, personal preoccupations so far removed from the reality of his situation that they are forms of madness, but madness all the same."[7] And this in turn is a reworking of a similar idea expressed by Otto Rank, for as he makes clear, the neurotic (and the pessimist, for they are scarcely distinguishable here) "suffers, not from all the psychological mechanisms which are psychically necessary for living and wholesome but in the refusal of these mechanisms which is just what robs him of the illusions important for living."[8] The quandary, then, is either that of how we infinitely fortify and perpetuate the deception (and so take heed of the warning: take the contrivance seriously or else—or else there'll be nothing to do and no one to be), how we approximate something like living within the maddening drone of that deception, or alternatively how we might do away with the need for the deception altogether.

---

[7] Ernest Becker, *The Denial of Death* (New York: The Free Press, 1973), 27.
[8] Otto Rank, *Will Therapy and Truth and Reality* (New York: Knopf, 1936), 252.

Non-Terminator: Rise of the Drone-Gods

It is important to note, however, that, in Rank's terms, the true pessimist cannot "partialize": they cannot limit their eating to only their allotted slice of the existential cake. They are compelled to eat the lot, and it is this that makes them sick—or sick, at least, in the eyes of those who can comfortably nibble their own slice without needing to taste the whole from which it came. Reality is always too much for us to stomach. Health and worldly-belonging, like those judgements of beauty from Nietzsche's herd men, are inescapably *shortsighted*. For no true pessimist could ever sustain an experience of something as simply beautiful—although the possibility that such an experience could momentarily blindside them can never be completely ruled out—because such an experience necessarily partializes in a way that they cannot: "The neurotic type [the pessimist] makes the reality surrounding him a part of his ego, . . . has taken into himself potentially the whole of reality,"[9] and no judgement of beauty could hope to remain intact under such pressure. The need is for us to see more and not be damaged by it, to partake of not only the omnispection of gods, but to acquire the power to assimilate what they see. As Becker explains:

> Gods can take in the whole of creation because they alone can make sense of it, know what it is all about and for. But as soon as man lifts his nose from the ground and starts sniffing at eternal problems like life and death, the meaning of a rose or a star cluster—then he is in trouble. Most men spare themselves this trouble by keeping their minds on the small problems of their lives just as their society maps these problems out for them. These are what Kierkegaard referred to as the "immediate" men and the "Philistines." They "tranquilize themselves with the trivial"—and so they can lead normal lives.[10]

Here the objective would seem ridiculously grandiose if it weren't for the fact that the pessimist is part of the way there already and, relative to that part, incurable (unless we accept impairment as a cure and go about healing them of the truth), and so poisoned with the conditioning of gods merely as a result of their not being one. The task

---

[9] Rank, *Will Therapy and Truth and Reality*, 146–147.
[10] Becker, *The Denial of Death*, 178.

as it presents itself here is not so much how such a person might become a god, but how they might become just godlike enough to inoculate themself from the suffering attendant to their perspectival overreaching. Or else, were option 2 available, become a Drone-God: for a Drone-God does not drown in their depression, they drink it.

The very idea of our lives being extended indefinitely is at best a problematic one, at worst horrific; for while there may be some who would see no reason why we couldn't embrace such an opportunity without reservation, their optimism looks too much like ignorance or gross stupidity to be anything else. Whichever side one falls on (the problem to be solved/the inevitable horror), and most will probably tend to oscillate between the two, it will prove useful to consider whether we might possibly make ourselves worthy of immortality*, *become* the sort of beings to whom the prospect of an endless life is considered unquestionably beneficial, an endless life that might just prove transformative enough to have the pessimist actually become the gods they so often appear to mimic. It is, of course, highly unlikely that we could ever even approximate how such beings would need to approach themselves and their environs. Nevertheless, isn't this a goal worth having, if any goal is, whether it is achievable or not? Nietzsche quoting Dante writes, "[n]ot 'mankind' but *overman* is the goal . . . *Come l'uom s'eterna*—INF. XV 85 How man makes himself eternal,"[11] and it is this making-eternal of the human that's left—when after the death of God there is only our aesthetic creativity to fill the gap left by his destruction. And that we are made not merely infinite but eternal, a being stripped not only of end but beginning as well, reveals that by occupying the God-void we ourselves have become God. But ultimately it is eternity's future burden that is the test, the arena (the thought experiment of choice) in which we can ascertain our own value, if any value remains. About this Nietzsche is right, but as for the formulation of the test, there is work to be done.

Nietzsche's concept of the übermensch is essentially defined in terms of his notion of Eternal Recurrence, for only the übermensch is able to gladly welcome a doctrine that has us living the same life over and over. He is the yes-sayer, the one who can be as positive about his sorrow as he can his joy—all of his life approached with affirmation, as

---

[11] Nietzsche, *The Will to Power*, 519.

a united, perfected whole.[12] The great becomes greater, the horrors heavier, harder to pass over with the passing of time, all of history made more significant; and yet at the same time there's also the meaninglessness of history's endless repetition and our impotence within it.[13] As Brian Leiter sees it, there are two central flaws:

> [P]erfection is a matter of living in such a way that one is ready to gladly will the repetition of one's life, in all its particulars, in to eternity. This, too, seems both too thin and too severe as a criterion of perfection standing alone: too thin, because anyone suitably superficial and complacent might will the eternal return; too severe, because it seems to require that a post-Holocaust Goethe gladly will the repetition of the Holocaust.[14]

In light of this, what's required is a reformulation of Nietzsche's thought experiment,[15] in which the mechanism for gauging human character is not how one faces up to the prospect of their life being

---

[12] And while there is clearly more impetus if we believe that we are living our life for the first time in this endless sequence—as it gives what we do weight, and frees it from the ephemeral—the likelihood of this being the case is extraordinarily slim.

[13] There's a certain similarity here to the scenario (a religious parable of sorts) played out in the film *Groundhog Day*, in which Bill Murray's character is forced to live the same day over and over again. Although he can develop new characteristics, learn new things, and act differently, everybody else stays as they were, and the day repeats. The slavish routine of that one day can never contain enough meaning on its own, but must be shored up by days in the future that will bear its mark, and crucially your mark by virtue of your having lived through it. In the existence Nietzsche envisions, Bill Murray remains unaware that the day is the same, he does not change and he never escapes— the future (that has never happened) never happens. This makes meaning a matter of being rather than becoming, in essence not consequence, stagnant not flowing, completeness not incompleteness. And it's this that makes it an aberration: that any human life could complete itself satisfactorily, that it could internally justify its own sufferings, that it could lack nothing by not continuing outside what it already is, strikes us as fundamentally non-human. And isn't that the point?

[14] Brian Leiter, "Nietzsche's Moral and Political Philosophy," in the *Stanford Encyclopedia of Philosophy* (http://plato.stanford.edu/entries/nietzsche-moral-political/).

[15] The literal truth of which remains a matter of debate.

endlessly repeated, but instead whether or not one is prepared to choose immortality* over immortality. For even the most superficial or complacent person can appreciate the risk in the second option, a risk any benefits of which such a character could not possibly grasp. By utilising this reformulation, both the allegation of severity and that of thinness are resolved, there being no obligation to will the infinite replay of atrocities, and no easy escape for the superficial and the complacent, for even though such people might not recognise the potential strength of immortality*'s venom, the mere threat of its bite would most likely be enough to dissuade them.

Just as Nietzsche criticised Kant for emancipating himself from the theist cage only to then crawl back inside it, he too is criticised for laying the groundwork for a pessimist philosophy only to subvert it with his notion of "higher" humans, his "revaluation." But this accusation is misguided on yet another level: for just as acknowledging the possibility of extending human life is not necessarily to condone it, acknowledging elements that might make such an extension more interesting is, likewise, not to say the effort justifies itself. Without pain, life is sillier, less significant, ludicrous and shameful; and at the heart of this is the concept of pain as a creative force, a transformative fuel. But suffering need not be idealised as a result of this, for what is instead enshrined is the human requirement for meaning, without that required meaning itself being grounded in anything further, without its meaning being thought of as objectively meaningful. To transform the belief "it is thus and thus" into the will "it shall become thus and thus"[16] is to become creative and tragic, that which is encapsulated in our saying Yes to life, Yes to reality, that crucial "move beyond all terror and pity"[17] that rids us of the need to expunge them from human existence. Just to what degree Nietzsche believed this transformation to be possible is not entirely clear, but the dilemma itself is captured perfectly by Pessoa, who likewise managed to extract some threadbare gleam of meaning from what he took to be the self-evident truths of pessimism: "How tragic not to believe in human perfectibility! / And how tragic to believe in it!"[18] For what immortality* drives home is the need to transcend the negatively tragic and instead become actively tragic, to

---

[16] Nietzsche, *The Will to Power*, 324.
[17] Nietzsche, *On the Genealogy of Morals and Ecce Homo*, 273.
[18] Pessoa, *The Book of Disquiet*, 247.

Non-Terminator: Rise of the Drone-Gods

replace non-belief with belief; but a belief that is itself groundless and known to be groundless, a belief manufactured from nothing—the belief that floats. The trick is not to have belief make us ignorant, masking our faces after we've watched them disappear, but to transmute via belief into the reflective substance of that which is believed, to believe facelessness into a new type of face.

How is it, then, we might ask, that divine completeness can appear so utterly harmless, its propagation of filled lacunae so seemingly replete with comfort? The answer to which arrives in the form of a denial: because those gaps were never truly filled. Any paradise's possibilities and instantiations remain forever incomplete, forever unseen (spectrally so), something realised with admirable succinctness by Kinbote in Vladimir Nabokov's *Pale Fire*: "As St. Augustine said, 'One can know what God is not; one cannot know what He is.' I think I know what He is not: He is not despair, He is not terror, He is not the earth in one's rattling throat, not the black hum in one's ears fading to nothing in nothing."[19] If we follow this apophatic process we will find God, and at the same time all other bywords for human meaning, find him (or it) as the subject of an infinite conveyor belt of subtractions, but not a single addition—a nothing that holds minuses together. Can you imagine how light we become all the while we keep these subtractions apart? And how heavy once they start to mingle and breed with each other? "Time is *heavy* sometimes; imagine how heavy eternity must be,"[20] and imagine too, while you're at it, how we might come to build the muscles needed to bear it.

The reward of eternity (immortality*) must, then, remain free of detail, must resist anything bordering on a complete description. Some sense of mystery and one's future enlightenment (always to remain future) must exist for salvation to be possible, for immortality* to remain a welcome prospect. But can this perpetual speculation really offer anything resembling salvation, or is it just one more makeshift measure, one more distraction that will eventually falter, leaving us eking out our endlessness devoid of sustainable meaning? Wittgenstein claimed that what's required is not incompleteness but its opposite, and that "if I am to be REALLY saved,—what I need is *certainty*—not

---

[19] Nabokov, *Pale Fire*, 227.
[20] Cioran, *The Book of Delusions*, 63.

wisdom, dreams or speculation—and this certainty is faith."[21] However, faith is a particular kind of certainty, one that sustains itself through a curtailment of reservation or enquiry, a selective and cultivated blindness, and so always a combination of certainty and openendedness—however sublimated that openendedness might be. For certainty demands an endpoint, a horizon already reached, and as Williams reminds us "[n]othing less will do for eternity than something that makes boredom unthinkable."[22] Therefore a state of total absorption must be possible for immortal*s, and with it a loss of character, a loss of self; whereas certainty is the opposite of distraction and cannot absorb us: a transparency stripped of its power to engage and thereby divert.

Nonetheless, in the case of the self, the fact that it is taken for granted, a given from which to proceed, is precisely what allows it to fall into the background where it needs to be. Whereas making the self a focus of enquiry makes something akin to a presence of its absence, resulting in a detachment from worldly engagements, the found absence of a substantial self becoming an unwelcome intermediary in the way of losing the self in those activities that would absorb it, thus making its unquestioned something a transparency, a nothing. Although, following Descartes, an exacting system of disbelief can lead us where we need to be, to the surety that there is experience and that that experience presents itself as localised, and localised in a manner that implies some sense of ownership without ever finalising the owning party or that which is owned. This is a state, or a series of states, or a process (which we can choose to label "self" or not) that can proceed more or less pleasurably, more or less tolerably, depending on the nature and levels of its awareness of itself, so that while certainty can allow the self to disappear, outside of the self this exhaustive peeling away of analytical interest is wont to reinstate that very self as something apodeictically problematic.

Certainty (outside of this blinkered presumption of our own identities), though often sought as a resolution to our unease, is consoling only insofar as it remains aspirational: its achievement being inimical to life that is not already or destined to become a living death.

---

[21] Ludwig Wittgenstein, *Culture and Value*, trans. G. E. M. Anscombe (London: Blackwell Publishers, 1998), 38, original emphasis.
[22] Williams, *Problems of the Self*, 95.

Non-Terminator: Rise of the Drone-Gods

In an essay, discussing and undermining the supposed *sui generis* status of Kafka's writings, Idris Parry identifies the following thematic strain:

> In his essay *Ur-Gerausch* (Primal Sound), Rilke speculates on man's sensory capacities. At present, he says, each of our five senses covers its own sector, which is separate from the others. . . . May there not be gaps between them, mysterious chasms in man's perception, spaces of which we are ignorant—not because there is nothing there, but because our sensory capacity is incomplete? It is these gaps in our awareness, Rilke believes, that cause our human anxiety, for we fear the unknown. And it is to these gaps that Gogol and Kafka lead us. They are constantly straining beyond their known boundaries.[23]

However, while Rilke, and indeed Parry in his advocacy of this stance with respect to Nikolai Gogol, Kafka, and Nathaniel West, appear to present us with an observation so standard and abundant as to be platitudinous (our fear of the unknown, no less) it remains a glaring example of a half-truth, and how misleading they can be; for while we may fear the unknown, without it our lives would be saturated in fear's worst excesses: the claustrophobic sickness of being trapped in some airtight conviction with no possibility of escape. In the film *Spoorloos*, Raymond Lemorne offers Rex Hofman a choice between never knowing for certain what happened to his missing wife and the very real risk of finding out: is he to drink the coffee that he knows to be drugged and so discover his wife's fate, or else walk away and live with the knowledge that he will never find out what happened to her? After thinking it through, he chooses certainty over uncertainty (over the certainty of that uncertainty) and wakes to find himself buried alive, literally trapped, suffocated and sentenced to death by the very certainty he so craved. By way of cajolement, Lemorne had offered these words: "And the uncertainty? The eternal uncertainty, Mr Hofman? That's the worst."[24] And in spite of the obvious risks to his life, Hofman is of the same mind. Here we have the undoing of mystery as an asphyxiating confinement and expeditious death, and

---

[23] Idris Parry, "Kafka, Gogol and Nathanael West," in *Kafka: A Collection of Critical Essays* (New Jersey: Prentice Hall, 1962), 89–90.
[24] See *Spoorloos* or *The Vanishing*, directed by George Sluizer (1988; France: Argos Films).

uncertainty and incompleteness as nothing less than life itself, Lermone's experiment having revealed to Hofman the inherent tension and insolubility of all that isn't mind-crushing claustrophobia and death.

Related to these thoughts on certainty, we should also note that life is unquestionably easier to endure during periods of complete absorption than it is during periods of boredom and worldly detachment. And yet, without the capacity to consider ourselves in isolation from our activities, we would lose much (if not all) of what it means to have a sense of self, thereby forfeiting the attachment we might expect to have between ourselves now and ourselves at some future time—if, that is, we are to consider ourselves as continuing to exist in any way that we regard as identity-preserving. Otherwise, do we not just become the tools (however integral) in some activity or series of activities? The concern for Williams is that although boredom is most often a localised and temporary condition, existing for a short time only as the result of a particular type (or lack) of activity, immortality would see it change into a generalised and permanent condition, the very threat of which would sour experience irrevocably. Each of us has a limited number of pursuits that we regard as pleasurable, and it is, at the very least, uncertain that these would prove endlessly repeatable and endlessly pleasurable.[25] The balance to strike, once again, is between us retaining our identity, and that identity being malleable enough to allow us to sufficiently metamorphose into something, as yet, completely unrecognisable.

---

[25] And while it must be conceded that this depletion of pleasure needn't happen by necessity—for, as John Martin Fischer ("Why Immortality Is Not So Bad," *International Journal of Philosophical Studies* 2 [1994]: 261) and David Benatar (*The Human Predicament* [New York: Oxford University Press, 2017], 156) have claimed, there are a number of pleasurable experiences that appear to be robustly repeatable (providing there are breaks between them), and so there is no reason for them to prove any less pleasurable should our lives be permanently extended—it is also worth noting that expectations congruent to such experiences, and the returns they offer, are often thought to diminish over the course of our current (relatively short) lifetimes, so that to imagine the enactment of this repeatability on what is an almost unfathomable scale would occur without eventual detriment to the experiences themselves is perhaps wishful thinking.

Non-Terminator: Rise of the Drone-Gods

What the prospect of immortality* threatens us with is the potential toxin of the instant, the many imagined flavours of your existence cooked into a single sour reduction, a uniform and poisonous gloop: "When speaking of life, you say *moments*; of eternity, *moment*."[26] The urge to categorise and order and ultimately own your temporal being must be overcome. The instant must be allowed to reign and you must disappear inside it—disperse before you implode. The selves we've manufactured to live for only a finite period—and forever only within the perfunctory and whimsy-soaked afterlives of religious or mystic extrapolation—are unequal to the task, their partible form in the fully disclosed face of endlessness nothing short of the purest horror. If Cioran is right that "[t]here are no hopes or regrets in eternity, [and that to] live each moment in itself is to escape the relativity of taste and category, to break free from the immanence in which time has imprisoned us,"[27] then this dispersal of self, that in concurrence with Williams would appear desirable for the immortal, is also something that immortality* demands and must surely (eventually) actualise.

While death is not evil—William James' "worm at the core"—nor is it the gift that those of a more pessimistic persuasion would have us believe. The mistake made by both camps is to regard death as something that we are sufficiently acquainted with. To consider the necessity of death an evil is to decry the end of a sequential process, the meaning and value of which you do not understand. How is it possible to substantiate that it is better for the sequential process to continue rather than not, when the conditions of that very continuance would seem to imply that you (as you are, as you recognise yourself) no longer play a part in it? And likewise, how can you substantiate that it is better for this sequential process to end than for it to continue, when the adaptations that this continuance would impose have not (and as yet cannot) be accurately delineated? Nagel observes that our "experience does not embody the idea of a natural limit," due in part no doubt to man's practiced sublimation. But why, then, is the prospect of immortality* so knotty? For if we did indeed approach our lives as an inexhaustible continuum, then immortality* would surely be a straightforward corrective, rather than a cause for panic. But Nagel's point cannot be dismissed so easily, for there is a sense in which the days allotted us—those of us not terminally ill—are endured or

---

[26] Cioran, *On the Heights of Despair*, 65.
[27] Cioran, *On the Heights of Despair*, 64–65.

enjoyed with little or no attention paid to some diminishing quota from which they were consumed. Although, this does not amount to an underlying and inbuilt sense of one's conscious limitlessness, but instead to an orderly contrivance of time, whereby we segment our lives into paradoxes of endless presents, and like Zeno's arrow we come to rest in these instants, and so never move decisively closer to our final destination. That we get there eventually through a succession of these instants is not something of which we are unaware, some conscious preclusion, but something found incongruent to the instants as we occupy them. Our steady encroachment on death steadies us inside the paradox while leaving it for the most part intact.

How many pessimistic thinkers have the luxury of being only that, only thinkers of that worst of apparent self-evidences? They entertain, and often make powerful and convincing cases for the essential meaninglessness of human existence, but the acknowledgement and detailing of a sickness is not the same thing as contracting it. Carlo Michelstaedter is one of a few concrete exceptions, one who found he could not slip back into life's rhetoric once he'd revealed its spurious weave and so suicided. And where is there for the pessimist to go? For all the accuracy and acuity of pessimism, the strong stomachs and adamantine resolve of its adherents, it remains almost completely impotent. Whether diseased or merely a carrier, the pessimist is stymied. But given this persistent impasse, what is there to prevent the pessimist rewriting the deadening rhetoric of life instead of succumbing to it in a fit of self-loathing weakness and impotent disadvantage? Why not do what humans do so well and create a story, and then live it and have it be unique and have it be fantastical? Why not refuse to accept that the difficulties of doing so are insurmountable? Or better still, why not accept those difficulties as insurmountable and seek to overcome them anyway? Why not embark unflinching on that "search for the impossible by way of the useless"?[28] Pessimism would have us believe that it is the last word, and indeed it is difficult for some of us to believe that it isn't: it is the loudest voice in the heads of those awake enough to hear it, but the last . . . ? Never accept last words! Better to remake the world newly absurd than to passively embody its pre-existing sillinesses. "Life not only has no meaning; it can *never* have one," but exactly what it can and

---

[28] Pessoa, *The Book of Disquiet*, 206.

does have is *many* meanings, all of them contingent and decaying and failing and repeatable and ultimately replaceable. If maturity "consists in having found again the seriousness one had as a child, at play," then immortality* should be welcomed, as the opportunity to grow up.

In order for immortality* to become a rewarding prospect, we would need to become more profound beings. We would have to make ourselves important enough to justify our immortality*. We would have to consider ourselves important enough to deserve it. Who knows what psychological deviations an infinite life facing up to our infinitude might occasion—or what depravities? The person who "looks death in the face, real death, not just a picture of death,"[29] was, for Wittgenstein, nothing short of a hero. And while there is obvious courage in such a transparent facing up to one's irretrievable annihilation, as anyone "who pretends to face death without fright, lies,"[30] the truest of heroes is not someone who confronts their death without first obscuring it, but instead someone who looks immortal* life in the face, real immortal* life, not just a picture of immortal* life, someone who welcomes immortality* and all the terror and trial it brings with it.

A person's existence is made their own. The person who wakes every morning at six and stares into the mirror for twelve hours a day, breaking only for meticulously timed excursions to eat, drink, visit the toilet, and sleep does not necessarily live a life empty of meaning. But what could make such an existence meaningful? Control? Force of will? An unerring commitment to a self-prescribed order? The sheer bloody-mindedness of it? To sustain this behaviour for a week would be challenging, to sustain it without end would be an unfathomable achievement. The thought is that any life that doesn't end would come to look like this, not in the details necessarily, but then immortality* removes the details. Therein lies the corrosive power of a life without end, for it is also a life without detail.

Let us accept for the moment that whatever change is necessary to instil immortality* with meaning that that change must be internal, that external changes, however extreme, can never suffice. As a list of responses to be fortified, we might present this: irony, humour,

---

[29] Wittgenstein, *Culture and Value*, 58.
[30] Jean-Jacques Rousseau, *Julie, Or the New Heloise, The Collected Writings of Rousseau Vol. 6*, trans. Philip Stewart (New Hampshire: Dartmouth College Press, 1997), 128.

heroism, defiance, and artistry, or more specifically the art of metamorphosis. Art of course needs no further justification, defying all utility and meaning outside of itself; and it is this self-containment that might possibly incubate any prospective immortals*, providing an art equal to Thomas Bernhard's proclamation that "the art we need is the art of bearing the unbearable," a life made aesthetic, as prescribed by Nietzsche, free of those extraneous layers of transcendent meaning needlessly piled on top of it—a genuinely creative and valueless mutation.

Immortality* demands that we cultivate addictions, enduring ones that cannot see outside themselves. It is addictions that positively exude life-affirmation, even those to substances that slowly kill us. You have only to look at the living-death that often follows in the wake of a prolonged addiction—the faces of the men and women reintegrating with the newfound pointlessness of diluted impulse—to know that addictions allow for only a meagre existence outside of their parameters; but this is not only a testament to their destructiveness, but also to their nourishment, to the perfection of their internalised structures of sense-making. James Joyce on his deathbed asked, "Does nobody understand?" (Hegel, on his deathbed, knew well that they didn't), and this from a man who consoled himself with a future life made entirely of the enigmas and puzzles he'd laid like traps for the curious brains of countless professors of literature born and yet-to-be-born. The concern is for the most part disingenuous, for there is no desire to be completely understood, to have your elliptical core reduced to so many platitudes. What could these understandings be beyond a certain point but signs of atrophy, Beckettian stains on silence, a tensionless drone? For solutions to leave the subject vital they must be transitory, must themselves be ambiguous and open to supplementary faceting. What addiction wants to lose its mythology? What addictive substance worth the name allows itself to be sampled, its essence grasped, before then being summarily discarded? Like art, addiction only satisfies "when it leaves behind something that, in spite of all our reflection on it, we cannot bring down to the distinctness of a concept":[31] a reason to continue, and even a way to hear the drone of immortality* as the potential for a music that sustains and transforms, without ever being fully understood.

---

[31] Schopenhauer, *The World as Will and Representation Vol. 2*, 409.

Non-Terminator: Rise of the Drone-Gods

On the specifically elusive and yet transformative powers of drone music, Joanna Demers has this to say:

> It is exceptionally difficult to write about drone music. I say this as a person who likes a lot of it, so I lack the prejudices often seen in print about drone music being "boring" or "like listening to a dentist's drill." Technical descriptions of drones take only a few words to state that one tone or chord lasts minutes or hours, leading to a rather sizable imbalance between the minimal number of words required to describe a drone and the maximal amount of time a drone takes. We also lack specific terminology for conveying exactly what goes on during a drone. "Sustained" and "held for a long time" are practically our only means of communicating what drones do, even though drone activity is often more complicated than these descriptions let on. Another approach would be to reflect on the ways in which drones affect the listening process. Drones impose a kind of sensory deprivation through effacing the variation we take for granted, the ebb and flow of acoustic data that occur not only in music but in daily life as well. Like other types of sensory deprivation, drones eventually sharpen other modes of perception by refocusing the listener's attention on the subtle fluctuations in timbre or pitch that accrue greater importance against an otherwise static background.[32]

She also notes how drone music is "dominated by tension between stasis and action, or between limitlessness and constriction [and so] appreciable as maximal only in the presence of boundaries, when we know that the music will at some point come to an end."[33] But the drone we are concerned with will not come to an end, and yet remains maximal in the absence of any boundaries, where by maximal we mean "a quality of excess, something appreciable only after long stretches of time."[34] The point being that while drone music may aestheticise a timeless catastrophe of sorts,[35] it only does so on the promise that its

---

[32] Joanna Demers, *Listening Through the Noise: The Aesthetics of Experimental Electronic Music* (Oxford: Oxford University Press, 2010), 93.
[33] Demers, *Listening Through the Noise*, 92.
[34] Demers, *Listening Through the Noise*, 92.
[35] See Joanna Demers, *Drone and Apocalypse* (London: Zero Books, 2015), 17.

timelessness is never made permanent, that its endlessness remain only an appearance. In order to make music of an immortal* drone, to enact in perpetuity some Bernhardian aestheticisation of the drone of ourselves, an exalted form of addiction is required, the substance of which can never be exhausted: an addiction wherein the returns do not wane but instead accentuate, destroying the addicted party only in order to refashion them in the likeness of the substance to which they are addicted: the noise of ourselves mutating in excess.

If the want is there for immortality*, it is a conflicted want, for who wishes themself into Hell? Attempting to excavate a residence in immortality* is not the problem of how to fill time, but how to become something else while remaining yourself: each of us built from the weaknesses we will destroy in order to survive. The problem is how to solve the paradox and occupy the ellipsis, or, in other words, how to become a Drone-God. And maybe "the only ultimate value of human life is to be found in this Promethean madness, . . . a value that is religious, not political, or even moral."[36] What's more, it is suicidal: this being at home without death, itself a thinly veiled manifestation of death, transformed into the sole remedy for the insomnia of life. Recall Blanchot's recounting of "The Hunter Gracchus," in which

> Kafka relates the adventure of a Black Forest hunter who, having succumbed to a fall in a ravine, has not succeeded in reaching the beyond—and now he is alive and dead. He had joyously accepted life and joyously accepted the end of his life—once killed he awaited his death in joy: he lay stretched out, and he lay in wait. "Then," he said, "the disaster happened." This disaster is the impossibility of death, it is the mockery thrown down on all humankind's great subterfuge, night, nothingness, silence. There is no end, there is no possibility of being done with the day, with the meaning of things, with hope: such is the truth that Western man has made a symbol of felicity, and has tried to make bearable by focusing on its positive side, that of immortality, of an afterlife that would compensate for life. But this afterlife is our actual life.[37]

---

[36] Bertrand Russell, *The Scientific Outlook* (London: Routledge, 2009), 69.
[37] Maurice Blanchot, *The Work of Fire*, trans. Charlotte Mandell (Stanford: Stanford University Press, 1995), 7–8.

Non-Terminator: Rise of the Drone-Gods

We too are dying in the life we want. And we do not want more of life. We merely want more. More of something for which we have no name, and more of that something for something else that we have not yet become. To be done with all this—all the suns and moons and values and desires—is to glimpse for just a second the life we want sequestered somewhere in the obscurity of death. All the while we can keep death ambiguous we can make a life for ourselves there—a life fashioned from the apparel of death, and modelled by us, the wide-eyed cadavers of this new life, the Drone-Gods of the as-yet-unliveable life.

Chapter 5

Smithereens: Depressed Survival in Robert Walser's *Microscripts*

Drilling down into Kōbō Abe's observation that only through a concentrated focus on the small, on the details of this world, can we escape the corrosive effect of the bigger picture, in which our own insignificance is brought into sickening relief, complications inevitably arise. The problem being that any such rigorous attention to the minutiae of this world must impose on itself a threshold beyond which it will not look. For without such a threshold the world once again expands beyond our comprehension, beyond our significance, beyond all our paltry constructs of human meaning, into the atomic and subatomic realms, where space is once again uncertain and merciless in its distance.

Where no additional space exists, the best way to make space is to shrink the occupying object. Where you cannot stretch confines, you make room by condensing that which is confined. This process of micromanagement can reveal arcades and vaulted ceilings in the details of a tomb. But having performed this act of dimunition, why then restrict the shrunken form's working area? Why cut and tear away at those spaces made larger through shrinkage? Why make space only to unmake it? But this dimensional insecurity, this shift in being—from claustrophobia to agoraphobia—is really just part of the overall process of self-imposed restriction. First the person is reduced, then the world they inhabit.

Walser's choice of spaces is significant: the occupations he effects with his accelerated deployment of cramped insectile markings—coagulating into blocks of blurred uniformity—are scratched for the most part into dead areas, flat holes obscured by near illegible characters desperate to fill the space they created when they shrank themselves. These are spaces resigned to emptiness, spaces abandoned

On the Verge of Nothing

to the meaning-void eye-sleep of a single uniform tone, spaces made up of blank frames and the undersides of business cards (spaces homaging commerce), of used postal wrapping and envelopes (quietly militating against the importance of destination), of the hidden underside of a penny dreadful cover (regurgitating sensation as a small patch of swamp mould crawling along the bottom of a soiled blankness), of pages torn and dissected from glossy lifestyle magazines (where men like hogs are butchered for their choicest cuts), or of the backs of old calendar dates (detailing the return of the past in the insulated creatures of routine).

The characters, for all their elegant observations and pseudo-clinical diagnoses, disclose themselves like persons meticulously partitioned from the world, incomplete and fractured zombies devoid of the tools necessary to achieve genuine emotive residence, those irrevocably detached from certain standard human conditionings: back in the world like curios exhaled from an electroconvulsive therapy ward, reconditioned casualties declared fixed following programmes of highly-selective neuron annihilations. His people talk over the silence of themselves. Like lonely residents in a nursing home, they relate facts and empirical data for the sheer honest and healthy wonder of it—the listener (and the teller to some extent: "My activity is superior to me")[1] is an irrelevance.

As to the genesis of Walser's fictional figures, Walter Benjamin pinpoints a single source:

> [H]is favourite characters come from . . . insanity and nowhere else. They are figures who have left madness behind them, and this is why they are marked by such a consistently heartrending, inhuman superficiality. If we were to attempt to sum up in a single phrase the delightful yet also uncanny element in them, we would have to say: *they have all been healed.*[2]

The truth of this is plain, and once acknowledged profoundly felt, for only once we've realised what has happened to them and where they might have come from can we recognise how their success might be

---

[1] Robert Walser, *Microscripts*, trans. Susan Bernofsky (New York: New Directions, 2010), 43.
[2] Walter Benjamin in Walser, *Microscripts*, 112, original emphasis.

considered a crisis, their cheerfulness, and the cheerfulness of others, a sweetened suffering of the same pathology. Even the distractions of art and literature are regarded as essentially crisis-prone; and any contentment found, a progenitor of lament (verl-aCH). Walser's "Demanding Fellow" tells of how "the happiness he achieved was a sort of calamity," so that he finds himself—with a painful sense of inevitability—sucked down into a condition in which "his longing, how he longed for it again."[3]

If we are to follow Benjamin's appraisal, Walser's characters have achieved what Gérard de Nerval and his "Aurelia" could not: the latter being a story with which he intended to convince his custodian in Passy, Dr Blanche, of his impeccable sanity, his status as a cured man, a man at home in life and free of all but the threat of death. But ultimately the sharp line Nerval sought to establish there, between the misery of madness and the happiness of health—the former replete with illusion and decayed senses, the latter with vigour and nourishment—was drawn too absolutely, the fabled "real world" that he claimed to have finally accessed, too distorted by the sickness of longing and denial, his story lacking the matter-of-fact robotism of Walser's.

The man in "Radio" eavesdrops on a public broadcast, acutely conscious that the announcer, as he feels the need to point out, "had not an inkling of my listenership or even of my existence."[4] This interplay of intimacy and alienation, of being both included and ostracised, is typical of Walser's conflicted instruments. The outside world, exhaustively marked with history and human intention, is subjected to a tempered fuzzing, like when "interesting buildings that had played a role in history were mirrored in the still, color-suffused water of remote canals."[5] That narratology, that historiological grounding, made ever so slightly out of focus, like the appearance of the very script in which they struggle to breathe.

In "Swine" we are asked, "Does not the endlessly endearing drag us down?"[6] For there's an interest in it all, loving and swinish—all the banal details laid out like jewels to be pondered in their natural state with no need for further embellishment. There's an acceptance—a

---

[3] Walser, *Microscripts*, 39.
[4] Walser, *Microscripts*, 23.
[5] Walser, *Microscripts*, 38.
[6] Walser, *Microscripts*, 28.

healthy one, maybe. This is what there is, let's look at it. Let's see it. Let's attempt to see and for once not see-as. But this concentration engenders its own mysteries: an un-edited purity where narratives lay uncoupled and attentions shift. For this bleakness of happiness is a meandering state, and so confusions are best left alone—as confusions. Where solutions are proffered they remain. They sit and exist as what they are: momentary reactions that were once in context. This way they seek to avoid the complications of truth and falsity. Where details muddy what goes on, they are omitted.

When in "The Train Station (II)" there is talk of "useful money,"[7] where the use of the extraneous adjective reveals a remoteness that is so explicitly contrived, and also when marvelling at the alien naivety of a comment like, "I myself am sometimes well-known, sometimes a stranger," we are forced to confront the interspatial complexities realised by Walser's cured narrators, how they are fundamentally disassociated not only from the world around them, but from themselves as encounterable things within that world. Like the microscopic scrawl that inhabits the space between the concrete of names, addresses and postal markings—some textual fungi or creeping vine leaching what life it can from flat, empty surfaces—his people are removed from those false (humanised) stories, and naturalised and haunting "sillinesses" reign in their place, something captured by Joyce some twelve years earlier in 1920:

> When travelling you get into those waggons called railway coaches, which are behind the locomotive. This is done by opening a door and gently projecting into the compartment yourself and your valise. A man in an office will give you a piece of cardboard in exchange for some money. By looking at it attentively you will see the word *Paris* printed on it which is the name of this stop.[8]

Although "unable to feel at ease anywhere at all"[9] (as is that foremost man), most of Walser's people try desperately to exist

---

[7] Walser, *Microscripts*, 42.
[8] James Joyce, *Selected Letters of James Joyce* (New York: Viking Press, 1975), 267, original emphasis.
[9] Walser, *Microscripts*, 40.

"somewhere and somewhen," and in the story underneath that title the best is seen as always missing, always nowhere and nowhen—a dream of the sick, bones dressed in a ragged couture of failing muscle and thinning skin, of airless places in which only words can breathe—"the present as the eye of God"[10] in which men and women can only exist as glossed reflections.

Walser's disenfranchised onlookers (self-fleshed contraptions of iatric absence) can only see other androids, see their automated aimlessness, the terrifying and yet ridiculous automatism of their daily encounters, the one difference being that their existences have not yet been exorcised of the pleasure that makes the world sticky: "People who are refined visit other refined people and confide in them, chattering and babbling out precisely what they have experienced and whether they found the experience indigestible or pleasing."[11]

In the revealingly titled "Usually I first put on a prose piece jacket," the ease of transition from sillinesses to self-confessed horror suggests that there is nothing substantial keeping them apart, almost as if each were already encroaching on the other's territory. The writer confesses that he hopes his automated prose piece "pleases you [the reader] so much it will make you tremble that it will be for you, in certain respects, a horrific piece of writing."[12] But why horrific? Wherein lies the horror for a healthy mind? In the lines preceding this, we are told of the mechanistic gesture of a woman, Rosalinde, who in dispensing bread to an underling does so with a movement at once utterly machine-like and beautiful, like the gallop of a horse—an animal that runs through her like blood (for as we see with Mr Brown and Mrs Black,[13] names colour Walser's figures indelibly and all the way down). The horror, then, is in the juxtaposition of beauty and the machine, in the essentially un-personed qualities of grace.

About ghosts, Kafka writes: "You'll never get a straight answer out of them. Talk about vacillation! These ghosts seem to doubt their own existence even more than we do, which given their fragility is hardly surprising."[14] On this basis, all Walser's figurines are bordering on the

---

[10] Walser, *Microscripts*, 54.
[11] Walser, *Microscripts*, 70.
[12] Walser, *Microscripts*, 62.
[13] Walser, *Microscripts*, 71.
[14] Franz Kafka, "Unhappiness," in *Franz Kafka Stories 1904–1924*, 41.

spectral: an ontological status befitting the almost wraithlike text that constitutes their true flesh.

The father and son shut up inside "Jaunts elegant in nature" like trinkets in an oak display case, the wife and mother invisible but for youth, beauty and a legacy of curls (no trademark frustrations or shrewishness, no meat there "longing for viper bites"[15]), present two opposing facets of man's ailing health: the progenitor flattened and stripped of pulse by an overbearing sense of duty and stoicism—for although desires would surface, "he found it his duty to disregard them," and when gripped by isolation and insomnia "befriended loneliness"[16] and the nights from which he could not remove himself—and his progeny, devoid of such concerns and so scarcely present at all, but for an alteration in air current, an olfactory pleasantry, in fact too insubstantial a being to breed even the slightest of adversaries ("he was forbidden to become something to which breath and a form belonged")[17] and so never quite a man, his illness and subsequent death ushering him away like something (un-thing-like) becoming itself again, a ghost fading from view like some lightly-sketched portrait left out in the sun. (The son is not in the world, but neither is he in his own story—for "characters in books stand out better, I mean, more silhouettishly from one another, than do living figures, who, as they are alive and move about, tend to lack delineation."[18] He is instead a poetical hypothesis on the possibilities of corporeal minimalism, an exercise in existential subtraction.)

The residence of this faintly-realised son (blessed with not only his mother's curls, but her figmental ontic status as well) is a place rich with alluring detail. But one detail is worth noting more than the others: "The air appeared to be the bride of the garden, and the garden its bridegroom."[19] That the second half of this sentence should have been thought requisite is itself something deserving of a book-length treatment, for it is not there by accident, and it is not mere pleonastic clutter. That a relation that is axiomatically two-way should be documented so comprehensively allows the reader to see the degree to

---

[15] Walser, *Microscripts*, 91.
[16] Walser, *Microscripts*, 31.
[17] Walser, *Microscripts*, 33.
[18] Walser, *Microscripts*, 43.
[18] Walser, *Microscripts*, 49.
[19] Walser, *Microscripts*, 32.

which Walser's worlds are atomised: no matter what the relation between objects and people, they remain intrinsically separate, inassimilable entities that are somehow fundamentally remote. Even a man who would be a wretch, and who, enslaved by his desire, attaches himself to a woman who would make him one is not truly united with her, for even this seemingly harmonious reciprocity simmers with the imminent threat of rupture. Even the man who orates on the evils of schnapps is so distant from his words that he must do so while under its influence. And even though one's own goodness may be considered contingent on others, that goodness is never duly transferred, but merely a requirement that leaves its subject empty. All are disconnected in a way that no brutality of kindness can alleviate, disengaged like the nun we find in the company of soldiers, or the city man persecuted in the quiet country village.

The robustness of Walser's figures resides in their ability to accept the precipitous frangibility of human life. They are the ones who are no longer "too frail to disclose [their] own frailties,"[20] the ones cracked and mended, those "strong at the broken places."[21] But what Walser compulsively details is the price of this strength: the ever-present uncertainties, the safety of a cold dead eye, the self-imposed strictures that are required in order to just approximate pleasure. Concerning the inception of the title for his most famous novel, William Burroughs writes: "I did not understand what the title meant until my recent recovery. The title means exactly what the words say: NAKED Lunch—a frozen moment when everyone sees what is on the end of every fork."[22] This is the aftermath of recovery, a state in which nothing is taken for granted, or glossed over, or just consumed—the world comes to these convalescents raw and unseasoned, no longer greased human for the palate. And happiness is no exception, its paradoxical nature haunting the microscripts: "[T]he shakiness of things and yet also the most solid."[23] An observation illustrated by Kafka in his four-sentence story, "The Trees": "For we are as treetrunks in the snow. They appear to lie flat on the surface, and with a little push one should be able to shift them. No, one cannot, for they are fixed firmly to the ground. But look, even that is mere

---

[20] Walser, *Microscripts*, 57.
[21] Ernest Hemingway, *A Farewell to Arms* (New York: Scribner, 1997), 225.
[22] Burroughs, *Naked Lunch*, 7.
[23] Walser, *Microscripts*, 57.

appearance."[24] Perhaps, though, the only place for victory and approbation, for completion and stability, is, as the *"Cheib"* of microscript 50 discovers, in a future into which we disappear to be remade in stone.

Walser's people are trying to set up home in autumn, and to ignore the seasons that precede it. For autumn has rightly put aside the false promises and gibbering inanities of spring (knows that "Not only under ground are the brains of men / Eaten by maggots"),[25] and has shrugged off the glare of a summer that had its eyes squinting half-blind. It has confidence in a worse state, a darker, colder place, and so finds some solace there—if only in its postulation, as seen in Walser's mansion-dwelling beggar who "was constantly taking his autumnalities for granted, as though there were such a thing as precisely nuanced gradations of life."[26] These demarcations are the stripes of their sanity. But habitation is never less than precarious, for though fortified those fortifications demand constant attention and renewal. A similarly anthropomorphic treatment of autumn can be found in the work of Georg Trakl, whose poems are haunted by the creeping manifestations of this starkly contemplative season. He could have been addressing Walser's creations when he wrote: "More pious now, you know the meaning of the dark years, / The cold and autumn in lonely rooms,"[27] been commenting on their fragile happinesses when describing the "Autumn sun, thin and unpredictable,"[28] or the inauguration of their perspectival insulation by warning that "When autumn arrives, / a sober brightness appears,"[29] describing their new topography of "Bare trees in autumn and stillness,"[30] their status as peripheral autumnal stains, those "black footsteps on the edge of the forest."[31]

The cartographer of facets and incidentals does not risk being consumed by the whole. The minutiae pile up like fragmented

---

[24] Kafka, *Franz Kafka Stories 1904–1924*, 37.
[25] Edna St. Vincent Millay, "Spring," in *Second April* (Whitefish: Kessinger Publishing, 2004), 2.
[26] Walser. *Microscripts*, 89.
[27] Georg Trakl, "Childhood," in *Autumn Sonata*, trans. Daniel Simko (New York: Moyer Bell, 1989), 77.
[28] Trakl, "Whispered in the Afternoon," in *Autumn Sonata*, 43.
[29] Trakl, "Helian," in *Autumn Sonata*, 67.
[30] Trakl, "Sonja," in *Autumn Sonata*, 97.
[31] Trakl, "Transformation of Evil," in *Autumn Sonata*, 125.

Smithereens

specimens on a shattered slide; incomplete and detached from their once rightful context, they take on new existences that resist the pain of conclusions and the demented dreams of completeness. The convalescent hides in the moment, languishes in a present that never completes, and in documenting it documents themself: consciousness now stripped of the threat of any prolonged confrontation with itself. And so when the Blue Page-Boy says, "I have not yet ever experienced anything worth mentioning except that now and then, i.e., relatively seldom, I glance into a little mirror,"[32] he has already indicated that the subsequent question, concerning whether or not he at some time kissed at a woman's mouth through a spoon, might be best left hanging, his proposed informality with the questioner left perpetually unconsummated.

Mistrustful of life and the blind integrations of humanity, Walser's characters, like his script, are instruments of precision used to perform localised surgeries, glass-eyed eviscerations of shrunken and necrotised anatomies, whereby the aggregate tissue of life is left nebulous and alive: a mechanism of defence, for, as Cioran explains, while "depressions pay attention to life, they are the eyes of the devil, poisoned arrows which wound mortally any zest and love of life. Without them we know little, but with them, we cannot live."[33] Walser's people have managed to isolate the poison, and are careful—a lifeless care—not to let it spread, to dissect life's corpse into enough pieces that it may never be put back together.

The work is only worth it when it isn't, like surgical precision honed on a corpse.

---

[32] Walser, *Microscripts*, 53.
[33] Cioran, *The Book of Delusions*, 75.

Chapter 6

Incompleteness as a Tunnel: Death, Escape and Paradox

Disbelief originates in possibility before becoming its own faith. And God's epistemological distance, while not exactly an endorsement of this condition, has all the hallmarks of one. "Everything I sought in life I abandoned for the sake of the search,"[1] and what is claimed here of life will now be claimed of death: the end abandoned for the sake of the quest to discover what it means to end.

We invest in our identities, our lived existence, and are strongly disinclined to leave that work somehow incomplete, while also being vaguely aware that even immortality would not solve the problem, would not make anything more comprehensive, but would just serve instead to make this sense of incompleteness more pronounced. Lauding the comforts of personal extinction, Schopenhauer presents us with a tellingly gothic scenario: "If we knocked on the graves and asked the dead whether they would like to rise again, they would shake their heads."[2] And when they shake their heads they do so as people (peopled corpses)—the head-shake being a human gesture—and are saying "no" to some proposed return from the nothingness they've found, a nothingness not replicated in life. That these graves are not yet tunnels is evidenced by their occupants' casual interactions; for if they were to respond in a manner befitting tunnellers, they'd surely disintegrate on the spot at the mere suggestion.

Despite the sting of futility that relentlessly pervades our thoughts and our bodies, all proclamations of objective meaninglessness never actually complete: they are left hanging, for all their credibility, because it is in the nature of meaning that it continually extends beyond its reach—projecting itself precariously onto things and times and

---

[1] Pessoa, *The Book of Disquiet*, 189.
[2] Schopenhauer, *The World as Will and Representation Vol. 2*, 465.

outcomes and beings whose existences in no way depend on these speculative anticipations. For however much we may be convinced of our insignificance, the problem remains within us (as a problem), and no world outside us, it seems, can alter that. We embody our absurdity; it follows us everywhere—even into death.

We see this situation played out in the H. P. Lovecraft story "The White Ship," in which a lighthouse keeper, Basil Elton, boards a mysterious white ship that transports him to anomalous and psychologised lands. The first of these lands is Zar (a place inhabited by man's forgotten dreams of beauty), on which they do not set foot, as leaving is said to be impossible; second is the walled city of Thalarion (a place inhabited by man's unfathomed mysteries) which once again they do not enter for fear of never being able to leave; third is the foul-smelling Xura (where man's unattained pleasures reside) which they pass by in a panic; fourth is the idyllic non-spatial, non-temporal, and deathless Sona-Nyl (a place of fancy) where they reside for many aeons; and last is that of Cathuria (the land of hope), the promise of which incites Basil to leave the perfection of Sona-Nyl, to find only an abyssal whirlpool filled with tortured men and unidentified creatures.

The most obvious conclusion to be drawn from this is the somewhat platitudinous one concerning our need to always want more than we have, to always be seeking progress just for the sake of progress, even if we have no idea what that progress or improvement might be. That Cathuria could never satisfy the wants of this quest is plain, for no place could: hope has no end-state, it is not land but abyss. However, this brief overview, while helpful, is still deficient in detail; and so a more comprehensive breakdown is required in order to truly examine the intricacies of the story's many connotations:

- Zar, despite being a place of immense beauty and bountiful promise, is never visited. It is never visited because the possibility of ever leaving is removed. (Once the trap is set we start to look for a way out, even if that trap is life itself, and a perfect life at that.)
- Thalarion represents a faithful embodiment of the mysteries of man, a city "fascinating yet repellent," a location replete with madness and demons; and once again, a place that once entered is never left. (When *only* mystery and uncertainty are

Incompleteness as a Tunnel

on offer, insanity and dehumanisation follow, and from this no possibility of extrication.)
- Xura is the concentration of man's thwarted desires, and so is, in Schopenhaurian terms, a realm of pure suffering, suffering without reprieve—a hell of unfulfilled wanting. (This land's smell alone is enough to drive them on to the next without stopping. But that its poisonous odours are associated with death, with plagues and open graves, is something of an anomaly. For desires, disenchanted or otherwise, are the very stuff of life. The smell of endlessly copulating bodies would have been more fitting.)
- Sona-Nyl is a place of paradisiacal attributes, a place inhabitable yet devoid of spatio-temporal location. Here there is no death and no facility for suffering. (It is no surprise that Sona-Nyl is referred to as a place of fancy, but still it lacks that one thing that Basil needs to sustain him: incompleteness and the mystery immanent to it. And in this lies paradox, for Sona-Nyl by virtue of its very completeness is found to be incomplete.)
- Cathuria, when found, becomes a land without land, its manifestation a descent embodied with shrieks. (It is a place never meant to be found, an end-state conscripted into a continual process of collapsing back into itself for want of an exit.)

In these five mythical lands, we have laid out for us the central themes of our struggle with meaning, and so any possible expansion of that meaning, into immortality. The first thing to note is that the closed system cannot satisfy—the story itself is an embodiment of this message; for at the end, once Hope has been visited and found to be empty, the bird (the driving force of the journey) is found dead. Incompleteness is not a possible destination, but a destination of possibility—and to remain possible it can never be found. Sustainable meaning always exceeds any list that might be collated to detail it: man's collective capacity to recognise and create beauty is insufficient if there is nothing outside it (Zar), but even when a list is completed, and recognition of an outside provided for (Sona-Nyl), we will it seems always find our home in the suffering of its non-preclusion of elsewhere, in the accessibility of the postulated beyond. To sustain us,

On the Verge of Nothing

Sona-Nyl would have to have an integrated incompleteness, lacunae within itself instead of those only made external to it, and an incompleteness that is not simply coextensive with hope, for what are hopes but ideals, and "[w]hat are ideals but an admission that life is worthless"?[3]

Aside from being a receptacle for hope, a lacuna's function in these cases, is to act as a bare possibility. In short, it is breathing room. However, possibility is not hope, although hope can and does attach itself to it, and room to breathe is not the hope to do more or other than you're already doing, not a longing to breathe more or better or something other, but the requirement that the breathing that's already going on will be allowed to continue, that the air will not be forced into recirculation and suffocate its breathers. And though we might be mistaken for thinking it, this does not translate as a hope for the sustainability of breathing, but a justificatory prop to the breathing we're already engaged in. Likewise, possibility here is not the hope for something other, something to be aspired to or achieved, as much as it is a recognition or vindication of the other or the external in what is otherwise thought to be contained—that which in both cases makes possible the possibility of unencumbered belonging and the complimentary possibility of non-belonging: a transcendental argument, then, for the architectures of meaning already erected. That said, wouldn't a state of belonging without the possibility of it ever being otherwise be a more economical and yet equally satisfying prospect? Here we only have to look at the example of Zar to see that this will not suffice: a place where residents will be swallowed up by beauty is a cage that we will refuse to enter.

In the Philip K. Dick novel, *The Three Stigmata of Palmer Eldritch*, we're confronted with the following scenario: an enigmatic space traveller (the eponymous anti-hero), long presumed dead, returns (physically at least) with a drug, by the name of Chew-Z, offering its users immortality. As it transpires, Chew-Z-users enter an entirely different universe, one of Eldritch's creation, and one from which there appears to be no escape, at least not one that you can ever be entirely sure of, such is the verisimilitude of his ersatz universe. Although Dick eventually offers his characters a likely reprieve, the way in which he does so is telling: first he claims that even if Eldritch is

---

[3] Pessoa, *The Book of Disquiet*, 158.

Incompleteness as a Tunnel

God, albeit a hostile one, then he could well be a lesser and inverted version of a greater, loving God; and secondly, that the real unclosed world of dull actualities and unfathomed potential still exists as a possibility for them. The hope of an outside remains. For although Leo Bulero's "boundaries" and beyond are seemingly eaten up and forever tainted by Eldritch, he replaces them with his character's list of possibilities. What is so nightmarish about this novel is that, should Eldritch's plan prove successful, his control would be complete, and there would be no room for salvation. The reader's imaginative project would be at an end, the knots would be tied, and Dick would have left his characters in Eldritch's manmade hell. On the penultimate page, Leo reflects on his predicament:

> It's nothing more than faith in powers implanted in me from the start which I can—in the end—draw on and beat him with. So in a sense it isn't me; it's something *in* me that even that thing Palmer Eldritch can't reach and consume because since it's not me it's not mine to lose. I feel it growing. Withstanding the external, nonessential alterations, the arm, the eyes, the teeth—it's not touched by any of these three, the evil, negative trinity of alienation, blurred reality, and despair that Eldritch brought back with him from Proxima.[4]

I proffer that the "something *in*" him that not even Palmer Eldritch can reach, that something that grows inside him but which is not him or his to lose, is a gap in what appeared to be a closed system. Bulero might see that void as the Christian God working through him, but the fact remains that someone has gifted him the possibility of a breach, a chink in the hermetically sealed and labyrinthine universe in which he believed himself captive for an eternity. The gap grows as he invests more of his self into its existence. It is not him or his to lose because it is only an absence and his attempt to characterise it in some way—an absence that cannot be eradicated by his attempts to detail it, because those attempts will always ultimately fail.

Nonetheless, it is Barney who best expresses their predicament, with a mixture of conviction and confusion: "An evil visitor . . . offering us what we've prayed for over a period of two thousand years

---

[4] Philip K. Dick, *The Three Stigmata of Palmer Eldritch* (London: Grafton, 1978), 203, original emphasis.

[eternal life]. And why is this so palpably bad? Hard to say, but nevertheless it is."[5] It is so palpably bad because Eldritch's universe and his dominion within it is, they are told, complete. There is nothing left for them, or rather the marked absence of a nothing for them, no air holes left through which they can breathe, in which that part of themselves of which they are ignorant can remain unmolested by knowing. Dick's fictions regularly rely on incompleteness in the hero's knowledge, and from there they invariably come to see that this incompleteness reflects a longing for some revelatory discovery that will free them, without freeing them from incompleteness altogether. Time and again he rejoices in his character's partial knowledge: *Time out of Joint*, *Flow My Tears, The Policeman Said*, *Do Androids Dream of Electric Sheep?*, etc.

Similarly, throughout Kafka's writings we see the gilded curse of incompleteness in many different guises. *Amerika* is riddled with gaps and remains incomplete, its final chapter a testament to unboundedness. In *The Trial*, Joseph K dies without knowing the offence for which he has been persecuted throughout the novel. *The Castle* sees K floundering after answers that he never finds. Kafka realises that incompleteness is an essential part of our intellectual lives, at times frustrating, frightening and disorientating but always enthralling—intelligence persisting only in absence of its object. Like Dadaism and Surrealism, eventual failure is acknowledged as being integral to human existence.

In a letter written on December 16, 1911, Kafka writes: "I am divided from all things by a hollow space and I don't even push myself to the limits of it."[6] There is nothing else but this sentence. All of Kafka is there. The world is not his. It is something he sees, something forced on his senses, but no home can be found there: however deep he attempts to dig inside it there is only ever the hollow space he brings to it, the boundary he cannot touch, that which exists outside the boundary stretching outward forever. And we see here how incompleteness is not synonymous with hope, as connections and possible ends are sought with scant expectation of success, existing as little more than means to acknowledge one's human lot: "Life, said

---

[5] Dick, *The Three Stigmata of Palmer Eldritch*, 135–136.
[6] Franz Kafka, *Diaries, 1910–1923*, ed. Max Brod (New York: Shcoken Books, 1948), 140.

Incompleteness as a Tunnel

Tarde, is the search for the impossible by way of the useless. Let us always search for the impossible, since that is our destiny."[7]

Being-a-whole was, for Heidegger, the mark of authenticity. For only by truly grasping death as one's "uttermost possibility" can Dasein, no longer lost in the they-self, be itself, individual and complete (or whole): "The existential projection in which anticipation has been delimited, has made visible the *ontological* possibility of an existentiall Being-towards-death which is authentic. Therewith, however, the possibility of Dasein's having an authentic potentiality-for-Being-a-whole emerges, *but only as an ontological possibility*."[8] And so death completes, but the completion it enacts is forced and arbitrary—so much so that it completes without actually completing. Immortality on this picture becomes nothing more than the perpetuation of possibility, and so of incompleteness—and so the sustainability of this all-too-human precariousness.

For Heidegger, "death reveals itself as that *possibility which is one's ownmost, which is non-relational, and which is not to be outstripped*."[9] But what does truly confronting one's own death, and the associated anxiety that ensues from such a confrontation, have to do with completeness? Consider Paul Celan's poem "You Were My Death": "You were my death: / you I could hold / when all fell away from me."[10] The similarities here are clear enough, especially when you consider the weight that death is made to carry in Heidegger's oeuvre, that is, nothing short of replacing God as our ultimate frontier. But the problem here is manifest: how do we make sense of the mineness of this death? And from what conception of ownership does this derive?

This conundrum puts us in mind of Wittgenstein's observations about the confusions surrounding notions of ownership. For instance, as a point of logic, how can my death be mine if it could never be anyone else's? What alien notion of possession is this? The death that arrives for any of us can never be owned, for there is no sense of possessing that from which you cannot get outside. I do not possess my cell, even if my cell is my house, if I have no possibility of ever

---

[7] Pessoa, *The Book of Disquiet*, 206.
[8] Martin Heidegger, *Being and Time*, trans. John Macquarrie and Edward Robinson (London: Blackwell, 1962), 311, original emphasis.
[9] Heidegger, *Being and Time*, 294, original emphasis.
[10] Paul Celan, *Selected Poems*, trans. Michael Hamburger and Christopher Middleton (Middlesex: Penguin Books, 1972), 90.

leaving it and no one else can possibly enter. Consequently, there can be no way of ever "holding" the death that arrives for me. For no death can ever be mine in this sense, and is as such always out of reach, unattainable, elusive.[11] And this can equally well be said of existence too, which likewise can never be mine: authenticity is not to accept the mineness of existence and that mineness's end in its correspondingly owned death, but rather to accept the very lack of any such possibilities for ownership. That there is this strange intimacy, one so often mistaken for ownership, only serves to reinforce the intractable possibility of death (as of life) as that which ends without ending, as that which must incorporate me without my ever being able to incorporate it, leaving that wholeness forever out of reach for the identity thus assimilated. In this way incompleteness is maintained even in death. My authentic aloneness in the face of death's possibility (the possibility of my own impossibility) does not make me the true proprietrix of the death that comes my way, but instead reinforces the lacuna at the heart of this intimacy (with life and with death), this inability to grasp, and so forces me to occupy it as the only possibility left, that is, the impossibility of identifying wholly with that which can be thought to own either a life or a death.

Heidegger argues for the mineness of existence (in which my life is mine and so is my death), but he does so at the expense of that mystery, that epistemic gap, around which my entire existence and its conclusion arranges itself: the possibility-of-my-impossibility's retaining its possibility in my absence, or rather through my absence. Death, then, becomes the possibility of no longer being me, no longer the disorientating weight that existence has so far accumulated. And from this gap, in the otherwise solid edifice of death, a tunnel is made—keeping in mind that the fissure and its excavation must still be undertaken in life, for to do it at the point of death is to find yourself crushed by life at the advent of death. The point is to escape life while supposedly in its thrall; the point is to take all the foul mutilations of the world and from these fragmentations of Hell construct a narrow egress, less a turning away and more a complete immersion and

---

[11] And perhaps should the opposite state pertain there would be no solution to this quandary, if "[t]o possess is [also] to lose" (Pessoa, *The Book of Disquiet*, 235).

Incompleteness as a Tunnel

subsequent falling through—where "Hell is the paltry notion God involuntarily gives us of Himself."[12]

That death so easily lends itself to narratives of escape is both inevitable and problematic; for even when death itself is formulated in such a way that its distinction from life is constituted in little more than terminological divergence, this death-as-life is regarded as a legitimate form of flight, if not *the* legitimate form of flight. What it is that's so compelling about the escape narrative is not simply that there is an out, a direction in what otherwise might be directionless, but rather that there are so many outs, so many directions, and all of them moving away (in varying degrees) not only from some particular location but from the things we'd become there. It allows us to imagine ourselves like water embodied in its tributaries, diversified into myriad tunnels for which we, crucially, cannot yet lay claim. That this flight's connection to leaking[13] is decisive is demonstrated by the escapee's fixation on those points of least resistance through which they can vanish via acts of repeated vanishing. The would-be-escapee, the tunneller, has already partially disappeared before they are anywhere close to completing their means of escape. Already the persecutions, squalor and debasements of the place-to-be-escaped is to some degree alleviated by their not being fully present to experience them. However horrific the conditions one is seeking to escape, escaping is always just as much about leaving yourself behind as it is about leaving the specific locale of your current suffering.

In the preface to "Madame Edwarda," Bataille writes of the protagonist: "[H]unting for a way out, and realising that he seals himself all the more inextricably into the impasse, he searches within himself for that which, capable of annihilating him, renders him similar to God, similar to nothing."[14] The way out does indeed involve equivalences of excavation and emptiness between the void made and the void-maker: the hole that is dug in the earth is commensurate with the hole made in the fabric of the one who digs. As a would-be-

---

[12] Bataille, "Madame Edwarda," 143.
[13] As made clear by Brian Massumi in his "Notes on the Translation" of Deleuze and Guattari's *A Thousand Plateaus*: "*Fuite* covers not only the act of fleeing or eluding but also flowing, leaking, and disappearing into the distance (the vanishing point in a painting is *a point de fuite*)," in Deleuze and Guattari, *A Thousand Plateaus*, xvii.
[14] Bataille, "Madame Edwarda," 142.

escapee takes soil out of the ground, or panels from a door, or bricks from a cell wall, they are also dismantling and discarding themself as the being who is contained. More and more the tunneller occupies the nothing they have created, until the time of escape is reached and both tunnel and tunneller occupy each other's excavated space. Before the tunneller has escaped through the tunnel, the tunnel has already escaped through them.

This breakout, however, cannot be achieved if the direction of the tunnel takes precedence over the possibility of the tunnel in and of itself. If the tunnel is seen as anything more than a conduit for escape, if it is only some part of some larger logistical plan to arrive at destination X, then no such mutual voiding will be achieved. There must only be *the way out*; there cannot also be *the way to*. In this sense the escape tunnel must be rhizomic: with no beginning or end, no centre or periphery, made up only of shortcuts and detours, unforeseeable, contingent, with endless new beginnings, and the negation of any one direction in favour of the proliferation of countless directions—the inexhaustible opportunity for getting and being lost.[15] (This is why Rumi, even when he settles on a destination settles on an expanse of water, and all the disorientation that implies: "For those of us still living, the grave / feels like an escape-hole back to the ocean.")[16] And it's in this going and going nowhere that the escape tunnel reveals itself as unequivocally philosophical; for there is no terminus, only myriad ways of getting there without ever having to get there, without its ever having to exist.

The anxiety of your tunnel being discovered before you have managed to escape through it overwhelms all others. The anxiety of not having properly disappeared until it is too late, of being witnessed only partway-gone and having to suffer the immediate reintroduction of all the sickening accoutrements of your containment: this now is your one remaining nightmare and the last part of you to go, the last

---

[15] The world keeps us busy and keeps us stupid, so if you are wondering whether your planned escape is just more of this banal business, the answer lies with what you envisage taking with you and where you imagine ending up, so that if you have a concrete answer to either of these questions, then your concern was justified and, should you even manage to enter it, the tunnel would surely spit you out.
[16] Rumi, *The Essential Rumi*, trans. Coleman Barks (New York: Harper Collins, 2004), 304.

Incompleteness as a Tunnel

visible remnant as you descend into the tunnel—the revenant of the revenant. As you fully embody this fear time will slow down, and will be felt more acutely than before, will become excruciating for the remainder that anticipates with such vividness the eventual timelessness of the tunnel.[17] "Plans and peace! These two can never go hand in hand,"[18] so while it is prudent to plan your escape—draw up diagrams of the tunnel, meticulously organise its excavation and construction, conceal its entrance, etc.—you do not take the plans with you when you enter.

In *Otherwise Than Being*, Levinas identifies transcendence as passing beyond being, passing beyond being and not-being to become being's other—a void marked only by the "there is." "The task" then becomes "to conceive of the possibility of a break out of essence,"[19] where essence is the realm of being and non-being, and going beyond is to establish subjectivity and humanity. But these notions it seems would themselves be reduced to extensionless points, subjective and human in only the barest and originary sense: the instantiation of the former ideals via the all but complete eradication of their content. For those seeking comfort, there is none, unless by comfort you can come to mean its no longer being required. For the only comfort lies in escaping into the other, forgetting your own life, now subdued, and so escaping its horror. The only comfort is its impossibility for you, and so too the impossibility of its opposite. The ataraxy of the tunnel is the irrelevance of comfort.

And what, now, of the darkness of the tunnel? Will light and its attendant play of images be extinguished there? These questions, while apparently pertinent, neglect the mutual excavation that prepared the way. For when we anticipate this absence of light we should at the same time recognise the integration of tunnel and tunneller that will precede it, and how these foreseen deprivations are the concerns of the seeing that will be made blind, and not the inevitable recalibration of what it means to see. Ultimately, if we must still talk of darkness, it should be that of Meister Eckhart, and so nothing other than a

---

[17] "Once we get beyond time and temporal things, we are free and joyous" (Eckhart, *Meister Eckhart*, 152). And again in Lispector: "I'm sad. An uneasiness that comes because the ecstasy doesn't fit into the life of the days. . . . The ecstasy must be forgotten" (Lispector, *Água Viva*, 84).
[18] Meher Baba in Masciandaro, *Sufficient Unto The Day*, 86.
[19] Levinas, *Otherwise Than Being*, 8.

"potential sensitivity,"[20] a possible receptiveness not before encountered when the lights were on and we saw everything at the expense of nothing. Or as Bataille puts it, in the first of his proposed exercises in "The Practice of Joy before Death": "I enter into peace as I enter into a dark unknown. / I fall in this dark unknown. / I myself become this dark unknown."[21]

Once in the tunnel there is no room to turn back, and no such thing as a dead end. And yet this is not the restoration of the same confinement, for there will be nothing left behind us, or else only what is already rotting, and that there is no destination or navigable direction to our continuance marks only the purity of what it means to truly escape, which is for escape itself to become the destination, and for the multiplicity of directions to model itself perfectly on our prior notions of what it meant to be directionless. When you are lost there is no need to seek a way out, unless you want to be found, in which case your way out is really a way in. To imagine deficiencies in the tunnel is to ignore the fact that the ultimate deficiency has already occurred, which means there is a deficiency even of deficiency.[22]

The escape tunnel is always a secret. Its entrance must remain hidden during its construction and for as long as possible after it has been entered. The standard reason for ensuring that a tunnel remains hidden indefinitely, long after its original user has made their escape, is so that others might effect further such escapes through the same tunnel. But for this last possibility of death no one will follow me, and so the requirement that it remain secret thereby serves an entirely different purpose: that purpose being that the tunnel does not actually represent an answer but a further question, the exact formulation of which must stay concealed in case the secret it reveals should retroactively destroy the acquired indifference that made escape possible and the tunnel along with it. Imagine that life revealed itself in this way, exhausting our capacity to know with some all-pervasive

---

[20] Eckhart, *Meister Eckhart*, 119.
[21] Georges Bataille, "The Practice of Joy Before Death," in *Visions of Excess*, 237.
[22] "If nihilism is the case then it does not lack anything, or more accurately, it does not 'lack in lacking'. This conundrum merely points to the obvious fact that nihilism may lack God, but it also lacks this lack of God" (Conor Cunningham, *Genealogy of Nihilism: Philosophies of Nothing and the Difference of Theology* [New York: Routledge, 2002], 170).

Incompleteness as a Tunnel

disquiet, and through this unwanted dissemination of its secrets made us long again for its silence:[23] what of escape then? and what of tunnels built and exoduses made? The ground would be too hard to dig new routes, and the escapees already in their tunnels (now prematurely ended, as all endings must be premature) would suffocate on the bad air. "The horrible duty is to go to the end,"[24] but a worse fate still is this second end for the sake of duty to the first.

The only thing worth doing, worth piling your days upon, is to search for hidden things, things that the day-to-day world tells you can't/won't/shouldn't exist, non-existent things that only a misguided (and ostensibly futile) hunt will uncover: digging for its own sake and that self-justifying state making a secret of itself. For, like Pessoa, we must "prefer a defeat that knows the beauty of flowers to a victory in the desert,"[25] and what is a secret but the failure of what is to become known, a known unknowing, a defence of knowledge at its own expense. However, when it comes to death, it is best to prefer a defeat (of knowledge in the secret) that knows the beauty of the desert, the beauty of the world running through our fingers, the beauty of our impossible tunnels made of sand—and death "like beauty passing through a nightmare."[26]

At this stage it should be noted that existence in the tunnel does not equate to timidity (a mole that when faced with what's outside, the myriad dangers aboveground, uses the tunnel as little more than a hiding place), for the tunneller does not wear the earth around them like some protective skein; but rather the tunnel, being their maximal possibility, is that over which they are the protector, a role enacted by their perpetual and unerring construction of it. Every new branch of the tunnel is the secret I've forgotten reminding me to keep searching for what I already know.

To adopt a Pessoan sentiment, I'm envious of the tunneller I'll become because he is not me, is not anyone, and yet he represents the death I consider worth living.

The as yet unspoken inconsistency in all this—in this distaste of life, in this fuzziness of death, and in all their various recombinant forms, and in the exuberant apathy/apathetic exuberance of the

---

[23] See Cunningham, *Genealogy of Nihilism*, 73.
[24] Lispector, *Água Viva*, 47.
[25] Pessoa, *The Book of Disquiet*, 175.
[26] Pessoa, *The Book of Disquiet*, 415.

disseminators—concerns the trade-off that occurs between clarity and vagueness, and the inability or unwillingness to side unequivocally with either. It is there in Pessoa:

> To make a decision, to finalize something, to emerge from the realm of doubt and obscurity—these are things that seem to me like catastrophes or universal cataclysms.[27]

> Anything, even tedium—anything but this general blurring of the soul and things, this bluish, forlorn indefiniteness of everything![28]

And it is there in Lispector:

> But I do know what I want here: I want the inconclusive. I want the profound organic disorder that nevertheless hints at an underlying order. The great potency of potentiality.[29]

> That brave thing that will be handing myself over, and which is like grasping the haunted hand of God, and entering that formless thing that is a paradise. A paradise that I don't want![30]

Here we see two instances in which indefiniteness and lucidity are both desired and shunned; and these are not accidental or peripheral contradictions, but are instead deliberate and integral. This is the paradox of their envisaged peace, the idealised, paradisiacal conclusion to the life that refuses to conclude. The predicament is impossible just as death is impossible: inexorable and yet unworkable. The conclusion that must be drawn is that this insoluble impasse is itself the solution, so that "what seems like a lack of meaning—that's the meaning."[31] Both sides of the paradox are requisite: the blurring of clarity and the clarity of the blurred. In other words, what presents itself as distinct and ordered must be subject to doubt and experienced obscurely, and what is obscure and formless must be approached with clarity and

---

[27] Pessoa, *The Book of Disquiet*, 397.
[28] Pessoa, *The Book of Disquiet*, 319.
[29] Lispector, *Água Viva*, 20.
[30] Lispector, *The Passion According to G.H.*, 10.
[31] Lispector, *The Passion According to G.H.*, 27.

precision. To understand in this way we must know our unknowing inside out, until the only thing left unknown is what it is to know. Such is the understanding we don't understand, the understanding that "closely resembles an acute incomprehension."[32]

A further inconsistency concerns our apprehension at the existence of a self and the apprehension that attends that same self's absence. For if "fear is not only entirely in you, but *is* you,"[33] a position endorsed by both Lispector and Pessoa—the latter (who spent his writing life fragmenting and compartmentalising that self into a less burdensome multiplicity) stating that "[t]here's no escape possible, unless I were to escape from myself"[34]—then how do we come by the facility to fear the very eradication of this source? Lispector talks of her fear becoming "[s]o much broader," and how this expanded version "was fear of [her] lack of fear."[35] That fear and the self are intertwined does not, it seems, prevent the self's eradication throwing up a new fear in its wake, that is, the fear of one's own disappearance. But if in the grip of such a fear there as an existential constant regardless of selfhood, what possibility is left for any kind of viable escape? Pessoa delineates this paradoxical state of terror as arising from, what he admits, is a confused terror of death: "I fear this nothingness that could be something else, and I fear it as nothing and as something else simultaneously, as if gross horror and non-existence could coincide there."[36] This fear, then, of both presence and absence seemingly coinciding, is one that crosses the boundary of death, but which might yet be transformed by the tunnel. To be active in your own disappearance: that is the solution, the juncture of appeasement.

If some residuum of fear should remain (or resurface) in the tunnel, it will be directly commensurate with the presence therein of self-awareness, of the "me" of the tunneller who suddenly finds their escape has been compromised. In the parlance of such excavations, this is tantamount to a fall, a cave in, a collapse, where only a further death will clear the way, a death subsequent to death—and maybe it will be necessary to die multiple times in this way before the tunnel

---

[32] Lispector, *The Passion According to G.H.*, 8.
[33] Lieut. Nab Saheb of Kashmir, *Bergmetal: Oro-Emblems of the Musical Beyond* (New York: Hworde, 2013), 43.
[34] Pessoa, *The Book of Disquiet*, 447.
[35] Lispector, *The Passion According to G.H.*, 95.
[36] Pessoa, *The Book of Disquiet*, 149.

On the Verge of Nothing

accommodates its pauses and the tunneller learns to breathe his own soil. This is the continuing conundrum of the tunnel: you have left yourself behind to be present there, a non-reflexive presence that nevertheless must still substantiate the metaphysical logistics of escape. I go without leaving, I leave myself behind in order to escape: my dying well is the paradox it had to be and I must follow suit. Oh, "to make a system out of delusions"[37] and have those delusions anesthetise their becoming true. And it is this openness to dying again, to dying as a threatened continuum, that sustains the possibility that would otherwise be forfeited, and is that in the face of which fear (in our presence to ourselves or its lack) becomes adrenalised in the service of the tunnel, in the service of its (and our) own lostness, its (and our) own abandonment, becoming thus assimilated (in its positive and negative aspects) so that we can "inhabit it like vermin, [so] it can be our space, [so that] our violent openness to the sacred death will protect us against their exterminations, driven insane by zero, we can knot ourselves into the underworld, communicate through it, cook their heavenly city in our plague."[38] For indeed we will through these exterminations become many, become plague, as we time and again become zero; but this is what it means to tunnel into death, to keep going, towards nothing and away from that arbitrary conclusion, that mantrap of the one completing death.

The endgame of existence is to find a cure for itself, a cure that cannot be death *simpliciter*, for death has been appropriated by the lives it closes, so much the inside of the door we pass through that we never see anything but the bad health of this exit. Death is hard because we are so often facing the wrong way. The cruelty to ourselves is always our compulsion to say goodbye.

---

[37] Cioran, *The Book of Delusions*, 78.
[38] Land, *The Thirst for Annihilation*, 132.

Chapter 7

Pessimism and Performance Art: A Speculative Contract

This is not the disquisition it might have been. How like itself. How like art without being art, which is where the future of art lives—and turns sour.

What is left after the performance is done: some photographs, some video footage, some words—some commodities that are not the artwork itself (although they increasingly become indistinguishable from it). But then, of course, the performance is never really over.

For all its obvious physicality—with its roots in the vigour and propulsions of Futurism and a reimagining of what was cabaret and variety theatre—a prevailing and demonstrably elemental strain of performance art is perpetuated in endurance-based works that explore nothing more frenetic than the frontiers of human inertia. And it is in these works that the artist's physical limitations are questioned most severely, and where the very physicality of human life is stretched out on the marble for all to see.

Pessimism is already performance art. Not only does it have all the elements of the freak show we have come to expect from the performative arts, from Joseph Beuys to Santiago Sierra, but its stake in endurance and self-mortification, in the collapsing of life and art as two distinct realms, is unparalleled. It could be argued that the pessimist's greatest performance is as a living paradox: how/why is the pessimist still alive when they have sucked all the vigour from existence? It is the one performance that unites life and art in a way that is indelible, trivialising both while also accentuating their combined seriousness. The only way they come apart is through catharsis or death. If the performances of Lee Lozano (her *Boycott Piece* lasting till she died, almost 30 years after its inception) and Tehching Hsieh (with works ranging from one to thirteen years) represent the pinnacle of endurance-based art, then the life of the pessimist must be offered in response. The pessimist's performance lasts as long as the pessimist. Nobody invests more time and effort into the art, into the pure and indelible pretence of being alive.

If a pessimist is not an artist, is not contextualised by the art world in some way, their existence-as-art will no doubt be considered ad hoc at best, spurious at worst; but the pessimist that persists (the tolerance of their intolerance in harmonious paradox) is by default already an artist. There is no need for them to be legitimated much less canonised: they would balk at the very suggestion. However, by enacting the beyond of that which has no beyond, by establishing non-meaning as meaning, and by stretching to near-breaking the logic of the very theoretical underpinnings they endorse, the pessimist is not only already partaking in performative art practice, but progressing art's agenda more than most of its established practitioners.

Having passed through a pseudo-mystic or shamanic stage, the future of performance art is pessimism, the future of pessimism is performance art—the now of pessimism is already performance art. To endure as a pessimist is already to perform. We might ask what the difference is between the pessimist that endures and the non-pessimist that endures, between the pessimist that performs and the pessimist that does not perform. To the first, the answer is knowing: knowing the context in which your life is a performative act of continued self-harm. To the second, the answer is that there is no difference, because there is no such distinction: every pessimist performs their pessimism, for life for the pessimist *just is* the performed life—there is that or there is death. And that we all perform our lives to some degree is no counter, for once again the art is in the knowing, in the conceptual apparatus behind the scenes, and what's more in the very collapse of that distinction.

Performance art moves from the speed and kinetic import of Futurism to the accentuated inertia of Hsieh and Marina Abramović. However, the central role that simultaneity played in both Futurism and Dada— the din of simultaneous noises, the blur of coincident images, the accidental confluence and dissonance of simultaneous movement, the essential abstraction of it all—can still be felt in modern performance art and indeed in pessimism. But whereas those foundational movements sought to capture and exploit what they considered to be the frenetic truths of human existence, these later examples see only distraction. It is not that these elements are simply missing from their works, but that they have been integrated in such a way that the original sense of dissonance and rapidity has been lost in the repetitive blur of ordinary lives, in the paradoxical simultaneity of a life lived and the rejection of that life.

"As art sinks into paralysis, artists multiply. This anomaly ceases to be one if we realise that art, on its way to exhaustion, has become both impossible and easy."[1] Impossible because no amount of talent can produce anything but the same old tired meanings, and easy because any amount of talent, however scant, can fail in the same old tired ways. Impossible because there's nothing left but existence itself and existence is empty, pointless and excruciating, and easy because anyone can exist (especially when you're not aware of doing it).

Susan Sontag observed that "[m]ost of the interesting art of our time is boring."[2] If we are to bear the unbearable boredom of existing, we must depict ourselves doing it, taking refuge in our fortitude: us bored with ourselves making art bored with itself, with humanity and art continuing to identify themselves in the process. In Heideggerian terms: "[B]oredom emerges as our own fundamental attunement."[3] It is our coming to terms with time: art as both exemplification and distraction from the profound emptiness of being and thus of itself.

Although the importance of space to an art form so reliant on the four-dimensionality of the human body may seem too obvious to mention, it is time, from the Futurists to contemporary performers, that has arguably been more crucial to performance art through the

---

[1] E. M. Cioran, *The Trouble with Being Born*, trans. Richard Howard (New York: Arcade Publishing, 1976), 51.
[2] Susan Sontag, *As Consciousness Is Harnessed to Flesh: Journals and Notebooks, 1964–1980* (New York: Farrar, Straus and Giroux, 2012), 136.
[3] Alina N. Feld, *Melancholy and the Otherness of God: A Study of the Hermeneutics of Depression* (Plymouth: Lexington Books, 2013), 127.

decades. Time is in some ways the one abiding subject. And nobody knows, feels and stages time like a pessimist.

The Futurist painters insisted that art must depict "activity" and "change," depict the speed, mechanisation and dynamism of the world around them. As a consequence of this they quickly deviated from painting and looked to a more representative medium, turning "to performance as the most direct means of forcing an audience to take note of their ideas."[4] For the pessimist, action and change are merely distractions from the horrific truth of existence: we act so as not to think, and see change so as not to see our pitiful condition, which does not change. It seems somewhat counterintuitive, then, to equate pessimism with any mode of expression that gives itself over to the act. As Cioran puts it: "If we do not regard ourselves as entrusted with a mission, existence is difficult; action, impossible."[5] What pessimist worth the name could turn life into a performance, transform our existential predicament into some comprehensive routine, some disagreeable enactment? But what of the purposeless performance, the performance of purposelessness? Can this lack of a mission not itself suffice as a mission? If action is impossible, then why not let inertia take its place? The pessimist thus inverts these naïve origins, and makes a non-performance of their performance, a true dream of the false activity, and through this oneiric possession acts out their own inaction; for, after all, "the dreamer is the true man of action"?[6]

In his manifesto on "The Pleasure of Being Booed,"[7] F. T. Marinetti advocated that Futurist writers and performers should cultivate a loathing for the audience, which ideally would then be reciprocated. For only booing signalled that the performer had done their job and that the audience was conscious to its affront, and not merely fawning in its sleep. Any applause or adulation from the audience was to be regarded with disdain, as it indicated only that the work performed was

---

[4] RoseLee Goldberg, *Performance Art: From Futurism to the Present* (London: Thames and Hudson, 2014), 14.
[5] Cioran, *The Trouble With Being Born*, 195.
[6] Pessoa, *The Book of Disquiet*, 87.
[7] F. T. Marinetti, "Manifesto of Futurist Playwrights: The Pleasures of Being Booed," in F. T. Marinetti, *Critical Writings*, ed. Günter Berghaus, trans. Doug Thompson (New York: Farrar, Straus and Giroux, 2006), 222.

Pessimism and Performance Art

all too palatable, quotidian, and bromidic.[8] And what more impactful affront to human existence is there than pessimism? Whose message is likely to be greeted with anywhere near the level of disapprobation as that of the pessimist? If the pessimist takes pleasure in anything they take pleasure in truth, however displeasing and unpleasant that truth might be; and what else could provide the soundtrack to that truth but a relentless cacophony of boos?

Marinetti's co-opting of variety theatre for the purposes of Futurism in the early 20th century was remarkably prescient, setting the tone for much of what was to become performance art (around the mid-1920s) for the next century and beyond; for what he found to admire in it, especially as a model for the Futurist project, was its dynamic embodiment of "the whole gamut of silliness, idiocy, gawkiness, and absurdities, which drive intelligence imperceptibly to the edge of madness,"[9] which can be seen as a proto-template for the performance art/performance of pessimism we recognise to this day.

Evoking a Futurist noise music performance from 1913, in which the audience was reported to issue "pathetic cries of 'no more',"[10] that predictably went unheeded, the pessimist continues to transmit their message however much those listening do not want to hear it. If the direction of travel all along has been for the audience and the performer to become interchangeable, what more effective way than for the performers themselves to be booing and pitifully screeching for an end, and for the audience to join in, wanting an end to the wretched requests of the performers and as a consequence (and perhaps even in sympathy) an end to existence itself?

Edward Gordon Craig and Enrico Prampolini (and the Constructionists, and members of the Bauhaus community that followed them)

---

[8] A tendency that would inevitably turn comedic, the droll potential of the unfunny played deliberately for boos, for the inherent humour of collective censure, until ultimately the boos turned to amusement and the game was up, or became a new game, the pleasure of being booed superseded by the dissemination of uneasy laughter: think Andy Kaufman reading *The Great Gatsby*, or Ted Chippington telling his One Mile joke.
[9] F. T. Marinetti, *Critical Writings*, 227.
[10] Goldberg, *Performance Art: From Futurism to the Present*, 21.

solicited for the eradication of the performer, for the performer's replacement by something mechanised, an automaton, a supermarionette. And so we present the ultimate supermarrionette as none other than the pessimist themself, that self-confessed human puppet extraordinaire. After all, what could be better than the puppet that knows it's a puppet, whose existence has embraced, nay absorbed, that role?

Oskar Schlemmer speculated as follows: "Might not the dancers be real puppets, moved by strings, or better still, self-propelled by means of a precise mechanism, almost free of human intervention, at most directed by remote control."[11] Might we imagine the pessimist's response as follows: the dancers are already real puppets, self-propelled by means of a precise mechanism minus a self, remote from who they are, each one a nobody.

Spontaneity has been exalted in performance art from the time of the Futurists to the present day. Whether it's Yves Klein or Zhu Ming, the unrehearsed, the random, and the impulsive have been factored in to bring performance art closer to life, for it to more successfully assimilate that which it is attempting to clarify. The idea, ultimately, is to have art become artless and the artless become art. In response, the pessimist will inform you that for all the vicissitudes of life, for all its many contingencies and whims, its abiding truth is an inescapable monotony from which no amount of surface variance or perceived novelty can compensate or distract. The pessimist will also tell you that your agency is a myth, so that any performer's controlled environment is likely to be not only artificial but flawed—artificial in conception, flawed in execution. With this in mind, the call for spontaneity is both superficial and redundant. The possibility of extemporaneous events cannot be eliminated, but nor are they anything but integral to what was already the work. The very idea that you could exclude them in the first place emanates from the same delusory reasoning that distinguished you from the puppets so they could be employed in your service.

---

[11] Goldberg, *Performance Art: From Futurism to the Present*, 107.

Pessimism and Performance Art

Marinetti claimed that "a time will come in which life will not be simply a matter of bread and toil, nor of idle existence, but *a work of art*."[12] After all, inertia is not idleness, but the hardest work imaginable.

Russian Futurist artist Vladimir Burlyuk lugged a twenty-pound pair of dumbbells around seventeen cities in the name of art. But what is twenty pounds compared to the weight of existing in any one of those cities for any time at all? And the question goes, but didn't he exist at the same time? And if he was a pessimist, the answer is yes. But if not, no; for only the pessimist truly exists.

The burden of the performance artist and the pessimist alike (to paraphrase John Cage): nothing new to say or do and the compulsion to say and do it anyway.

The everyday world of the pessimist is Fortunato Depero's vision of a new theatre of performance made from human flesh: "[E]verything turns—disappears—reappears, multiplies and breaks, pulverises and overturns, trembles and transforms into a cosmic machine that is life."[13] And the machine does not care about you and you in turn should not care about the machine—beyond the fact that you are part of it, when it would be better if you were not.

Hugo Ball, co-founder of the Cabaret Voltaire, explained that "all living art will be irrational, primitive, complex: it will speak a secret language and leave behind documents not of edification but of paradox."[14] Consciousness, according to Zapffe, is "a breach in the very unity of life, a biological paradox, an abomination, an absurdity, an exaggeration of disastrous nature."[15] If anything is to qualify as *living art* it must first live. The pessimist at least does this. All others, as Zapffe points out, occupy the rather more nebulous status of undead. And not only can the pessimist only talk in paradoxes (in a *secret language* of paradoxes), they can only live as one as well.

---

[12] F. T. Marinetti, *Critical Writings*, 402, original emphasis.
[13] Goldberg, *Performance Art: From Futurism to the Present*, 48.
[14] Hugo Ball, *Flight Out of Time: A Dada Diary* (Berkeley and Los Angeles: University of California Press, 1996), 49.
[15] Peter Wessel Zapffe "The Last Messiah," in Ligotti, *The Conspiracy Against the Human Race*, 23.

On the Verge of Nothing

Berlin Dadaist's demanded "the introduction of progressive unemployment through comprehensive mechanisation of every field of activity, [for] only by unemployment does it become possible for the individual to achieve certainty as to the truth of life and finally become accustomed to experience."[16] The censure of all that distracts us from the horror of existence is the very staple of pessimism. Diversions and recreations are the contagions at the root of humanity's almost wholesale zombification. It's small wonder that the Dadaists were considered adherents of nihilism. How embarrassing to be employed, worse still usefully employed. How disingenuous to make a difference. Unemployment is the only valid response to the truth of what there is that is worth doing, worth achieving. If you must be employed be employed with your boredom. Recall Cioran's terse lesson to those weary with the consequences of indolence: "To that friend who tells me he is bored because he cannot work, I answer that boredom is a higher state, and that we debase it by relating it to the notion of work."[17]

The young nihilist soldier, Jacques Vaché, a close friend of André Breton, in refusing to "produce anything at all" ought to be considered responsible for producing one of the first significant works of performance art, one so ahead of its time it almost went unnoticed, an anti-work that stands as a direct precursor to the works of Lozano and Hsieh,[18] despite there being over half a century between them. And that he thought art "an imbecility"[19] is only further proof of its credentials. Roger Gilbert-Lecomte's *The Odyssey of Ulysses the Palimped*, which militated against its being performed by having lengthy sections that were to be "read silently," although audacious in its own right, looks downright timorous in comparison.

Dada, for the Parisian Dadaists, was a destructive end point, an obliterative swansong: they were not interested in producing something better than what had gone before, only in destroying what they found already consecrated as art. This is the essence of pessimism: the end

---

[16] Goldberg, *Performance Art: From Futurism to the Present*, 70.
[17] E. M. Cioran, *Drawn and Quartered*, trans. Richard Howard (New York: Arcade Publishing, 2012), 78.
[18] Most notably his final *One Year Performance, No Art Piece* (1985–1986).
[19] Goldberg, *Performance Art: From Futurism to the Present*, 81.

that keeps on giving, once it has taken everything else. Pessimism does not seek to replace the philosophical and religious theories that have so far sheltered us with their illusory structures, but only to undermine them to the point of collapse. There are no subsequent plans to rebuild anything new or improved from the rubble; for the rubble is already something improved, in that it is no longer the architectural lie that had arranged it to look like truth.

Dada promoted transience, pitched it against the infinite. Most pessimists do the same. Those that don't (Bahnsen for instance), those with a much crueller vision of our predicament, merge the two: all the paltry stuff of transience made to last forever, because the sickest joke of all has no punchline.

Bauhaus exponent Josef Albers claimed that "art is concerned with the HOW and not the WHAT; not with literal content, but with the performance of the factual content. The performance—how it is done—that is the content of art."[20] Living art must be about the living, the art of what it is to live, and so the core subject matter of pessimism no less. (As Marina Abramović has stated: "[T]he performance is all state of mind"[21]—there is nothing else.) Consider the artist Morton Viskum: can we really say his work is there in his finished paintings, or instead in how they were created, by using a dead human hand in place of a paintbrush? If this is painting it is Action Painting. If pessimism is an art form, it is the challenge of inertia undertaken so as to delineate the integrality of futile gesture, and of failure.

In John Cage's famous silent work *4' 33"* (1952), everything heard is music. The work in this way makes way for itself: it disappears so it can exist. I leave you with this silence. Fill it with the noise of listening for what isn't there in order for it to arrive. Fill it with the non-existent music of life. Fill it so it can remain forever empty, forever waiting, forever what it is not. Fill it with the music of doomed expectation.

Cage's silent work incorporates no real silence. Genuine silence is unbearable. It drives you mad. It quickly becomes excruciating. We

---

[20] Goldberg, *Performance Art: From Futurism to the Present*, 121.
[21] Matthew Akers, *Marina Abramović: The Artist is Present* (Music Box Films, 2012), 1:19.

might think of nihilism as the anechoic chamber of the soul, and the post-pessimist as one who exists in such a chamber, albeit one in which the faintest murmur of some unidentifiable and impossible thing can still nevertheless be heard.

In 1961, for *Living Sculpture*, Piero Manzoni signed each of his live sculptures as follows: "This is to certify that X has been signed by my hand and is therefore, from this date on, to be considered an authentic and true work of art." In the same year he inflated balloons and exhibited them as *Artist's Breath*, and had his faeces sealed in ninety thirty-gram tins to be sold as *Artist's Shit* at the then current price of gold. These pieces constitute a sustained send-up of the artist as conveyor of value and meaning. The artist is the same as you, the same as anyone else, and yet somehow different because of an idea, or a set of ideas. We breathe, we shit, we sign things; and yet when the artist does it the abstract contextualisation of art imbues a cryptic significance that is otherwise missing. This is the narrative, and it is one that Manzoni was all too willing to simultaneously critique and exploit. The pessimist's penumbral positioning—when it comes to rejecting existence while continuing to exist, and at the same time making theoretical currency out it, out of the same tired routines quietly endured by everyone else—is not dissimilar to Manzoni's. The pessimist says: here is my signature, it identifies nothing in the same way that your signature signifies nothing, only it does so from a place of concentrated absence, an always felt spasm of vacuity. The pessimist says: here is my breath, and much like yours it happened without consent, but I have registered my displeasure, my disgust, and you have not. The pessimist says: here is my shit, and while I acknowledge we all defecate, only mine was used to decorate a life.

In 1965, Joseph Beuys made *Twenty-four Hours*, for which he remained in a box for the titular duration. Although he allowed himself to stretch out at intervals, his feet never left the container. In 1974 he made *Coyote: I Like America and America Likes Me*, for which he swathed himself in felt and shared a room with a wild coyote for seven days—to, as he claimed, highlight the American Indian's persecution. Despite the laudable sentiments attached to the second performance, both are little more than templates for two far more interesting performances that never happened: *Twenty-Four Years*, in which he was sealed in a

Pessimism and Performance Art

wooden box for the titular period; and *Bear: I Hate America and America Hates Me*, in which he shared a room with a starving Black Bear.

In *Command Performance* (1974), Vito Acconci made a performance of his absence: placed inside an otherwise empty area is an empty stool underneath a spotlight and a video monitor, where the viewer is encouraged to inaugurate their own performance. A year earlier, Dan Graham used mirrors and video so that each audience member also became the performer. Both these artists attempted to bring the performer and the audience together in an uncomfortable unity. To perform who you are for yourself is a self-portrait, but not just any self-portrait: a self-portrait of a person disappearing, or failing to be born, the anonymity of being alive—"the anonymous work of an anonymous reality only justifiable as long as . . . life lasts."[22]

Just as performance art is as much a disavowal of art as it is an art form, pessimism is as much a disavowal of philosophy as it is a philosophical position.

It is often claimed that Vienna Actionist, Rudolph Schwartzkogler's "artistic nudes—similar to wreckage" led to his death in 1969, when he castrated himself and bled to death. The reality is he fell from a window and died from his injuries. If I had to pick the story I liked best I would pick both, just as they are: the apocryphal tale of the artist dying for his art juxtaposed with the pathetic reality of his expiring as the result of some banal accident. If I *had* to choose one as Schwartzkogler's final work of art, a summation of his career, I would choose the latter.

Marina Abramović and Ulay's *Relation in Movement* (1977) comprised Ulay driving around in circles for sixteen hours while Abramović counted off the number of circuits. All I can think is, why sixteen hours? Why aren't they still there? I want to hear all the justifications for imposing that limit on themselves (all the other less mindlessly cycloidal things they had to do), so I can laugh myself to sleep.

In 1972, Stuart Brisley made *And for Today, Nothing*, for which he reclined fully-clothed in a bath filled with dark, filthy-looking liquid,

---

[22] Lispector, *Água Viva*, 16.

strewn with assorted debris and congealed scum resembling lily pads, for two weeks. The scene looked like some home-grown biological experiment gone wrong, or the aftermath of some intensely squalid murder. But perhaps something else was going on. Perhaps the liquid and its congealed floaters were excesses of Hippocratic black bile and phlegm, Brisley's dynamic mind having produced the former, his excessive torpor the latter? Submerged but for his mouth and nose, he lay there stricken by the unholy confluence of an intense vitality of thought and a prolonged indolence, each causing and perpetuating the other: I think therefore I undermine all reason to move; I refrain from moving therefore accentuating my capacity for thought. And to think without action is always to be on the brink of drowning, of sinking below the surface of the world outside you and never again coming back up for air.

Imagine Gilbert and George's 1969 performance piece *Meal*—in which a thousand people were invited to watch Isabella Beeton and Doreen Mariott cook a meal for Gilbert, George and David Hockney, with Richard West as their waiter—where instead of food, they were served and ate only shit. What if it wasn't just any shit? What if it was Manzoni's tinned shit? What if this *ne plus ultra* of coprophagic indulgence would not go down, that regardless of its value they found its taste repulsive? Some would argue, of course, that the value is irrelevant to its flavour, because art-value is not gustatory-value, and that artworks as a rule are not meant to be eaten. And yet what would such a performance represent if not art eating itself, or rather art attempting this act of autophagy only to find itself inedible? Imagine an art this squeamish, this fixated on good taste having anything to say. Imagine Manzoni's shit consumed and then puked back up to be repackaged for sale at the current price of platinum. Imagine the value of anything improved that thing. Imagine there is any such thing as the inherent value of value. Imagine the entire human experiment squeezed into a tin. Imagine who or what might esteem such a thing.

Jannis Kounellis considered the whole history of art as a series of "frozen performances." He maintained that each and every painting or sculpture since art began has told the same story, that of "the loneliness of a single soul."[23] The only thing left is to dispense with the soul, and more importantly the story.

The integration of life and art only leads one place: the pessimist in a room, outside a room, in fact anywhere, doing anything (instead of doing nothing, or as a way of doing nothing).

Robert Wilson sourced the psychological traits of an autistic teenager, Christopher Knowles, to use as material in his performances. The symptoms of autism include social isolation, trouble abiding by the rules of conversation, trouble understanding group dynamics, a profound dislike of talking about oneself, problematic spontaneity, inappropriate honesty, trouble understanding emotions common in others, a disinterest in what is going on around you, disproportionate focus on only one or two topics, and an inability to understand the motives behind other peoples' actions. Wilson might have used a pessimist to equal effect.

The impossibility of the beyond of pessimism: this is the only subject left. And this equates perfectly with the impossibility of the beyond of art itself.

In the 1980s and 90s, the activist group ACT UP performed "die-ins" on the front steps of prominent pharmaceutical companies. How about self-inflicted wounds, immolations, endurance and fatalities for no cause whatsoever? How about dying for no reason at all, like everybody else?

For his 1994 piece, *12 Square Meters*, Zhang Huan sat in a public latrine in Beijing's East Village slathered in fish oil and honey. The performance lasted one hour, and by the end of it Huan was completely covered in flies. To prematurely turn yourself into an enticement for creatures hardwired to exploit decay, to become a living lure for all those devotees of rot, was to engage in a new strain of forensic entomology in which the decomposition of the living is determined, and the crime of life itself meticulously and clearly substantiated. How easy it is to be dead in life, and how hard to be anything else. What Huan succeeded in doing was performing both the

---

[23] Goldberg, *Performance Art: From Futurism to the Present*, 170.

On the Verge of Nothing

frenetic veneer of existence (his membrane of flies) and the quiet collapse of the interior, the hidden ruin, the decomposed core, the death that feeds the life you see, the putrefaction and inertia at the heart of all the squirming multiplicities of living, all those myriad vitalities struggling to mask the all but perished substance within: the identity, the person, the artist.

What if Sun Yuan and Peng Yu's blood brought that conjoined fetus back to life, or if those eight American pit bulls confined to treadmills died of exhaustion? Maybe then we'd be closer to something. The audience wants to see skin in the game—even if the skin is only the artist's by proxy, and even if the game can only ever be lost. Imagine if art was both miraculous and egregious in this way; imagine if art was the birth of a child. Did Costa Rican artist Guillermo Vargas really starve a dog to death for an art exhibit? If we knew either way, what difference would it make for art? Imagine if, in line with a not uncommon if suspiciously hyperbolic claim, art really did make life worth living. What a miracle that would be, and how patently disappointing into the bargain.

Sigalit Landau's *Barbed Hula* (2000) is said to be about the glaring inadequacies of Middle Eastern politics. But it is an even more accurate visual representation of the flagrant self-abuse of those naïve enough to believe in any of our political solutions to human existence.

Pessimism is the reverse trompe l'oeil of performance art: where there were four dimensions there are now three, for you cannot touch emptiness. The pessimist flattens everything: the ostentatious edifices of the human project are consummately razed.

With *Challenging Mud* (1955), Kazou Shiraga progressed beyond his earlier action paintings to establish an even closer intimacy between artist and material, eschewing the customary hierarchy. During the performance, Shiraga and his material shared the same status: the artist was mud and the mud was artist. For the pessimist and his materials to become similarly familiarised, he would have to exemplify the cold indifference of the universe as the universe in turn exemplified him. The personal would become process and the process personal, inner

Pessimism and Performance Art

and outer ceasing to demarcate what becomes a universal vacuity of purpose.

Yayoi Kusama's first performance piece *Narcissus Garden* (1966) used 1,500 reflective balls, which distorted the features of anyone who looked at them. Ostensibly an attempt to puncture vanity by revealing its inherent distortions, pessimism might instead have used 1,500 normal mirrors, and sold them as self-portraits of anyone and so no one.

Kusama's *Infinity Mirrored Room—The Souls of Millions of Light Years Away* (2013) gives the illusion of endless space, a blinking cosmos stretching on forever, with us looking out into it, irrelevant. Only one visitor at a time is permitted, reinforcing that sense of loneliness and abandonment. A deep space perforated with light. An installation work, it could just as easily have been a performance work (in the mould of Acconci's *Command Performance*) in which members of the audience one by one enact the live aspect. Maybe the pessimist should replicate the room under a new title: *If You Need This to Feel This, Your Consciousness is Impaired*. The post-pessimist has already found this dark unfeeling cosmos inside their own head, knows that "[t]he problem with introspection is that it has no end,"[24] and knows too, more importantly, how that problem is also a solution.

For *Marking Time V* (2014), Marilyn Arsem occupied a room at the Palazzo Mora for twenty-four hours over seven days as part of the Venice International Performance Art Week. For *100 Ways to Consider Time* (2016) she was present in Gallery 261 of the Museum of Fine Arts in Boston for six hours a day, for 100 days. At those times during which she was absent a recording of her voice was played inside the gallery. About her work, she has said it explores "how to fill time that feels too empty." If a pessimist had made these works, they would have said that they explore, "how to *feel* time that feels too empty." And you only feel time by expressly refusing to fill it.

During *Transfiguration* (1998), Olivier de Sagazan sculpts clay all over his head, obscuring his face, coating himself in the claggy material, all the

---

[24] Philip K. Dick, *The Transmigration of Timothy Archer* (Boston: Houghton Mifflin Harcourt, 2011), 187.

time gouging it, layering it, slowly transforming himself into some human/animal/alien hybrid. It is through concealing his given human face that de Sagazan demonstrates how the mask goes all the way back, beyond the clay, beyond his now hidden face. As with Mr Okuyama in Abe's *The Face of Another*, he becomes someone/something else by trying to become himself: the attempt to fashion a new face over one's old face is to acknowledge not only a multitude of faces but an ultimate facelessness. The very idea of a face is a mask. The idea that you are seen, presented to the world and to others via some arrangement of material features that somehow identifies you, is itself both abhorrent and disingenuous. And of course the problem is not the face, or that the face is a mask, but that there's nothing behind it.

In order to make *Testicle Banquet* (2012), Japanese artist Mao Sugiyama volunteered to undergo a surgical procedure to remove his genitals. He then organised for the removed flesh to be cooked and served to five dinner guests. As an effort to spotlight the plight of x-gender and asexual people, Sugiyama's performance might appear to patently frustrate the pessimist's attempt to universalise our miserable human predicament. However, what is this repudiation of gender and sex but a rejection of life as it is given, an attempt to modify and correct some universal mistake of nature. And while this is a discrete and localised rejection of the imposition of one's prescribed existence, the refusal to just accept what has been "gifted" feels similarly audacious and exploratory.

In 1975, for a piece called *Search of the Miraculous*, Bas Jan Ader attempted to cross the Atlantic in a sail boat. He set out from Cape Cod and was never seen again. It puts us in mind of Dadaist Arthur Cravan, who having left the coast of Mexico in a small yacht in 1918 never arrived at his destination in Buenos Aires, and was also never seen again. To leave and yet never to arrive, to depart as a prelude to disappearing: how like the pessimist, who having absconded from life never arrives anywhere else, who having turned their back on life, disappears inside it.

Nailing your testicles to the ground to protest against Vladimir Putin's authoritarian government (a la the artist Pyotr Pavlensky [2013]) is

Pessimism and Performance Art

puerile; nailing your testicles to the ground to protest the puerility of protest is also puerile, but profoundly so.

What role does the audience play in pessimism as performance art? It could be said that the audience becomes the performance's perpetuation-in-waiting, which brings us to the actual duration of any particular performance. For if this "duration refers not only to the length of time in which a performance initially unfolded, but also to the extended time of the work's reception, then the duration of performance might be seen as the time in which an audience might be transformed into something else."[25] The audience is the material to be converted, potential acolytes to their own disintegration, and the performance lasts until that conversion takes place. Thus the pessimist's performance never ends.

Frazer Ward asks: "Can there be any art when the artist keeps that art secret?"[26] The pessimist answers with a sigh, because they know, alas, that there are no secrets. However, the post-pessimist also knows that the absence of secrets is itself a secret, and that it is in this slenderest fissure of secrecy that the art of the other resides. The possibility of art without an audience is the possibility of art. Like Lovecraft—who though he often wrote of discoveries of hidden knowledge and creatures that are too much for his scientifically-minded protagonists to bear, also wrote of the opposite psychological trauma inflicted when our scientific methodologies fall short, and we cannot come to understand some alien phenomenon—we find ourselves impaled on both horns of a dilemma: undone by the absence of secrets and undone by their recalcitrance.

Doomed (1975) involved Chris Burden lying under a pane of glass leant against a gallery wall. It finished on the third day, when a carafe of water was placed alongside him, compromising the work. But, crucially, Burden had abdicated responsibility for when it would end. Something external to the work would be required to conclude it. This in-built open-endedness, that nevertheless factored in the necessity of its eventual termination, combined with its title, produced what could be

---

[25] Frazer Ward, *No Innocent Bystanders: Performance Art and Audience* (New Hampshire: Dartmouth College Press, 2012), 13.
[26] Ward, *No Innocent Bystanders*, 3.

considered a proto-pessimist performance. It is not down to the pessimist to end what was started without their consent. They may be doomed, but the responsibility for that state lies elsewhere. All they need do is erect some transparent veneer between themself and others (that fundamental yet unseen difference occasioned by self-imposed segregation), and wait out their own performance.

Against the idea that performance works are intrinsically event-centric and non-repeatable, Frazer argues that "it is a viable claim that the afterlife of performance is as important as the initial moment, insofar as that is when and where its meanings unfold, and that is where it generates transformations of the audience that are not strictly event-reliant."[27] And this is prevalent not only with regard to individual transformations, but to the possible transfiguration of what it means to be an audience: after all, the endgame of pessimistic performance art is to eradicate the distinction (between audience and performer) altogether.

As Acconci, for one, advocated, we should move away from seeking answers to the works of some performer within the subjectivity of that performer; for while the perspective of the pessimist may seem paramount, the object is not to reveal a personal truth but a human one. Insofar as one is human and condemned to remain that way, autobiographical content is an irrelevance. The pessimist performer is not so much divulging themself as the lack thereof, and nor are they divulging their experiences but rather experience itself. They are not performing so that they may be captured, but in order to avoid capture:

> In line with the argument that performance is as much concerned with the evasion or critique of subjectivity as in articulating it, they might best be described as escape attempts, insofar as they disarticulate artistic subjectivity from the artists' own presence in their works, which are in turn disallowed from being seen as complete in themselves. The overall effect is of an ironic form of self-liberation.[28]

---

[27] Ward, *No Innocent Bystanders*, 14.
[28] Ward, *No Innocent Bystanders*, 22.

Pessimism and Performance Art

For his 1972 performance *Seedbed*, Acconci installed a ramp inside a gallery underneath which he masturbated. Stimulated by the sounds of the visitors walking on the ramp above, he broadcasted his lewd fantasies to the room above via a speaker. By doing so, he brought the private sphere into the public sphere and vice versa, which is precisely what pessimism as performance art does: you might think this way but you do not develop these ideas in public, you keep your dirty little secret to yourself. Like masturbation, pessimism is something virtually everyone indulges in (at some time or other), while only very few are willing to advertise this participation.

Acconci and Burden have an obvious debt to minimalism: "Acconci referred to his performance work as 'a last gasp of minimalism,' and twenty years later said that minimalism had been 'the father art' for him."[29] Don't let the, at times, prolific output of pessimistic thinkers or the occasional ornateness of the prose fool you into thinking they are anything but minimalists. For all the pages produced the message is always the same. They are self-admonishing schoolboys doing their lines. The experiment is never with the message, the philosophical position, but with the delivery system: how can I say this so they'll see I mean it?

Minimalism makes meaning and subjectivity public: there is no private headspace conveyed via the medium of the performer. It is a rejection of the Cartesian model: more Heideggerian porousness, less interiority. The pessimist is minimalist in the sense that their hell is also your hell, the only difference being that you might not have come to realise it yet.

Abramović's *Rhythm 0* (1974) involved her standing in a gallery in Naples for six hours and submitting to the whims of the audience, whatever they might turn out to be. In front of her was a table with 72 objects on it that included razor blades, a scalpel, scissors and a loaded gun. She was the object and they could do with her as they wished. She was interfered with sexually but wasn't raped; she was cut but no more than shallow nicks. She was threatened with the gun but wasn't shot. Those audience members who sought to exercise their freedoms in increasingly violent ways came into conflict with those who conversely sought to protect her. As a rejoinder to pessimism this could be

---

[29] Ward, *No Innocent Bystanders*, 28.

On the Verge of Nothing

interpreted as reinforcing the notion of degrees of passivity, making the pessimist's notion of the human as a puppet seem overly simplistic. But look at the audience: even as a work of art its members can only gently lean against the boundaries of their conditioning. If the audience members could not escape the ethical implications of either their action or their inaction, which seems safe to assume, then their status as facets of a work of art unearthed no more than the predictably timorous automatons to be found anywhere. I can't help wondering what it would have meant (what it would mean now) if Burden had turned up to Abramović's *Rhythm 0* and shot her between the eyes.

Ward states that "performance art may issue a very contemporary call to think about what 'we' are prepared to put up with, and in what name."[30] What more fundamental, and fundamentally accurate, answers could there be than these: life itself and anonymity?

The framing conditions of pessimism can appropriate the entire history of art. It is the ultimate parenthetical disease.

In *Five Day Locker Piece* (1971), Burden occupied a locker in an art school for 120 hours. The space inside was two feet by two feet and three feet deep. The locker above him contained five gallons of water and the one directly underneath an empty five gallon container. But Burden was not separated from the audience like some would-be gymnosophist; for though ostensibly isolated, he conversed with visitors for thirteen or fourteen hours a day, making his private space very much public. His remoteness from others was presented as essentially superficial, his interiority, in the mode of Beckett, was no more than voices without faces. He was performing his own failed privacy, his inability to be separate from what he was, from the curse of that.

Earnestness and Asininity: the poster boys of performance art and pessimism.

In *Following Piece* (1969), Acconci followed a series of random strangers. When they went inside a building, he stopped following them and

---

[30] Ward, *No Innocent Bystanders*, 21.

moved on to someone else. The people he followed (unwittingly) escaped the work by retreating to their pre-established interiors. Acconci had no such option: he had what was publicly available, what could not be hidden nor hidden from. The pessimist likewise has no home, no refuge from the fate of everyone: they have only the empty pursuit of movement because the work of existence necessitates it.

For *Second Hand* (1971), Acconci hung a clock on a wall and stared at its second hand for one hour. He spoke of disappearing inside the clock, becoming it, becoming time itself. However, this is not to experience time but to attempt to escape time, to not feel time by sublimating that which feels into pure processional absence, to sacrifice inertia at the altar of a desensitised sequence. The colloquialism that would have us believe that to watch time is to slow or stop time, ignores the fact that at the apex of the concentrative scale a self-annihilative absorption occurs, whereby the threat of time is simultaneously embraced and evaded. With our thought occupied elsewhere we too are elsewhere, however banal that other place. To exist inside time in this way, is to have time act as a proxy for the debilitating relentlessness of your own thoughts, it is to have the clock think for you.

For *Hand and Mouth* (1970), Acconci repeatedly placed his hand inside his mouth until he gagged and was forced to remove it. For *Soap and Eyes* (1970), he repeatedly poured soapy water into his eyes. For *Waterways* (1971), he repeatedly filled his mouth with saliva until he couldn't contain it any longer and let it pour into his cupped hands. These repetitive tests of physical endurance are deliberately ordinary, deliberately trivial: there is nothing of the sensational threat to life that we find in the work of Burden or Abramović, only self-inflicted discomforts and the body's automatic responses. His gag reflex, his blinking eyes, and his salivating are all outside of his control, his autonomy restricted to the contriving and performing of this series of trials. As such, these works comment on just how much of any given performance is under the artist's control, how much is always contingent on crude human and physical realities. We might compare this realisation to that of the pessimist, who despite all their theoretical underpinnings are still subject to the instinctual physiological attachment to life. However much the pessimist repeats their self-destructive mantras, their performance will always be subject to the basic human drives to perpetuate their own unwanted state at all costs. The body endures the performance and the performer endures the body, and so the stalemate goes on, for the stalemate *is* the performance, after all.

Shoot (1971) involved Burden being shot in his left arm by a friend. The bullet was only intended to graze his arm, but instead it caused significantly more damage, taking a chunk out of his bicep. While the audience could identify with Burden, they didn't get to feel what it was like: their experience was vicarious and distant. Each had their own experience, their own version of what it must be like, but they could not grasp the sensation of the bullet entering their flesh, only the general sense of apprehension previous to it. Burden later spoke of *Shoot* as having inculcated in him some special kind of knowledge (unique to those who have been shot), a rarefied insight that set him apart from others. The pessimist's performance would have insisted the audience too submit its arms to the bullet. For the pessimist's knowledge is not singular or exclusive in the way Burden describes; it is only that they abjure distraction from it, while most others suffer a (healthy) dependency on such distraction, existing as they do almost completely within its parameters. The performance could not allow for each audience member to have their own take on what it must be like: they must be made to feel the universality of what it is that a bullet imparts, as it decimates the many frivolous variances of diversion— something no pessimist has ever achieved.

According to Ward, "Burden's account [of *Shoot*] resonates with Donald Judd's single requirement that a work of art be interesting."[31] The persistence of the pessimist is interesting because it's conceptually and psychologically problematic: it should not be possible to exist stripped of all human illusion (as far as such a state is possible) and yet it happens anyway. It is interesting in the way that Roger Penrose's experiments with four-dimensional impossible objects are interesting. When we materialise the theory, add dimensions to a representation, we come to see just what adjustments or malformations are necessary in order to achieve it. Likewise, pessimism is not in itself a theory that is particularly interesting (its status as a philosophical theory is

---

[31] Ward, *No Innocent Bystanders*, 86.

Pessimism and Performance Art

notoriously dubious, limiting and rendering void as it does so many other fields of intellectual endeavour), just as a gun being fired into a person's arm is not of any special note; however, what is of considerable interest is the context of the performances, the conditions under which a theory is enacted or a person's arm shot. The most interesting thing about pessimism is not its relatively unsophisticated, if nevertheless compelling, claims and arguments, but that it ends without ending, destroys life without bringing about death.

Burden's *220* (1971) took place in the F Space Gallery in Santa Ana, California. After lining the gallery with plastic and arranging four wooden ladders against the walls, he submerged the floor under twelve inches of water. He and three other participants then climbed to the tops of their respective ladders, at which point Burden dropped a 220-volt electrical cable into the water. The performance started at midnight and they remained there for six hours. Once the allotted time was up, the current was switched off and they safely made their descents. The take home point would seem to be that we are all clinging to structures that keep us from falling into the void, that life is precarious and the architecture of our deaths quite literally all around us. The pessimist's predicament is that however much they might doubt the legitimacy of the ladder—its meaning, its reality even—for want of an alternative, they cling to its rungs same as everyone else.

For the pessimist performance artist, resilience is the primary medium/product/market.

For *TV Hijack* (1972), Burden agreed to do a cable TV interview with Phyllis Lutjeans, during the course of which he held a knife to her throat and threatened to kill her if the live transmission was interrupted. He also told her of his plans to force her to execute obscene acts in front of the camera. She had not been forewarned of this hijack and was genuinely scared for her life. What for Burden was performance was for Lutjeans very real, and the room for contingency meant that there was always something at stake. What, though, could possibly be at stake for the pessimist? Hasn't everything already been lost? What is left to be risked? Then again, while there might appear to be nothing remaining that could feasibly be put in jeopardy, there is still that inviolable principle that maintains that, whatever else, the beyond of pessimism cannot be a retreat. There is no return to illusion as a form of truth, only the escapade of truth as a form of illusion. What is at stake, then, is the stark lucidity of the pessimistic position. It is not the knife at their throat that unduly concerns the pessimist, but that they might come to see that knife as a threat to something of seemingly irreplaceable importance.

During the 1975 version of *Thomas' Lips*, when Abramović was about to cut yet another five-pointed star into her belly with a razor blade, someone called out: "You can stop. You don't have to do this." In response, a second member of the audience shouted: "Yes she does." And, of course, the first person to call out was right: she did not have to do it—but she did it anyway. And so the second person to call out was also right: she did have to do it—what else was this self-harming automaton going to do? What else is the non-suicidal pessimist going to do but perpetuate their own self-harm? One might as well entreat Jordon Wolfson's *Female figure* (2014) to stop gyrating.

How does the audience know that the pessimist is a pessimist, that it's not just a stunt? Answer: because nobody pretends to be a pessimist (or if they do, they don't need to pretend for long, for the requisite pretence will soon evaporate); it would be like pretending to be a leper and in so doing living alongside them in a colony, or like Johnny Barrett in *Shock Corridor* (1963).

By submitting herself to various tests of endurance, Abramović seemed to be arguing that any sense of human identity she might arrive at would resemble less and less the (bodily) material she exploits. Who could fail to ignore the mystical qualities to Abramović's performance, *The Artist is Present* (2012), which she describes as going "through the door of pain" and entering "another state of mind," an experience that is both unexplainable and "holy."[32] This habit of utilising the physical in order to get beyond it is yet again prevalent in her new work, to be revealed (in 2023) at London's Royal Academy of Arts. The show will include an artwork that employs virtual reality, and she describes this immersion in the virtual as "a very shocking experience—the feeling

---

[32] Matthew Akers and Jeff Dupre (dirs.), *Marina Abramović: The Artist is Present* (USA: A Show of Force, 2012).

that I was there and not there at the same time."[33] The artist is present but is not present: she sits at a table as if vacated of agency. The artist mutilates her body as a way of distinguishing herself from it: self-mortification as an othering of self. Her realities have always been virtual, there and yet not there, material and yet floating. This paradox of being is the pessimist's default state, a felt condition, a roleplaying of the flesh (or rather a roleplaying of a roleplaying of the flesh, for the disconnect is itself a ruse), a machine in a ghost, suffering without a sufferer.

Wittgenstein claimed that "[t]he philosopher's treatment of a question is like the treatment of an illness."[34] The pessimist, however, only has one question left, and it asks: why am I still here? And the question is indeed the manifestation of an illness. Only, the pessimist seeks no treatment for the question/illness, because they know there is no such treatment: all there is is waiting for the question to resolve itself through the eventuality of its no longer being possible to think. The only option available is whether to acknowledge your illness or not. That most choose to medicate on ignorance (imagining the question resolved in whatever arbitrary manner) and so feign health is no surprise when the alternative is to ask the same question over and over with no hope of ever receiving the answer you want.

For *House with an Ocean View* (2002), Abramović lived for twelve days on a raised platform that could only be reached by three ladders, their rungs made of butcher's knives. Suspended above her audience, the knives (as means of escape) remind her that if she attempts to leave she will materialise—she will arrive by going. And conversely, by remaining she will gradually become more and more intangible. The pessimist too knows that a way out is in view if they only choose to take it, while also knowing that their philosophical position, as yet ethereal, will have to come into contact with the sharp edges of any escape route in order to achieve it.

---

[33] Marina Abramović, "Frieze News," *Frieze* (07 February 2019) (https://www.frieze.com/article/serpentine-performance-marina-abramovic-appear-augmented-reality-very-shocking-experience).
[34] Ludwig Wittgenstein, *Philosophical Investigations*, trans. G. E. M. Anscombe (London: Blackwell, 1994), 91.

On the Verge of Nothing

From 1971 till her death in 1999, Lee Lozano performed *Decide to Boycott Women* or *Boycott Piece*, during which time she refused to talk to or directly interact with any other women (although it is rumoured that this proscription may not have included her mother). She'd originally intended the performance to last for just a month, but ended up continuing it for nearly thirty years. What began as an attempt to improve her relations with other women ended up eradicating those relations altogether. She cut women out of her life and developed a taste for it. If only she had extended the boycott to herself, she might have bifurcated into an even more impressive artist: the refusing-self refused, the superposition of boycotted and boycotter, the pessimist's creed of *I want no part of this nothing that is me*.

Pessoa advocated paring life back to its barest minimum, abjuring the diversionary embellishments of human living so that from this elemental existence we might find a solution to our tedium—in tedium. He writes: "Wise is the man who monotonizes his existence, for then each minor incident seems a marvel. . . . Monotonizing existence, so that it won't be monotonous. Making daily life anodyne, so that the littlest thing will amuse."[35] This wittingly vacuous asceticism is present in every one of Hsieh's performances, for which he time and again meticulously embraces the potentialities of abject boredom, the creative reserves of repetition, and the hypothetically infinite space of banal detail.

Hsieh claims that leading up to the first of his *One Year Performances*, *Cage Piece* (1978–1979), he was "frustrated and depressed," and that the work "was a way of making a form of how [he] felt." That form was a wooden cage (11.5 x 9 x 8 feet) equipped with nothing but a sink, lights, a bucket and a single bed. Throughout that year he did not speak or read or write, watch television or listen to the radio. As an illegal alien, Hsieh was performing the necessity of remaining hidden, making a show of his disappearance. His asceticism was the asceticism not of transcendence but of occupation: he was instantiating a mood as a set of circumstances in a bid to accentuate them. He gave his predicament and his state of mind a definite and prescribed location and a definite and prescribed duration. He compartmentalised what for the pessimist

---

[35] Pessoa, *The Book of Disquiet*, 153.

is fundamentally inseparable from human existence—something that, as we will see, Hsieh's later works seem to acknowledge. This work, then, does not so much dissolve the line between art and life, as construct four lines around a tiny subsection of life and have art be that cordoned area. Life is only art if it has lines drawn round it.

For the second of his five *One Year Performances*, *Time Clock Piece* (1980–1981), Hsieh punched a time clock every hour on the hour. Each punch of the clock activated a camera which took a picture of him from the waist up, the clock to his right recording the time. Placed in sequence, the images form a six-minute film in which his head goes from being cleanly shaven to swathed in shoulder length hair. The steady lengthening of his hair shows the passage of time, the growth of that dead matter standing as a proxy for the life lived in between. As with *Cage Piece*, this performance would appear to conflate art and life congruous to a well-established paradigm of such attempted conflations. As Ward elucidates:

> One reading of Hsieh's work would see it in a long line of avant-gardist attempts to bridge the famous gap between art and life. But given that Hsieh could never leave the immediate vicinity of the time clock (so as to be back in time for the next punch), it cannot help but seem deeply ironic that the undocumented alien's attempt to bridge this gap should collapse both art and life into an intense process of documentation and discipline.[36]

However, while the irony of Hsieh meticulously documenting his existence in a country in which he remains undocumented should not pass without mention, there is something more elemental, more axiomatic, at work here. For what is pivotal in this piece is Hsieh's imposing a structure where there is none, where the very severity, lengthy duration, and arbitrariness of his self-imposed incarceration serves to floodlight his regimen's artificiality, and in turn the artificiality of the act of documentation itself. This performance, as with all Hsieh's performances, acknowledges first and foremost the human nonsense of prescriptive existence, while at the same time acknowledging that its playful yet rigorous appropriation is perhaps the last residuum of human meaning. What are Hsieh's self-imposed and

---

[36] Ward, *No Innocent Bystanders*, 142.

perversely doctrinaire impediments to spontaneous existence if not test cases for undermining the very legitimacy of personal freedom, of any unfettered and aleatory bedrock for human meaning? His performances are a palimpsest of human significance, as exemplified by artistic creativity, erasures of accentuation, sedimentary agitations repurposed as if by some enlightened automaton.

Hsieh's third *One Year Performance, Outdoor Piece* (1981–1982), involved him spending an entire year outside, living itinerantly around New York City and sleeping in a sleeping bag. During this time he did not permit himself to enter a building or shelter of any kind, not even short trips in vehicles. By stripping himself of even the most rudimentary and impermanent forms of residency, Hsieh enacted a state of hyper-homelessness. He became the complete alien, the ultimate placeless being. For although most of the year was spent in lower Manhattan, as evidenced by his scrupulous daily reports (which documented everything from his location at any one time and expenditures incurred, to his ablutionary and toilet habits), the only marks he left were urine and faeces. Someone living on the streets will usually have either a tent or at least regular places in which to seek shelter, abandoned properties and the like. A fox will have its den, a rat its nest, and yet Hsieh shunned this most basic of creaturely conventions. A man without a country or even the most rudimentary accommodation, Hsieh mimicked the precarious truth of human abandonment with all the tenacity and fastidiousness of a votary of that original abandonment.

To identify some thing or some event as art is to say that there is no reason for its existing other than its contextualisation as art. To categorise something as art is to label it useless and pointless, as a thing created from and for that void. By exploring the hidden spaces within life's constricted limits, this is what Hsieh has done for human existence, or as he puts it: "Life is a life sentence; life is passing time; life is freethinking."[37] And while, as Camus advised for Sisyphus, we

---

[37] Tehching Hsieh, "Interview: Tehching Hsieh and Marina Abramović in conversation," *Tate Etc.* (17 June 2017) (https://www.tate.org.uk/tate-etc/issue-40-summer-2017/interview-tehching-hsieh-marina-abramovic).

needn't imagine Hsieh happy in his self-inflicted trials, we do nevertheless imagine him contortedly content: imagine him elsewhere, absent, lost in the work, gone in the futility of the living and of that living's contrived futility as art.

Hsieh performed his fourth *One Year Performance, Rope Piece* (1983–1984), with fellow artist Linda Montano, during which they occupied a single room tied together with an 8-foot-long rope. Despite this proximity no touching was permitted. Although their verbal interactions were recorded throughout the performance, the tapes have never been heard. The tapes now sealed up and bearing the artists' signatures will never divulge their contents: like Manzoni's tins of shit, this waste product has nothing more to say than has already been said by the performance that produced it. And of course you could break the seal on the tapes and listen to them, just as you could open Manzoni's tins, but what would you find inside to replace the aura of mystery and significance conveyed to them by their quarantine? What could you reasonably hope to find? Hsieh is making clear that beyond the artificial limits (of both performance and product) there is no value to be found. There is only value (only escape, release, identity) in those artificial and absurdly capricious strictures themselves.

For his fifth and final *One Year Performance, No Art Piece* (1985–1986), Hsieh observed twelve months of complete artistic abstinence. Not only did he refrain from creating any art, but he avoided art in all its possible forms. There was the artistic statement of intent and that was it. Apart, that is, from the very artwork he was creating, which makes for a truly delicious paradox. With this piece, Hsieh surely joins Lozano —who with the revolutionary works *Untitled (General Strike Piece)* (1969) and *Dropout Piece* (1982–1999) is the undoubted pioneer of such renunciant art—at the apex of performance as non-performance, of art divested of art. Without any documentation, all focus falls on the artless life as art, on the eradication of art as art, on a life lived deliberately ostracised from artistic endeavour. Thus art becomes immaterial, becomes paradox, becomes bafflingly elusive, becomes exactly that "something that, in spite of all our reflection on it, we cannot bring down to the distinctness of a concept."[38] Ultimately, Hsieh's intention was to "just go in life," but it is through this going,

---

[38] Schopenhauer, *The World as Will and Representation Vol. 2*, 409.

this departure from art to a place artificially voided of art's artificiality, that Hsieh managed to collapse both art and life into a single amorphous vacuum, around which he drew a decisive yet impossible line.

Hsieh's next work, *Thirteen Year Plan* (1986–1999), extended his previous work's isolation from the art world, while allowing him to partake in artistic creation. Hsieh would create art but would not exhibit it. On the day after the work's completion, January 1st 2000, he issued the following statement, constructed from letters cut from magazines in the form of a ransom note: "I kept myself alive. I passed the December 31st, 1999." The art world celebrated his return and prepared itself for whatever commodities might surface from this extended absence. According to Ward, "the *No Art Piece* and *Thirteen Year Plan* together stretch the membrane between art and non-art to the point where it still exists, but no longer serves as a legitimating framework for behaviour."[39] The membrane stretched into the thinnest of lines has been drawn, and yet we cannot see it: the line is an act of imagination, of conceptual will. This is the exact same structure as the theoretical atoll on which the pessimist subsists, their life in defiance of life, their performance of that life too marginal in its method to be seen.

In *No Art Piece*, Hsieh gave us art as the performance of the non-performance of art, followed by *Thirteen Year Plan* in which he gave us art as the non-performance of the performance of art. The former interrogated the definition of performance art through the eradication of art, while the latter did so via the eradication of the performance, a performance without a public. And it is both these works together that encapsulate the pessimist's performance: the pessimist's work is both a performative non-creativity, a creative absence, while at the same time being a ghettoised performance, a performance without an audience.

Hsieh has said that with *Thirteen Year Plan* he was attempting to disappear, to enact a "double exile," severing communication with art as both something reliant on audiences and contemporary content. However, this exile is once again paradoxical in conception, for Hsieh

---

[39] Ward, *No Innocent Bystanders*, 148.

remains an exile from within, a refugee from a place he never leaves, an art émigré of an art world where he is still embraced, an outsider whose conceptual agenda permits of no outside. As Ward explains:

> Hsieh's gesture to abandon or refuse art is made from within art (it is made as an artist, from within the art world, in relation to an art audience). The secret work of disappearance, Hsieh has acknowledged, involved driving from New York to Seattle ("I tried to get to Alaska but didn't make it that far"): "I went to a totally strange place to start a new life. I felt like an illegal immigrant again, living just for survival, doing jobs."[40]

Claire Bishop argues that contemporary performance artists "do not necessarily privilege the live moment or their own body. Rather, they engage in strategies of mediation that include delegation, re-enactment, and collaboration."[41] Performances are increasingly being "outsourced" to performers other than the artists; and while this is clearly nothing new, and performers have outsourced the performative element to audiences and even puppets for decades, Bishop, while also acknowledging these forebears, nevertheless feels there is something distinctive about the current shift, in which "[a]uthenticity [is] relocated from the singular body of the artist to the collective authenticity of the social body," more and more frequently achieved through financial transaction.[42] Santiago Sierra has, for example, since the turn of this century, paid "people to stand in a line, to have their hair dyed blond, to receive a tattoo, or to sit inside a box or behind a wall for days on end."[43] (Paying them only minimum wage, Sierra has been accused of exploiting the poor, of perpetuating the capitalist injustices he is supposedly attempting to critique.) By making the transactions an integral part of the work (like some real-life Guy Grand),[44] using economics as a medium—now his trademark—Sierra distinguishes his works from earlier examples and sets a precedent for future performance art. As Bishop puts it:

---

[40] Ward, *No Innocent Bystanders*, 148.
[41] Claire Bishop, "Outsourcing Authenticity? Delegated Performance in Contemporary Art," in *Double Agent* (London: ICA, 2009), 111.
[42] Bishop, "Outsourcing Authenticity?," 111.
[43] Bishop, "Outsourcing Authenticity?," 112.
[44] See Terry Southern, *The Magic Christian* (New York: Random House, 1959).

On the Verge of Nothing

In recent years, this financial arrangement has become increasingly essential to the realisation of delegated performance: Elmgreen and Dragset paid twelve unemployed men and women to dress as invigilators and guard an empty gallery (*Reg(u)arding the Guards* [2005]), Tino Sehgai paid children to describe his back catalogue of works at the Frieze Art Fair (*This is Right* [2003]), Tania Bruguera paid blind people to wear military uniforms and stand in front of the Palace of Culture in Warsaw (*Consummated Revolution* [2008]).[45]

Bishop claims that one of the most significant differences between contemporary delegated performance and the body art of the 1970s is that where the earlier examples involved the artist working inexpensively with their own body, the current trend presupposes some degree of affluence (both of the artist, who must finance it, and the audience, whose cultural tastes reflect a predominantly wealthy demographic). Where we have ended up, then, is at a mediated authenticity/a staged immediacy, in which people are economically incentivised to impersonate themselves, "to signify a larger socio-economic demographic, for which they stand as an authentic metonymic fragment."[46] Just how this trend ties in with the performance of pessimism can be best explained by revisiting the proposed shift from pessimism to post-pessimism, and recognising that the latter's outsourcing of the burdensome futility of our existence to other abstract placeholders—whereby each creative act of lucid illusion is exploited for its mimetic effect, and in which oneiric proto-personages are incentivised with the pseudo-currency of some diminutive share in the overall negative utility realised—matches this contemporary model almost exactly.

*

In sum, I can see no way out and yet the prospect of that impossibility enthrals me. The reason, as I see it, is that I can escape without ever having to escape. I can plan my future lives in meticulous detail

---

[45] Bishop, "Outsourcing Authenticity?," 114.
[46] Bishop, "Outsourcing Authenticity?," 117–118.

Pessimism and Performance Art

without ever having to go through the disappointment of enacting them. I can perform the impossibility of living.

In sum, with the telling question yet to be devised, the pre-emptive answer is the only thing it can be: vain, absurd, insanely impractical, and logically sound.

In sum, no sum.

Acknowledgements: I'd like to thank Edia for all her help and support getting this book into shape, Scott for his insightful foreword, Eugene and Stuart for the kind words, and Chip and Nine-Banded Books for the astute comments and for getting it out there.

Gary J. Shipley is the author of numerous books, including *Bright Stupid Confetti* (11:11, 2021), *Terminal Park* (Apocalypse Party, 2020), *You With Your Memory are Dead* (Inside the Castle, 2020), *30 Fake Beheadings* (Spork, 2018), *Warewolff!* (Hexus, 2017), and *The Unyielding* (Eraserhead, 2017). His monograph, *Stratagem of the Corpse: Dying with Baudrillard*, was published by Anthem Press in 2020. He has contributed to various magazines, anthologies, and academic journals. More information can be found at Thek Prosthetics.

Scott Wilson is former Professor of Media and Communication at Kingston University, London. He is co-editor (with Fred Botting) of *The Bataille Reader* (Blackwell, 1997). Other books include *Scott Walker and the Song of the One-All-Alone* (Bloomsbury, 2020), *Great Satan's Rage: American Negativity and Rap/Metal in the Age of Supercapitalism* (Manchester University Press, 2016) and *Cultural Materialism: Theory and Practice* (Blackwell, 1995).

Caveat Lector.

www.NineBandedBooks.com